Cost and Management Accounting

An Active Learning Approach

2nd Edition

T Lucey
M.Soc.Sc., F.C.M.A., F.C.C.A., J.Dip.M.A.

Terry Lucey has been an accountant and consultant in industry and has had over twenty years examining and teaching experience at all levels of professional studies and for diploma and degree courses in business studies. He was previously Head of Department of Business Studies at the University of Wolverhampton and is now a consultant and Visiting Fellow at Aston Business School, Aston University.

Amongst his other published works are:

Investment Appraisal: Evaluating Risk and Uncertainty, Accounting and Computer Systems (co-author), *Quantitative Techniques, Management Information Systems, Management Accounting, Costing,* and several ACCA and CIMA Study and Revision manuals.

DP Publications Ltd
Aldine Place
London W12 8AW
1995

Acknowledgements

Examination questions

The author would like to express thanks to the following for giving permission to reproduce past examination questions.

Association of Accounting Technicians (AAT)

Chartered Association of Certified Accountants (ACCA)

Chartered Institute of Management Accountants (CIMA

London Chambers of Commerce and Industry (LCCI)

Royal Society of Arts (RSA)

A CIP catalogue record for this book can be obtained from the British Library

ISBN 1 85805 127 4

Typeset by
Elizabeth Elwin, London

Printed in Great Britain by
The Guernsey Press Co Ltd

Preface

Aims

The aim of this book is to provide an activity-based introduction to Cost and Management Accounting. It will be found most useful on those courses where students are encouraged to be active participants in the learning process.

Typical courses on which it can be used include:

- BTEC courses in Business Studies and Finance
- Association of Accounting Technicians
- Access Courses
- Open Learning Courses
- RSA and LCCI courses

In conjunction with the author's other titles, *Costing* and *Management Accounting*, it will also be of value to ACCA and CIMA students on discovery learning courses.

Approach

The book has a practical approach and is carefully structured to support and encourage the students to discover and to learn by doing.

There are two sections: Section I – Discovering Cost and Management Accounting; Section II – Developing Knowledge and Skills.

Section I – Discovering Cost and Management accounting

This section contains 12 topics which together cover all the essential principles of cost and management accounting (CMA). Each topic presents the teaching material via:

(a) Scenarios, Quick Answer Questions (QAQ's) and Tasks

(b) Supporting study text, summaries and further reading references.

(a) Scenarios, Quick Answer Questions (QAQ's) and Tasks

Students are encouraged to learn through the experiences of Alan Irwin, a management trainee, the questions he faces and the tasks with which he has to deal. In this section there are *Scenarios* relating to some aspect of Alan's experiences, followed by *Quick Answer Questions (QAQ's)* to draw out of students the key objectives and features of the managerial problem being considered (answers are printed upside down immediately following the question). In addition there are also one or more *Tasks* within each topic which are more involved than the QAQ's and are expected to require the student to study the appropriate text or refer to the suggested additional reading (answers to Tasks are at the back of the Section).

The Scenarios, QAQ's and Tasks are the driving forces of the discovery and learning process and for easy identification are shaded in the same manner as this paragraph.

(b) **Study text, summaries and further reading references**

Cost and management accounting principles are presented concisely and placed in the text immediately following a task.

Note: The topics should be tackled sequentially as they build on knowledge and techniques already covered.

At the end of each part (i.e. after Topics 4, 8 and 12), reference is given to Section II (see below) to enable development of knowledge and skills.

Section II – Developing Knowledge and Skills

This section contains a mixture of multiple choice questions, cases, assignments and examination questions both with and without answers. The section enables the student to gain practice and to deepen understanding. It may be used as directed by lecturers, as a diagnostic tool by students or as revision. Because CMA is universally applicable there are questions, cases and assignments relating to service industries, government, hospitals etc. as well as manufacturing applications. For ease of use, this section is in the same sequence as Section 1.

Note for lecturers

This book may be used in a variety of ways. For example as a classroom work-book, as a basis of supported self-study, as a follow up of formal teaching or a mixture of the above.

A comprehensive Lecturers Supplement is available free to lecturers adopting this book as a course text. The Supplement contains:

- ❐ Guidance on alternative ways of using the book
- ❐ Guidance notes for the cases in Section II
- ❐ Answers to those Questions in Section II where no answer is given in the book
- ❐ Suggestions for role play, group work, etc.
- ❐ OHP masters of key diagrams

Note to the Second Edition

The text has been reorganised to make it simpler to use. It also contains numerous detailed improvements and extensions of coverage. There is more material on activity-based costing and other current developments, and on management accounting in service functions and industries.

T Lucey
1995

Contents

Discovering cost and management accounting

Introduction

Section I consists of a number of Topics, each containing several single story line scenarios. Each topic illustrates some managerial problem or need or practice from which you can discover a part of the theory and practice of cost and management accounting. Each scenario is followed by a number of Quick Answer Questions (QAQs) which draw your attention to the key objective and features of the scenario. Always make some attempt at the QAQs before looking at the answers (which are printed upside down immediately following the QAQs).

In addition to the QAQs, there are one or more *Tasks* within each topic. These are more wide ranging than the QAQs and to deal with them, you will probably need to study the knowledge summaries and perhaps follow up the recommended reading, or carry out some form of investigation. Answers to tasks are found at the end of this Section (beginning on page 178).

The QAQs and Tasks are parts of the discovery and learning process and should not be ignored or skimped.

The topics and scenarios have been arranged in a sequence which progressively develops your knowledge and understanding and they should be worked on *in sequence* not in a haphazard fashion.

Background to the scenarios

The scenarios describe the experiences and tasks carried out by Alan Irwin. Alan is a management trainee who has joined the Hempson Group of companies. The Hempson Group has expanded rapidly largely through a series of acquisitions which have resulted in a Group of over 30 companies varying greatly in size. They range from a small specialist tool company making items to order to a large company employing over 3,000 people which makes standard building products such as window frames by repetitive production methods. The Group also includes a computer consultancy which provides expertise within the Group and also sells services to outside customers.

Alan has joined the Head Office staff but it is Group policy for trainees to spend time within various Group Companies to learn about their systems and problems and to gain experience. It has been decided that the first part of Alan's training will concentrate on the internal accounting systems within the Group. The Personnel Director made it clear to Alan that he will have to learn about routine, but important, day-to-day procedures as well as higher level things such as planning and decision-making. He also emphasised that Alan must continually question why things are done the way they are and find out what purpose they serve. The continual probing and questioning will enable Alan to learn more rapidly and completely.

Contents

Part 1

Cost analysis and cost ascertainment

Introduction

Topics 1 to 4 cover the elements of cost and management accounting (CMA). You will discover how to analyse costs and how to deal with the key cost elements; material, labour and overheads. You will also find out how to cost products, jobs and batches, what these costs can be used for and how CMA provides assistance to management.

The basics of Cost and Management Accounting (CMA)

CMA and its purpose are explained and the foundation of cost analysis are described. Some key definitions are given and the build-up of overheads and product cost is outlined.

Contents

The purpose of Cost and Management Accounting

1.1 What is Cost and Management Accounting (CMA)?

CMA is one specialised aspect of the whole subject of accounting. CMA is a key part of the internal financial information system of an organisation and is equally useful in manufacturing firms, in service industries such as banking, insurance and education, and central government, in hospitals and so on.

In summary, CMA provides vital financial information to management in three interrelated areas:

- Cost analysis and cost ascertainment (detailed coverage in Topics 1 to 5)
- Planning and control (detailed coverage in Topics 6 to 9)
- Decision making (detailed coverage in Topics 10 to 12)

CMA is not a complex highly technical subject. It is a collection of commonsense rules and procedures designed to be of practical help to Managers. The information produced by the CMA System should be; relevant for the purpose intended, understandable, and produced in time to be used.

Note that the subject of Cost and Management Accounting may be sub-divided into costing (or cost accounting) and management accounting. However any such sub-division is quite arbitrary and fulfils little purpose.

Scenario A Finding out some background

Alan starts at Hempsons Group Headquarters and is told that he will be based initially at the Precision Tool Company. Before leaving for the Tool Company Alan decided to see John Wellington, the Group Management Accountant, to ask him for guidance and advice.

John was very helpful and explained that each Group Company had some form of accounting system, analysing and recording expenditure and preparing financial information for management. That part of the accounting system which dealt largely with internal matters was called the Cost and Management Accounting (CMA) System.

Alan was puzzled to learn that the CMA System in each company was different in certain respects as he thought that the Accounts companies had to produce were defined in the Companies Act and other legislation.

Also, he confided in John, he was not too sure why he had to learn about accounting as he intended to become a manager, not an accountant.

Quick answer questions*

1. Can you think of any reasons why the CMA System in the Group Companies may differ from one another?
2. Why do you think Alan should learn about Accounting?

*Answers to QAQs follow, upside down. Always make an attempt at the QAQs before looking at the answers.

1. The CMA System must suit the type of production, the company structure and be able to supply the management of the company with financial information to enable them to run the business efficiently. This means that the system must be tailor made to suit each business and thus will differ in some respect from all other CMA Systems. However, certain principles and techniques are found in all CMA Systems, especially those in the same type of business. You will come across these as you work through the book.

2. There are two main reasons why it is useful for Alan to spend time learning about CMA Systems in the Group.

(a) The CMA System of each company is concerned with all aspects of operations e.g. production, stores, material and labour, administration and so on. Consequently, learning about the CMA System is an excellent way of finding out about each company and the way the departments and functions work together.

(b) Many factors must be considered by management, when carrying out a task e.g. social, behavioural, political and other consideration. However, an ever present factor is the financial effect. Will it be worthwhile? What will be its cost? Can we save by doing it this way? And so on. Thus managers, and intending managers like Alan, should have a good grasp of accounting principles, they should know the limitations of accounting information and they should know enough about accounting to be able to ask accountants the right questions.

Task 1 *(answer page 178)*

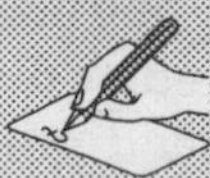

Give 6 examples of information that might be supplied by a CMA and what the information might be used for. Try to find examples from both manufacturing and service industries.

**Help in answering tasks is provided in the text immediately following tasks and/or will have been previously covered in the text.*

1.2 Why is a CMA system essential?

To run any organisation in an efficient manner it is essential that management are supplied with relevant information. Depending on the problem management may require information about Sales, Personnel, Production, Training, Equipment or other matters. In addition, they will invariably require information about the financial aspects of the problem. Information is produced to record some event or to answer a question or as a basis for some decision, i.e. it is always produced for a purpose.

Table 1.1 gives some examples of CMA information that might be produced and what it might be used for.

Examples of CMA information	Possible uses
Cost of producing a litre of paint	1. Factor in setting selling prices. 2. A help in monitoring production efficiency. 3. Stock and profit calculations etc.
Amount spent on salaries in the Marketing department	1. Part of the build-up of total administration costs used in profit calculations. 2. Control of salary costs. 3. Assessing efficiency. 4. Salary negotiations etc.
Comparative costs of refuse collection by own staff and contractors	1. Major factor in deciding between methods. 2. Means of assessing efficiency. 3. Factor in setting targets. 4. Assessing value for money etc.
Expected costs of starting a second shift	1. Major factor in deciding whether to increase production. 2. Factor in long-term investment planning. 3. Factor in short-term cash planning etc.
Cost of administering a customer's account in a bank	1. Factor in customer charging. 2. Cost control. 3. Aid in monitoring efficiency. 4. For internal/external comparisons.

Table 1.1 CMA information: examples and uses

Although external factors are often very important it is broadly true that the thrust of CMA is concerned with internal factors such as costs, activities, efficiency, control and so on. That part of accounting which deals with external financial matters and external reporting is known as financial accounting.

Scenario B The past and the future

On arriving at the Precision Tool Company, Alan was introduced to Margaret Holland who was the Company Accountant. She explained that the Precision Tool Company made tools, dies and specialist production equipment to customers' order. It was a company small enough to get a good grasp of the system and organisation quickly.

Margaret told Alan that their CMA System, like all others, could be thought of as having two aspects; one analysing and recording what had already happened, i.e. the historical view, and the other aspect, looking forward to what might happen in the future. She explained that the two aspects were inter-related and that the data base obtained from recording what had happened in the past was frequently used as the basis of predictions about the future. As an example, she told him about the information she was currently preparing for the Sales Manager.

A few months ago they had made a Blanking Tool for Smiths Presswork. Smiths now required a price for a new Blanking Tool which Precision had not made before but which was similar to the one made previously. Margaret was analysing the production records and production costs of the tool they made previously (i.e. the historical record) to prepare estimates of the costs expected for the new tool (i.e. the future aspect). The expected costs will be used by the Sales Manager as one of the factors he must consider in arriving at a selling price to quote Smiths Presswork.

Quick answer questions

1. The Precision Tool Company is called a Jobbing Manufacturer. What do you think are the characteristics of jobbing manufacturers?
2. Can you think of any other purpose which the production cost of the Blanking Tool made a few months ago could be used for?
3. Margaret is currently preparing information from the CMA System for the Sales Manager. Can you think what key principle this illustrates?

1. *Jobbing firms make products to order, usually to the customer's design or specification. Jobs tend to be different to one another and the firms tend to be relatively small. In contrast to a jobbing firm, a mass-production firm, e.g. a firm making televisions, makes standard products to its own design which the firm then attempts to sell. As mentioned, the CMA System must be tailored to suit the type of firm.*
2. *The product cost of a completed job can be used for many purposes but the one you may have thought of is to find the profit or loss made on the job. Other things it may be needed for include; a means of assessing production efficiency, as a basis for stock valuation etc. all of which you will come to later in the book.*
3. *The key principle is that the information or records must be relevant for some management need or purpose. This applies to all CMA records and information. The information must be useful for management otherwise it should not be produced.*

Scenario C **Expenditure analysis**

After their preliminary meeting, Margaret told Alan that he would now have to get down to detail. She thought that he should start with *expenditure analysis*, which is at the heart of every CMA System. In response to her query Alan said that he thought it meant that expenditure was analysed into various categories such as materials, labour, electricity, telephone etc. Margaret told him that he was partly right but for the CMA System more detail was required. Take as an example expenditure on salaries. The firm needed to know how much was spent on salaries but, in addition, for CMA purposes it also needed to know where or on what the salaries were spent. This means that all expenditure needs to be classified in two ways:

By type: e.g. salaries, materials, telephone and so on.

By use or location: e.g. in the Sales Department, in the product, for maintenance and so on.

Margaret explained that this two-way analysis was carried out by means of *coding* the information and she showed him Precision Tools code lists; an abstract of which is given below.

Code	*Expenditure type*
200	Wages
201	Overtime wages
250	Salaries
300	Stationery
301	Office sundries
310	Telephone
450	Advertising
500	Steel Category A

Code	*Location/use*
1000	Sales Department
1010	Works Administration Department
1070	Accounting Department
1200	Inspection and Testing
1250	Repairs and Maintenance
1500	Directly in the Product

Quick answer questions

1. Why do you think a two way expenditure analysis is required for CMA Systems?
2. Based on Precision Tool's coding system, what codes would you give these?
   (a) £2,500 expenditure on Office Sundries for use in the Accounting Department.
   (b) £1,100 of wages for people employed on Repairs and Maintenance.
   (c) £870 expenditure on Category A Steel used in a saleable product.
   (d) £262 expenditure on Stationery for Works Administration.

1. It is essential for management to monitor all expenditure so as to be able to control waste and improve efficiency. This can only be done if, in detail, information is recorded on what money has been spent, where it was spent and for what purpose. For some accounting purposes it is sufficient to have information just on the type of expenditure e.g. salaries, materials, etc. but CMA Systems require, in addition, details on the location and/or purpose of that expenditure.

The two way coding system determines into which accounts expenditure is recorded.

2. (a) Code 301/1070
(b) Code 200/1250
(c) Code 500/1500
(d) Code 300/1010

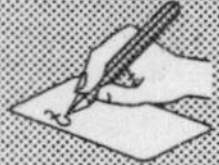

Task 2 *(answer page 178)*

At what point in Precision Tool's CMA System would the four expenditure examples given in QAQ B be coded? Classify them into direct and indirect costs.

Essential elements of CMA systems

1.3 Cost analysis and cost ascertainment

The foundation of any CMA System is knowledge about both the nature of expenditure, e.g. wages, materials, telephone charges etc. and the location or use of that expenditure.

This two-way analysis is achieved using a coding system with two distinct elements:

Nature of expenditure : location or use

For example, expenditure for salaries in the Planning department might be coded as follows:

Whereas salaries in the Accounts department might be coded thus:

The codes thus determine in which accounts expenditures are recorded and form the basis of all subsequent analyses. Expenditure is coded as early as possible, i.e. as soon as the type of expenditure and its location/use is known. This may be when an invoice is received, wages paid, goods issued from stores and so on.

In summary, that part of CMA dealing with cost analysis and cost ascertainment:

- analyses and records all expenditure by nature of the expenditure.
- analyses and records, the use and/or location of the expenditure.
- calculates the cost of running departments and operations and the cost of making the product or supplying the service using the previously analysed expenditures.

1.4 Key CMA definitions

Cost unit

Costs are always related to some appropriate object or function or service, e.g. a car, a hair-cut, a hip replacement, a kilowatt hour etc. These are known as *cost units*. The cost unit chosen is that which is most relevant for the particular cost exercise. This means that, in any one organisation, numerous cost units may be used in various part of the organisation or for differing purposes.

Direct costs

Direct costs are those that can be directly identified with the product or job or service. For example the steel in a car, the wages paid to a carpenter making a window, the fees paid to a surgeon and so on.

Indirect costs or overheads

Any cost which cannot be identified as direct is an *indirect cost* or *overhead cost*.

For example, the rates for business premises, although a necessary expenditure, cannot be identified with a specific product or service so they are *indirect* or *overhead* costs. In practice, most expenditure is overhead expenditure. Although overheads cannot be identified directly with a product of service they are nevertheless part of the costs of an organisation and have to be included in the cost of the product. This is dealt with in more detail in Topic 3 but in essence a Product Cost is found as follows:

Direct Materials in product + Direct labour in making the product + Share of overheads = Total Cost of product.

Note: The total of Direct Costs is known as the *Prime Cost*.

The above outline of Product Costing applies also to service industries, e.g. banks, hospitals, local authorities, etc., but naturally the type of costs vary widely.

Cost centre

By their nature direct costs can be readily identified but several steps are necessary to find out what overheads should be included in the product cost.

The first step is to divide the organization into *cost centres.* A cost centre can be likened to a 'pigeon-hole' in which overhead expenditure is accumulated. A cost centre may be a location (e.g. the Planning Department) or a function (e.g. quality control). All cost centres are given a code and it is this code which forms the second part of the two-way analysis mentioned above. (i.e. Nature of expenditure: Location of expenditure).

Some costs are specific to a cost centre (e.g. salaries paid to the people who work in the Planning Department) whilst others are general cost (e.g. Rates) which have to be spread over all the benefiting cost centres. This sharing out is known as *cost apportionment.*

Cost apportionment

This is the process of sharing a common expenditure over two or more cost centres; ideally in the proportions in which they receive benefits. The basis of apportionment varies from cost to cost and some typical bases are shown below:

Basis	**Examples of costs which may be apportioned on this basis**
Floor area	Rates, Rent, Heating, Lighting
Volume or space occupied	Heating, Lighting, Building Depreciation and Maintenance
Number of employees in each cost centre	Canteen, Welfare, Personnel, Administrative costs.

Example of cost apportionment

An organisation has total heating costs of £25,000 and wishes these to be shared out fairly over its 10 cost centres. It has been decided that space occupied is the fairest basis of apportionment.

Cost centre	**Space occupied (cubic metres)**	**Percentage of total**	**Share of heating costs £**
No. 1	750*	6.5%	1,625
2	750	6.5%	1,625
3	3,500	30%	7,500
4	250	2%	500
5	750	6.5%	1,625
6	250	2%	500
7	2,250	20%	5,000
8	1,000	9%	2,250
9	750	6.5%	1,625
10	1,250	11%	2,750
Total	11,500	100%	£25,000

* each apportionment is dealt with in the same way, e.g.

$$\frac{750}{11{,}500} = 6.5\% \text{ and } 6.5\% \text{ of } £25{,}000 = £1{,}625.$$

1.5. Finding the overheads for a cost centre

The total overheads for a cost centre are thus a mixture of those directly spent by the cost centre, for example, the salaries of the people employed in it and an appropriate share of general costs such as rates, heating and so on.

In a manufacturing company some cost centres are directly concerned with making the product and are known as Production Cost Centres, for example, Machining, Assembly, Spraying and so on. The rest, which are non-production cost centres, are usually grouped under titles such as Administration, Marketing, Finance, Design and others, to suit the particular organisation. Each classification of cost centre naturally has different types of overhead but the general principles of gathering overheads by cost centre are universal and apply to service industries, government departments, universities and colleges, retail organisations, etc., as well as to manufacturing companies.

Figure 1.2. summarises the build-up of overheads.

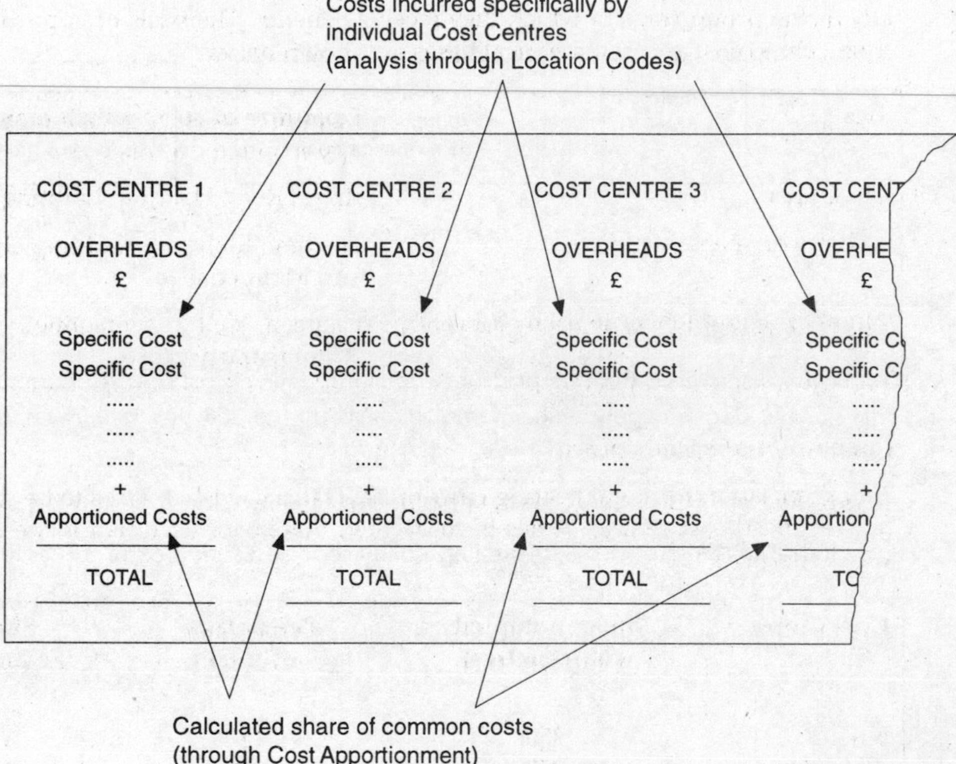

Figure 1.2 – The build-up of overheads by cost centre

1.6 Overhead absorption (or overhead recovery)

The total cost of a product includes its direct costs plus a suitable share of overheads. To ensure each product carries an appropriate share of overheads a two-stage process is necessary. Firstly, overheads are collected by the cost centre system shown in Figure 1.2. Then the overheads are spread over all the products passing through that cost centre by the process known as *overhead absorption* or *overhead recovery*. Ideally, each unit of product should receive that share of overheads which exactly reflects the load that producing that unit places on the cost centre. Naturally this ideal is difficult to achieve but if the time is recorded that a product takes to move through a cost centre and then overheads are absorbed in proportion to the time taken (measured in labour hours or machine hours spent in the cost centre), accurate results can be achieved.

Overhead absorption is dealt with in detail in Topic 3.

1.7 Product costing outline

Figure 1.3 shows the framework of product costing which can be thought of as the production units flowing through the organisation gathering overheads as they move along.

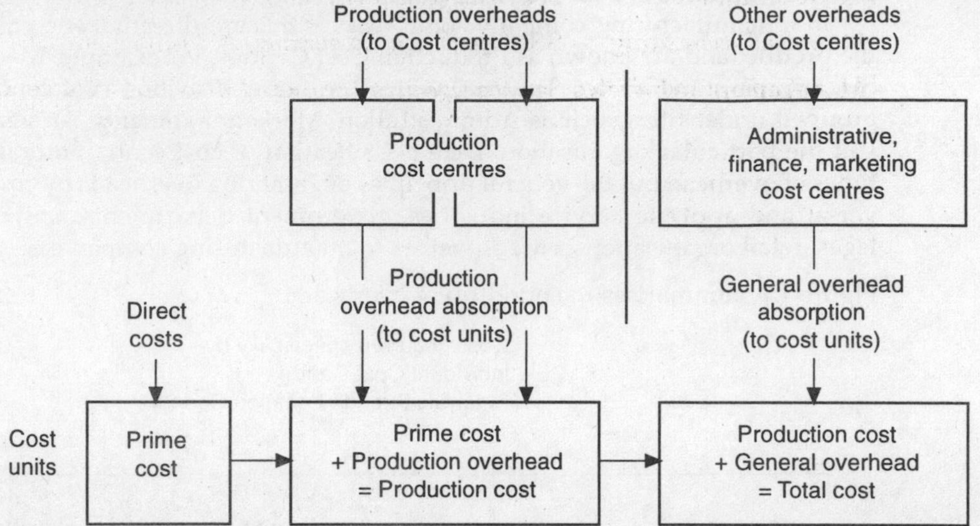

Figure 1.3 – Outline of product costing

Task 3 *(answer page 178)*

Alan has discovered that the part of accounting called Cost and Management Accounting (CMA) deals largely with internal matters but he still has a number of unresolved questions; as follows:

(a) Is the form of the CMA Systems that is used in Precision Tool defined by legislation?

(b) What is the aspect of accounting called that deals with external matters? Is it governed by legislation?

(c) What are the key external matters dealt with?

Key point summary

- CMA provides financial information to management, mainly about internal operations.
- CMA includes: cost analysis and the provision of information for planning, control and decision making.
- A primary requirement is knowledge about the *type* of expenditure and its *location or use*.
- Direct costs are those that can be identified directly with the product.
- Indirect costs or overheads are charged to cost centres using direct charging of specific expenses and apportionment of general expenses.
- A product costs comprises: Direct materials + Direct labour + a share of overheads.
- Overhead absorption or overhead recovery is a method of ensuring that each cost unit bears a suitable share of overheads.

Need more detail or want to pursue a topic further?

Basics of CMA	See *Costing*, T Lucey, DP Publications.
CMA terminology	See *Management Accounting Official Terminology*, CIMA.
Financial accounting	See *Foundation Accounting*, AH Millichamp, DP Publications
Management principles	See *Management Theory and Practice*, GA Cole, DP Publications.

Materials and labour

The types of materials are described and the major material pricing system are illustrated. Direct and indirect wages are explained and the main renumeration methods are described and illustrated.

Contents

Cost summaries

Scenario A The cost of jobs

By the end of his first week at Precision Tool, Alan was becoming more useful to Margaret Holland, the Company Accountant. She explained that the Works Director liked to have a Summary each week of the jobs completed during the week, showing their costs and the profit and loss on each job. Margaret had already prepared part of the Summary for the week and asked Alan to complete it for her. She passed over to him the following information.

Summary
Job completed week ending 25/10

Job no.	Wages paid	Materials used	Overheads	Total cost	Selling price	Profit (loss)
X107	£258	£482	£387		£1,400	
W556	£1,479	£3,010	£2,340		£7,200	
R803	£384	£775	£576		£1,650	

Quick answer questions

1. What is the total cost of each job?
2. What is the Profit or Loss on each job?
3. What is the total wages on these three jobs? Do you think this is the total wage bill for Precision Tool for the week?

1. Wages + Materials + Overheads = Total Costs.

Job no.							Total cost
X107	=	*£258*	+	*£482*	+	*£387*	= *£1,127*
W556	=	*£1,479*	+	*£3,010*	+	*£2,340*	= *£6,829*
R803	=	*£384*	+	*£775*	+	*£576*	= *£1,735*

2. Selling Price – Total Costs = Profit (Loss)

Job no					Profit (loss)
X107	= *£1,400*	–	*£1,127*	=	*£273*
W556	= *£7,200*	–	*£6,829*	=	*£371*
R803	= *£1,650*	–	*£1,735*	=	*(£85)*

3. Total Wages on the three jobs.

= £258 + £1,479 + £384 = £2,121

This is the total wages paid on completed jobs. Other wages will have been paid for work done on jobs not yet completed. The incomplete jobs are known as the Work-In-Progress (WIP). The wages (and all other costs) on these incomplete jobs will continue to be accumulated until the jobs are finally completed.

Task 1 *(answer page 179)*

(a) What are the Prime Costs of Job nos. X107, W556 and R803 shown in Scenario A?

(b) Job No X107 was made entirely in the Fitting Department where the fitters are paid £6 per hour wages. W556 took 152 hours in the Fitting Department and 81 hours in the Assembly Department. What is the wage rate in the Assembly Department?

(c) Why does the cost of each job have to include some overheads?

Materials

Scenario B Material costs

Alan next turned his attention to finding out how material costs were charged to each job. Margaret explained that materials were first taken into Stores and then issued, as required, to the various jobs. Each Issue Note contained details of the quantity or weight of materials issued, their description and code and the job number they were to be used on. The Issue Notes were then sent to the Cost Department where they were priced and the Job Card charged with the cost of materials used.

Having outlined the general system Margaret suggested that Alan visit the Cost Department to investigate further. Alan soon found that the objective of charging jobs with the cost of materials was complicated by the fact that materials in stock were often purchased at different times and at different prices. In consequence the Cost Department used an Issue Pricing System known as First In First Out (FIFO). Bill Randall, the Cost Clerk, showed Alan some recent examples of material pricing relating to l" diameter Tool Steel, code 508.

Material code 508 – 1" diameter tool steel

Stock at 1st July

200kgs	bought at	£12.50 kg
400kgs	bought at	£13.00 kg
300kgs	bought at	£13.20 kg

During July there had been the following issues:

			Material cost charged to job
Issue 1	100kgs to	Job No. S672	£1,250
Issue 2	50kgs to	Job No. X221	£625
Issue 3	120kgs to	Job No. L449:	£1,535
Issue 4	75kgs to	Job No. M208:	£975

Quick answer questions

1. Why do you think it is necessary to use an Issue Pricing System at Precision Tool?
2. How had Bill Randall calculated the material cost charged to each job?
3. What was the opening Stock Value of material code No. 508 and how many kilograms were in Stock at the end?

1. An Issue Pricing System is used where it is difficult or impossible, to identify the material or parts issued with any given purchase. In this case one piece of l" diameter tool steel looks like any other piece so it is impossible to track down the actual price paid.

2

Issue 1	*100kgs at £12.50*	*=*	*£1,250*	*charged to job S672*
Issue 2	*50kgs at £12.50*	*=*	*£625*	*charged to job X221*
Issue 3	*50kgs at £12.50*	*=*	*£625*	
	70kgs at £13.00	*=*	*£910 +*	
			£1,535	*charged to job L449*
Issue 4	*75kgs at £13.00*	*=*	*£975*	*charged to job M208*

Note how the earliest batches and prices are assumed to be used first, i.e. First In, First Out. This means that Issue 3 of 120kgs is assumed to come from two batches, i.e. the 50kgs left from Batch 1 at £12.50 kg and 70kgs from Batch 2 at £13 kg.

3 Opening Stock value is:

(200 × £12.50) + (400 × £13) + (300 × £13.20) = £11,660

Closing Stock Quantity

= Opening Stock Quantity	*900kgs*
– Issues	*345kgs*
= Closing Stock Quantity	*555kgs*

Task 2 *(answer page 179)*

1. What is the Closing Stock value of material code No. 508 at the end of July?
2. What are two alternative Issue Pricing Systems to the system used by Precision Tool?
3. Using one of the other issue pricing systems calculate the amount that would be charged to each of the four jobs and the value of the closing stock of material code 508.

2.1 Direct and indirect materials

Direct materials are bought in raw materials, parts, components and so on which are incorporated into the finished product. The cost of direct materials is charged to the cost unit. Examples include; sugar, milk, flavourings at a chocolate manufacturer, steel, tyres, headlights etc. at a car manufacturer and so on.

Indirect materials are any materials used in the organisation that do not appear in the final product. The cost of indirect materials is part of overheads and is charged to the cost centre using the material. Examples include; paper and stationery used in administration, fuel oil used for heating, paint used for maintenance.

2.2 Storage and issue

Most materials, especially direct materials, are taken into storage and then issued for use as and when required. An Issue note is raised for each issue which shows the quantity and type of material and on what or where it is to be used. This will be recognised as the two-way analysis mentioned earlier.

2.3 Pricing issues

This is a more complicated problem than it appears. This is because in practice, the stock of materials and parts is made up of numerous deliveries often bought at different prices. As a consequence, it is difficult or perhaps impossible to identify an item with its delivery consignment and hence find the actual price paid.

Accordingly, it is normal to price issues from stores using a *materials pricing system* rather than try to trace the actual price paid. The system used should charge issues on a consistent and realistic basis and should be easy to use. Numerous systems are possible and three important ones; First in – First out, Average Price and Standard Price, are described below, followed by a worked example.

First In – First Out (FIFO)

Using the FIFO system, issues are priced at the cost of the oldest batch in stock until all that batch has been issued when the cost of the next batch is used and so on.

This system reflects good storekeeping practice whereby oldest items are used first but it does mean keeping track or the number of quantity in each batch which causes extra clerical work.

(There is a complementary pricing system where the price of the newest batch in stock is used; this is known as the Last In – First Out or LIFO system.)

Average price

This is a straightforward system whereby the issue price is the average price of all items in stock. The average price is recalculated after each receipt.

The average price method makes cost comparisons between jobs easier and requires less clerical work than the FIFO system.

Standard price

A standard price is a planned price for a period which is used for all issues and returns. This is the simplest system to deal with clerically and is best suited to stable conditions otherwise there is difficulty in deciding upon an appropriate standard price.

Note: The choice of issue price also determines the value of the closing stock.

Example of issue pricing

The following data relate to Part No. X200 for the month of May

May	1st	Opening stock	1,000 items @ £4 each
	3rd	Issue	600 items
	6th	Receipt	400 items @ £4.20 each
	12th	Issue	500 items
	25th	Receipt	700 items @ £4.30 each
	26th	Issue	200 items

The firm is considering using a Standard Issue Price of £4.15 per item but wishes to compare this price with the issue prices if FIFO or Average Price were used. Also the firm wishes to know what the closing stock values would be using the three systems.

Solution summary

		Stock movements	Standard price (see Note 1)		FIFO (See note 2)		Average price (See note 3)	
			Issue prices and stock valuations					
May 1	Stock	1,000		£		£		£
3	– Issue	600	600 @ £4.15 =	2,490	600 @ £4 =	2,400	600 @ £4 =	2,400
New stock		400						
6	+ Receipt	400						
New stock		800						
12	– Issue	500	500 @ £4.15 =	2,075	(400 @ £4) (100 @ £4.20) =	2,020	500 @ £4.10 =	2,050
New stock		300						
25	+ Receipt	700						
New stock		1,000						
26	– Issue	200	200 @ £4.15 =	830	200 @ £4.20 =	840	200 @ £4.24 =	848
Closing stock		800	Stock value = £3,320		Stock value = £3,430		Stock value = £3,392	

Note 1:

All issues take place at the Standard Price of £4.15 per item and total:

£2,490 + £2,075 + £830 = £5,395.

The closing stock is also valued at Standard Price, i.e. 800 @ £4.15 = **£3,320**.

Note 2:

The FIFO system uses the price of the oldest batch first, until it is all used up thus:

	Batch 1			Batch 2
Opening Stock	1,000 @ £4			
600 Issue on 3 May	600 @ £4			
Balance	400 @ £4		Receipt	400 @ £4.20
500 Issue on 12 May is from 2 batches	400 @ £4	and	Issue	100 @ £4.20
			Balance	300 @ £4.20
			200 Issue on 26th	200 @ £4.20
			Balance	100 @ £4.20

Note that the FIFO system may require issues to be drawn from more than one batch which means that several prices may be included in one issue.

The Total issue value using FIFO is £2,400 + £2,020 + £840 = £5,260 and the closing stock value is found as follows:

Opening Stock + Receipts – Issues = Closing Stock

£(1,000 × 4) + (400 × 4.20 + 700 × 4.30) – 5,260 = 4,000 + 4,690 – 5,260 = **£3,430**

The closing stock valuation can be proved as follows:

Closing stock, 800 items made up of

100 from Receipt on	6th May	= 100 @ £4.20 =	£420
700 from Receipt on	25th May	= 700 @ £4.30 =	£3,010
		=	**£3,430**

Note 3:

The Average Price system uses the average price of stock and is recalculated after every new receipt thus:

3rd May Issue of 600 @ £4 (i.e. as opening stock) leaving a balance of 400 @ £4

6th May Receipt of 400 @ £4.20

∴ New average price = (400 × £4 + 400 × £4.20) ÷ 800 = £4.10

12th May Issue 500 @ £4.10 leaving balance of 300 @ £4.10

25th May Receipt of 700 @ £4.30

∴ New average price = (300 × £4.10 + 700 × £4.30) ÷ 1,000 = £4.24

26th May Issue of 200 @ £4.24 leaving a balance of 800 @ £4.24 = **£3,392**

Closing Stock Valuation proof

Opening stock + Receipts – Issues = Closing Stock

= £4,000 + 4,690 – 5,298

= **£3,392**

Labour

Scenario C Wage costs

Alan felt he now understood much more clearly how material was priced but he wanted to know more about how the job costs were gathered and how labour costs were calculated. Margaret explained that each job was given a unique Job Number and a Job Card opened for each job. On this was recorded the hours each department worked on the job, the wages paid and the material used. On completion, the overheads to be charged to the job were calculated in the Accounts Department and the total cost of the jobs found. Margaret thought that it would be useful if Alan now investigated the Wages System.

Alan was surprised to find that all the production workers in Precision Tool were paid by the hour because he had previously thought that most production workers were paid piecework. He found that each worker completed a Daily Time Sheet which provided the basic data for the CMA system and for the calculation of wages.

A summary of a days' time bookings for Harry Smith, a Fitter in the Fitting Department, follows:

Name: *Harry Smith*

Attendance Hours: 9½ *(including 2 hours overtime)*

Job no.	Hours worked
S552	*3*
J809	*4*
K221	*2 (in overtime)*

(½ hour was spent waiting for work)

Quick answer questions

1. Why do you think that the workers in Precision Tool are paid hourly?
2. What do you think is meant by piecework? What type of production do you think suits wage payment by piecework?
3. If the normal wage rate in the Fitting Department is £6 per hour and the overtime is paid at time and a half, what are Harry's gross wages for the day?

1. Workers in Precision Tool are paid hourly because all jobs are different, quality is all important, output is difficult to measure, and volumes are low.

2. Piecework means that workers are paid according to the amount they produce, e.g. 50p per item made. The production that best suits a piecework system is: repetitive (i.e. similar products are made continuously) easily measurable, where quality can be easily monitored and volumes are high.

3. Gross wages for the day.

Payment hours × rate = $7\frac{1}{2} + (2 \times 1\frac{1}{2}) \times £6 = £63$

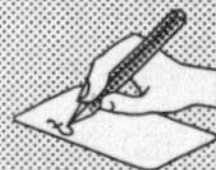

Task 3 *(answer page 179)*

1. Alan has been asked to calculate what wages would be charged to Jobs S552, J809 and K221 in connection with Harry Smith's work. What should he come up with?
2. What is the term given to the ½ hour Harry Smith spent waiting for work?
3. Does he receive wages for this ½ hour? If so, where are they charged in the CMA system? Why?

2.4 Direct labour or wages

Direct wages are those paid to people directly concerned with manufacturing the product. Examples include; machinists, assemblers, sprayers etc. The wages paid to people who support and organise production such as foremen, inspectors, maintenance and so on, are not direct wages but are classified as production overheads.

There are numerous methods of calculating direct wages but the various systems can be classified into those that are based on *time* and those that are based on *output*. These are explained overleaf:

Time based wages

At the simplest, wages are paid at a basic rate per hour up to, say 38 hours per week. Time worked above 38 hours would be classed as overtime and is usually paid at a higher rate, for example, 'time and a half' i.e. $1\frac{1}{2} \times$ basic rate per hour, depending on the number of hours worked and when the overtime was worked.

Time based wages are not dependent on the level of output but naturally output quantity and quality are still vital factors and it is normal for performance to be closely monitored. Time based systems are most appropriate where quality is all important or where output related schemes would be difficult or impossible to install.

Time based systems frequently also include bonuses and other payments. For examples, timekeeping and shift bonuses, good housekeeping bonuses, safety bonuses and so on.

Output based wages

Schemes in which wages are dependent on output are usually known as *incentive schemes.* There are numerous types of these schemes, some apply to individuals, others to groups, some have minimum earnings guarantees and so on. Properly organised incentive schemes can benefit both the employee and the firm. The employee from the extra wages arising from increased production and the employer from the reduced overheads per unit of the increased production.

Incentive schemes can increase production and wages and thereby improve morale, but some schemes are difficult to administer and there can be problems in deciding upon performance levels and rates.

The commonest wages systems based on output are Piecework Schemes and Bonus Schemes which are explained below.

Piecework schemes

At their simplest, the worker would be paid an agreed rate per unit or operation, for the number of units produced or operations carried out.

> *Example*
>
> A machinist is paid on piecework at the rate of £1.80 per 100 components produced. During a week he produced 9,140 components of which 60 were rejected by inspection. What were his wages for the week?

Solution

	Components
Output	9,140
Less rejects	60
Net good output	9,080

∴ Wages for week = 9,080 @ £1.80 per 100 = **£163.44**

Note that only good production is paid for.

Where, as in the example above, the same rate per unit is paid for all production, the system is known as *straight piecework.* On occasions, the rate is increased progressively at various output levels and this is then known as *differential piecework.*

Example

A worker is paid by differential piecework and the following rates have been agreed.

up to 500 units	25p per unit
501 – 600 units	27p per unit
601 – 700 units	30p per unit
701 and above	35p per unit.

During a week the worker produced 642 good units. What were his wages for the week?

Solution

Wages		£
500 @ 25p	=	125
100 @ 27p	=	27
42 @ 30p	=	12.60
		164.60

Bonus systems

There is a great variety of these systems which usually combine a flat rate per hour with a bonus for achieving a given output level. Often the bonus is based on the savings made between the actual time taken and the target time for a job.

Example

A worker with a basic rate of £5 per hour receives a bonus of half the hours saved on each job. In a 38 hour week he completes 2 jobs as follows:

Job	Target time	Actual time
A	32 hours	23 hours
B	16 hours	15 hours
		38 hours

What are his wages for the week?

Solution

Bonus hours		
Job A	$= \frac{1}{2}(32 - 23)$	$= 4\frac{1}{2}$ hours
Job B	$= \frac{1}{2}(16 - 15)$	$= \frac{1}{2}$ hour
Total bonus hours		5 hours
Total pay hours	= 38 + 5	= 43 hours
and wages	= 43 × £5	= **£215**

2.5 When direct wages may be classified as indirect

There are certain occasions when the wages paid to direct workers are classified as indirect, i.e. they become part of overheads rather than part of direct costs. Typical examples are:

(a) when overtime is worked it is common to charge overtime wages above basic rates to overheads rather than direct wages. For example, if the basic rate is £5 per hour and overtime is paid at 'time and a half' then £5 would be charged to direct wages and £2.50 to overheads. The reason is that it is usually accidental which job is done in overtime and that job should not be penalised.

(b) when workers are paid by an incentive scheme and an unavoidable production stoppage occurs, the period during which no production takes place is known as *'idle time'* and the workers usually revert to being paid at normal time rates. Idle time wages are invariably classified as overheads.

2.6 Changing wage patterns

Traditionally wages were expected to vary more or less in proportion to the amount produced. This was because most workers were paid according to output. For example, by piecework and because workers were engaged or dismissed in direct response to the order book.

Nowadays more workers are paid salaries or guaranteed weekly minimums. As a consequence, labour costs have become more fixed in nature (i.e. they do not vary directly with output).

Note: Costs which vary directly with output are known as *variable costs*. Those that tend to remain unchanged when output changes are known as *fixed costs*. Cost behaviour is dealt with in more detail later.

Key point summary

- ❒ Close control must be kept over all stages dealing with materials: Purchasing, Receipt, Storage and Issue
- ❒ The material cost of a product includes an allowance for unavoidable scrap
- ❒ Materials are charged out from stores using a pricing system rather than actual cost
- ❒ The First in – First out (FIFO) system prices issues at the cost of the oldest batch in stock. The LIFO system prices issues at the cost of the newest batch in stock
- ❒ The Average Price system uses the average price of all items in stock
- ❒ A standard price is a planned price for a period
- ❒ Time based wages include basic rates and overtime rates such as 'time and a quarter' and so on
- ❒ The simplest incentive scheme is Straight Piecework
- ❒ Differential piecework means that the rate per item is increased as output increases
- ❒ Numerous types of bonus scheme exist and are frequently based on the savings between actual and target time

Need more detail or want to pursue a topic further?

Material and wage systems:	See *Costing* , T Lucey, D P Publications
Stock valuations:	See *SSAP 9* (*SSAP = Statement of Standard Accounting Practice*)

Overheads

Overheads are defined and the conventional way they are absorbed into products is described. Depreciation is explained and details given of the more important methods. Finally, traditional absorption costing is contrasted with Activity Based Costing.

Contents

Overhead absorption

Scenario A Cost centres and overheads

Alan now understood how the direct costs, material and labour were charged to jobs so Margaret thought it was time he looked at the problems of indirect costs, or overheads.

She explained that overheads were analysed and recorded for numerous purposes including: cost control, as a help in keeping track of departmental performance; part of product costing and so on.

She thought that it would be better if he first concentrated on the way overheads were gathered and then used in finding the cost of a product.

The first problem Alan found was that overheads could not be identified directly with particular jobs or products. He had already realised that the cost of each job had to include an appropriate share of overheads but was not too sure how this was done. Margaret explained that this was done using a two-stage process.

The first stage collected all the overhead costs relating to each cost centre. These costs were of two types; costs spent directly by the cost centre (e.g. the salaries of the people working in it) and a proportion of common costs such as rates. When the total overheads were established for each cost centre every job passing through the cost centre would be charged a share of the centre's overheads by a process known as overhead absorption.

Margaret showed Alan a part of Precision Tool's overheads summary sheet with some sample entries. She explained that this represented the first stage of the overhead process, i.e. the accumulation of overhead costs.

Overhead Summary Sheet – Precision Tool

	Total cost	Production cost centres				Other cost centres		
		Grinding	Machining	Fitting	Heat treatment	Admin.	Finance	Marketing
Cost specific to CC	£	£	£	£	£	£	£	
Salaries								
Consumables								
Power								
Computer costs								
Maintenance								
Common costs								
Rates	18,650	3,800	4,300	2,450	2,950	2,750	1,800	600
Heating	14,200							
Canteen deficit	9,410							
Insurance	7,960							
Total								

Quick answer questions

1. What is a cost centre?
2. What do you think is the principle behind the way general costs are spread over the cost centres?
3. How are the overhead costs spent directly by each cost centre identified?

1. A cost centre is a location (e.g. Grinding Department) or a function (e.g. Marketing) against which overhead costs can be identified. They can be thought of as a pigeon-hole used to accumulate overhead costs.

2. The process by which common costs are spread over cost centres is known as cost apportionment. The general principle is that cost centres are charged with costs in proportion to the benefit received. Various bases are used depending on the cost concerned. As an example, the total cost of Rates paid by Precision Tool will be spread over individual cost centres on the basis of their floor area. Thus a cost centre twice as large as another will be charged with twice the amount of Rates.

3. By the Location Code. It will be recalled that each expenditure is given a two-way code; Type of Expenditure: Location or Use. Each cost centre has a unique code which is used as the means of accumulating the overheads for the cost centre.

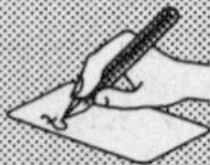

Task 1 *(answer page 180)*

The following information relates to the Overhead Summary in Scenario A.

Cost centres

	Grinding	Fitting	Machining	Heat treatment	Admin	Finance	Marketing
No. of personnel	23	37	18	10	14	6	8
Equipment value '000s	85	26	140	90	35	25	5

The total floor area for Precision Tool is 27,000 sq. feet.

(a) What do you think would be reasonable bases of apportionment for Heating costs, Canteen Deficit, Insurance?

(b) What are the floor areas of each of the 7 cost centres?

(c) Apportion the total costs of Heating, Canteen Deficit and Insurance over the cost centres.

Scenario B **Overhead absorption**

Alan saw that the accumulation of overheads by cost centre depended on the expenditure coding system for specific costs and the methods used for apportioning the common costs.

Margaret explained that the overheads were then charged to individual jobs using a process known as *overhead absorption or overhead recovery*, which could be thought of as the job passing through the various departments gathering overheads as it moved along. She explained that at the beginning of the period an overhead absorption rate per hour (OAR) was estimated for each department and this was used to calculate the overhead charge for each job passing through the department. Depending on the nature of the department, either labour hours or machine hours could be used as a basis. She showed him the estimates for the four production departments she had prepared at the beginning of the period.

	Estimated overheads for period £	Estimated hours for period	Overhead absorption rate (OAR) £
Grinding Dept.	23,500	3,133 labour hours	7.50
Machining Dept.	42,000	4,800 machine hours	8.75
Fitting Dept.	16,950	2,825 labour hours	6.00
Heat Treatment	34,500	3,000 machine hours	11.50

As an example of how these rates were used she showed him the records of two recently completed jobs:

Job No.	Prime cost £	Hours spent in Production Depts. Grinding	Machining	Fitting	Heat treat.
L522	482	12 labour hours	6 machine hours	–	4 machine hours
X913	1,738	–	24 machine hours	42 labour hours	–

Quick answer questions

1. What factors do you think Margaret has to consider when choosing between labour hours or machine hours as the base of the OAR calculation for a particular department?
2. What general objective does overhead recovery seek to achieve?
3. What are the production costs of jobs L522 and X913?

1. The basis chosen is that which most accurately reflects the incidence of overheads in a department. In a department where most overheads are machine related (e.g. depreciation, power, maintenance etc.) then machine hours would be most appropriate. Where there is relatively simple machinery, labour hours would probably be better.

2. Overhead recovery seeks to charge each job with a suitable proportion of the overheads of each department that works on the job. If a job takes longer in a department (i.e. uses up more of its resources) it is clearly fair to charge that job with more overheads than one which is only in the department for a short while.

3. ***Production Costs***

Job L522

			£
Prime Cost			*482.00*
+ Overheads			
		£	
Grinding Dept.	*12 × £7.50 =*	*90.00*	
Machining Dept.	*6 × £8.75 =*	*52.50*	
Heat Treatment	*4 × £11.50 =*	*46.00*	*188.50*
		= Production Cost	*£670.50*

Job X913

			£
Prime Cost			*1738.00*
+ Overheads			
		£	
Machining Dept.	*24 × £8.75 =*	*210*	
Fitting Dept.	*42 × £6.00 =*	*252*	*462.00*
		= Production Cost	*£2200.00*

Task 2 *(answer page 180)*

(a) Find the reasons why Margaret calculates the OAR at the beginning of a period using estimates rather than at the period end when the actual figures would be available.

(b) The Production Costs of Jobs L522 and X913 were £670.50 and £2200.00 respectively. Assuming that at the beginning of the period it was estimated that the total of all non-production overheads would be £50,000 and that the production cost of all jobs in the period would be £200,000, calculate a realistic Total Cost for Jobs L522 and X913.

3.1 Overheads defined

Overheads can be defined thus:

> "Expenditure on labour, materials or services which cannot be economically identified with a specific saleable cost unit." *Terminology* (alternative terms sometimes encountered are *on-cost* or *burden*).

3.2 Overheads build-up

As explained in topic 1 overheads are accumulated by cost centre using a two-way coding system. Expenses directly incurred by a cost centre can be charged direct to it, general expenses (e.g. heating, rates etc) have to be shared out or apportioned over the cost centres using some appropriate basis.

Overheads are just as much part of the costs of the organisation as the direct costs of the product and accordingly overhead cost must be included in the total cost of the product or service. This is done by spreading the overheads of a cost centre over all the products passing through the cost centre. The process by which this is done is called *overhead absorption* or *overhead recovery*. This has the objective of spreading overheads over production in a way which fairly reflects the loading a product or job places on the cost centre.

The usual way this is done is to record the time (in machine or labour hours) that a product is worked on in a cost centre and to multiply these hours by an *overhead absorption rate* (OAR). This gives the amount of overheads to be included in the cost of the product or job or service.

3.3 Overhead absorption rate (OAR)

OAR's are calculated using the overheads of a cost centre and the number of units of the absorption base considered most appropriate, say, labour or machine hours. Because the *actual* amounts of the overheads and the absorption base cannot be known until the end of a period and the OAR is required throughout the period it is normal to use estimated values for both factors and to make what adjustments are necessary later. Thus the OAR for a cost centre is:

$$\textbf{Predetermined OAR for cost centre} = \frac{\textbf{Estimated overheads for cost centre}}{\textbf{Estimated units of absorption base}}$$

Example 1

The assembly cost centre has estimated overheads for period 1 of £75,000. Labour hours are considered the most appropriate basis and it is expected that 12,000 hours will be worked in total during the period.

What is the OAR?

Solution

$$\text{OAR for assembly} = \frac{£75{,}000}{12{,}000} = \textbf{£6.25} \text{ per labour hour.}$$

3.4 How is the OAR used?

The factory or production cost of a cost unit comprises its direct costs (direct material, direct labour and any direct expenses) plus a share of the overheads of each production cost centre involved with the manufacture of the cost unit. The share of overheads is found by using the calculated OAR of the particular cost centre multiplied by the hours spent in the cost centre (assuming that time is considered the most appropriate absorption base).

Example 2

Job no. 525 is one of many jobs that pass through the assembly cost centre during a period. The only work done on job 525 is assembly work and its direct costs are

Direct materials	£65
Direct labour (5 hours @ £4)	£20
Total direct costs	£85

What is the total production cost of job 525 assuming that the Assembly OAR is £6.25 per hour as previously calculated.

Solution

Job 525	**Total production cost**
	£
Direct materials	65
Direct labour (5 × £4)	20
Prime cost	85
+ assembly overheads (5 × £6.25)	31.25
Total production cost	**116.25**

Note that the 5 labour hours are multiplied by the previously calculated OAR to find the total overheads of the job.

However, unlike example 2 most jobs pass through more than one cost centre and gather overheads from each of the cost centre involved in the manufacture of the job. For example:

Example 3

Job 854 is made in two cost centres. Assembly and Finishing, whose overheads absorption rates are £6.25 and £11 per labour hour respectively. The job details are:

		Assembly		**Finishing**
Direct materials		£120		£25
Direct labour	8 hrs @ £4	£32	14 hrs @ £5	£70

What is the production cost of job 854?

Solution

		Total production cost
	£	**£**
Direct materials (£120 + 25)		£145
Direct labour (£32 + 70)		£102
= Prime cost		£247
Overheads		
Assembly 8 × £6.25	£50	
Finishing 14 × £11	£154	£204
Total production cost		**£451**

3.5 Choice of absorption base

There are no hard and fast rules for deciding which is the most appropriate absorption basis; judgement is always necessary. What is required is an absorption base which realistically reflects the characteristics of the given cost centre and which avoids undue anomalies.

It is generally accepted that the time based methods (labour and machine hours) are more likely to reflect the load on a cost centre and one of these should normally be chosen. However, other absorption bases exist; for example, recovery on direct wages or materials or by cost unit, but these alternatives have numerous disadvantages and would rarely be chosen.

The characteristics of the time based methods are given below:

Direct labour hour basis

This is best suited to a labour intensive cost centre where simple (and inexpensive) machinery only is employed. The system is easy to use as the hours taken are normally recorded anyway for wage payment purposes. However as production becomes increasingly mechanised, this method of overhead absorption is likely to be less appropriate in the future.

Machine hour basis

This basis is most appropriate for mechanised cost centres. In such cost centres, overheads are related to machinery and machinery usage (power, maintenance, depreciation and so on) so absorption using a machine hour rate reflects the occurrence of overheads in a reasonably accurate way.

The machine hour OAR of a cost centre is calculated using estimates of the total machine hours and overheads expected in the cost centre, in a similar fashion to the labour hour method described previously.

Period end adjustments and depreciation

Scenario C Period end overhead adjustments

So that Alan had the opportunity to see the full overhead cycle, Margaret thought he should deal with the period end adjustments. She explained that because pre-determined overhead recovery rates were used throughout the period, based on estimates, it was unlikely that *absorbed overheads* would be exactly the same as *actual overheads*. She explained that the differences were known as *under-absorbed* or *over-absorbed* overheads and that these figures had to be calculated because the profit for the period was based on actual figures.

She showed him the overhead adjustment summary for the period which had been partly completed.

Precision Tool
Overhead Adjustment Summary For Period X

	Production cost centres				Other cost centres	Total
	Grinding	**Machining**	**Fitting**	**Heat treatment**		
Previously calculated OARs	£7.50 per Lab hr	£8.75 per MC hr	£6.00 per Lab hr	£11.50 per MC hr	25% of production cost	
Actual results						
Actual production cost					£210,000	
Actual hours	3276 Lab hrs	4728 MC hrs	2460 Lab hrs	3030 MC hrs		
Actual overheads	£24,750	£39,260	£15,475	£34,100	£54,750	
Overheads absorbed (under)/over absorption						

Quick answer questions

1. What are under-absorbed overheads; over-absorbed overheads?
2. Why is it necessary to calculate the net amount of over/under absorption?
3. What is the total amount actually spent on overheads by Precision Tool in the period?

1. *Under-absorbed overheads: Where the amount of overheads absorbed by the actual work done, using the pre-determined OARs, is less than actual overheads.*

   Over-absorbed overheads: Where the amount of absorbed overheads is greater than the actual overheads.
2. *Profits are calculated using actual sales and actual costs. The cost of jobs completed during the period so far include the actual prime costs plus an estimated share of overheads based on the predetermined OARs. The period end adjustment using the net under/over recovery is necessary so as to bring the amounts of overheads absorbed into line with the actual overheads spent.*
3. *This is simply the total of the actual overheads spent by each of the cost centres i.e.*

   £24,750 + 39,260 + 15,475 + 34,100 + 54,750 = £168,335

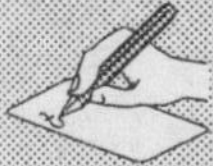

Task 3 *(answer page 180)*

(a) Complete the Overhead Adjustment Summary shown in Scenario C i.e. calculate the overheads absorbed and the (under) over absorption.

(b) Where is the net amount of (under) over absorption taken to in the Accounts?

(c) One of the items included in overheads is Depreciation. How does Depreciation differ from other overhead items and how is it calculated?

(d) What are the key differences between conventional absorption costing and Activity Based Costing?

3.6 Under or over absorption or overheads

Each job or cost unit passing through a cost centre absorbs, through the OAR system, some of the overheads of the cost centre. This happens progressively so that at the end of the period the total amount of overheads absorbed by production is known. Because the predetermined OAR's are based on estimates of production and overheads, invariably the total of absorbed overheads does not agreed with the actual overheads incurred.

If overheads absorbed by production are *greater* than actual overheads, this is known as *over absorption*.

If overheads absorbed by production are *less* than actual overheads, this is known as *under absorption*.

An example follows:

Example 4

Cost centre 210 data for period 8

	Estimated	**Actual**
Overheads	£85,000	£82,605
Machine hours	7,500	7,210
Prime cost		£126,500

The machine hour basis of overhead absorption is considered the most suitable for cost centre 210.

What is the amount of under or over absorbed overheads?

Solution

$$\text{OAR based on machine hours} = \frac{85{,}000}{7{,}500} = £11.33 \text{ per hour}$$

∴ overheads absorbed by actual production = 7,210 hours × £11.33 = **£81,689**

It will be seen that the total of absorbed overheads, £81,689 is less than the actual overheads of £82,605 so there is under-absorption in this instance.

i.e. £82,605 – £81,689 = **£916 under-absorption**

3.7 What happens to under or over absorbed overheads?

It is important to realise that it is actual costs and overheads which determine the final profit. This means that the total of actual costs must be used to find profit and not merely the calculated product cost; which includes actual prime costs plus absorbed overheads based on a predetermined OAR.

Thus the amount of *under absorbed* overheads should be *added* to total costs before profits is calculated and conversely the amount of *over absorbed* overheads should be *subtracted* from total costs. This is illustrated, using the date from Example 4.

Actual prime cost	+	**Absorbed overheads**	=	**Calculated production cost**	+	**Under absorption**	=	**Actual production cost**
£126,500	+	£ 81,689	=	208,189	+	£ 916	=	£ 209,105

↓

To profit calculation

Note: The under absorption has had to be added to the calculated production cost to bring the total up to the actual costs incurred. This may seem to be a long winded way of getting to actual costs but it is necessary because individual job costs are required right through the period and it would be highly inconvenient to have to wait until the end of the period before they could be calculated. Accordingly predetermined OAR's are used, based on estimates, and errors in the estimates are compensated for at the end of the period, using the under or over absorption process described above.

3.8 Absorbing non-production overheads

Many of the overheads of a typical company are incurred outside the production cost centres. They include overheads relating to: administration, selling and distribution, research and development, marketing, advertising, finance and numerous other non-production cost centres.

Naturally these general overheads must be included in the total cost of a product together with the prime cost and production overheads dealt with previously. Because of the difficulty of relating general overheads to individual products the absorption of general overheads is usually done by taking either a percentage of product cost or percentage of sales value. For the same reasons given earlier, predetermined OAR's are used.

Example 5

The general overheads of a firm comprise those relating to administration, marketing and research. For period 6 the following estimates were made:

Estimated total general overheads	£45,000
Estimated total production costs	£75,000

(a) what is the general overhead absorption rate assuming that absorption based on production cost is considered the most appropriate?

(b) what amount of general overheads would be absorbed by the following two jobs?

Job no.	**Total production cost**
168	£6,050
243	£2,900

Solution

(a) $$\text{general OAR} = \frac{\text{Estimated total general overheads}}{\text{Estimated total production costs}}\ \%$$

$$\frac{45{,}000}{75{,}000}\ \% = \mathbf{60\%}$$

(b)

		Job 168		**Job 243**
		£		**£**
Production cost		6,050		2, 900
General overhead	(60% of 6,050)	3,630	(60% of 2,900)	1,740
Total cost		9,680		4,640

3.9 Depreciation explained

Most assets decline in value due to wear and the passage of time. This decline in value is known as *depreciation* and the amount of depreciation in a period is included as part of the overheads of the period.

Although depreciation is an important item of overheads it differs from other overhead costs in two ways. Firstly, the amount of depreciation to be charged in a period is decided by the organisation itself. With most other forms of overheads, for example, electricity, telephones, rates and so on, the organisation has little or no control over the amount charged. Secondly, a typical overhead cost entails money being paid out from the organisation. Examples include: salaries, electricity, insurance and so on. In contrast, a depreciation charge does not cause a movement of cash; the charge being a book-keeping entry only. This does not mean that depreciation is unimportant. It would be unrealistic not to include the cost of expensive machinery and buildings in the cost of a product and depreciation is the most practical way this can be done.

3.10 Depreciation methods

Numerous methods exist but they can be grouped in two categories:

(a) where depreciation is based on *time*;

(b) where depreciation is based on *volume of production*.

Two of the more important time based methods; straight line and reducing balance, and the production unit method based on volume are described below.

Straight line depreciation

This method, also known as the equal instalment method, reduces the value of an asset by an equal amount each year thus:

$$\text{Depreciation charge per year} = \frac{\text{Asset cost}}{\text{Estimated life in years}}$$

Example 6

A welding machine costs £25,000 and is expected to last 10 years. What is the depreciation charge per year?

Solution

$$\text{Depreciation per year} = \frac{25{,}000}{10} = \textbf{£2,500 per year}$$

This means that £2,500 per year would be included in the overheads of the cost centre in which the welding machine was situated.

Each year the asset is assumed to decline in value by the amount of the calculated depreciation. Thus, the welding machine in example 6 would have a net value (known as the written down value or WDV) at the end of year 1 of £25,000 – 2,500 = £22,500.

At the end of year 2 the written down value would be £22,500 – 2,500 = £20,000 and so on. Thus at the end of 10 years, in each of which £2,500 had been charged, the welding machine would have a written down value of zero.

Reducing balance method

Using this method a *percentage of the written down value* is charged as depreciation each year. The percentage chosen would be sufficient so that, over the life of the asset, its original cost will be reduced approximately to zero.

The effect of the reducing balance method is that *decreasing amounts* of depreciation are charged each year, as compared with the straight tine method where *equal amounts* are charged each year.

> *Example 7*
>
> A boiler costs £30,000 and is expected to last 10 years. The firm uses the reducing balance method of depreciation and a rate of 40% is normal for this type of asset.
>
> What is the depreciation charge for each of the first 5 years?

Solution		£	
Year 1	Cost	30,000	
	40% of 30,000	12,000	Year 1 depreciation charge
		18,000	Written down value
Year 2	40% of 18,000	7,200	Year 2 depreciation charge
		10,800	Written down value
Year 3	40% of 10,800	4,320	Year 3 depreciation charge
		6,480	Written down value
Year 4	40% of 6,480	2,592	Year 4 depreciation charge
		3,888	Written down value
Year 5	40% of 3,888	1,555	Year 5 depreciation charge
		2,333	Written down value

And so on.

Note how the yearly depreciation declines each year, from £12,000 in year 1 to £1,555 in year 5. Naturally the process continues over the life of the asset and the reducing balance method thus produces heavy charges in the early years and much lighter charges later on.

One possible criticism of the two depreciation methods described above is that they do not take account of the amount of production in a year; the same depreciation being charged whether production is low or high or indeed non-existent. This is considered incorrect for certain types of assets, especially those directly concerned with production where volumes can easily be recorded. In such circumstances the production unit method of depreciation can be used.

Production unit method of depreciation

This method bases depreciation on the production volume in a period using a previously calculated depreciation charge per unit thus:

$$\text{Depreciation charge per unit} = \frac{\text{Asset cost}}{\text{estimated units of production over life of asset}}$$

> *Example 8*
>
> A blanking machine costs £25,000 and it is estimated that it can produce 1,000,000 parts over its lifetime. During the first two years, 110,000 and 155,000 parts respectively were produced.
>
> What is the depreciation rate per unit?
> What are the depreciation charges for years 1 and 2?

Solution

$$\text{Depreciation rate per unit} = \frac{£25{,}000}{1{,}000{,}000} = 2.5\text{p.}$$

Depreciation charges

Year 1	110,000 × 2.5p = **£2,750**
Year 2	155,000 × 2.5p = **£3,875**

Absorption costing and Activity Based Costing

3.11 Absorption costing

Absorption costing or total absorption costing is the name given to the method of finding product costs that have been described so far in this topic i.e. where total overheads are absorbed into production based on the volume of production (expressed in labour or machine hours). This is the traditional method and is still the most common so it must be thoroughly understood.

Alternative methods of costing exist. These include *marginal costing* (dealt with in topic 10) and *activity based costing* described below.

3.12 Activity based costing (ABC)

ABC is a recent approach to product costing and is an attempt to reflect more accurately in product costs those activities which influence the level of overheads. Traditionally, all overheads were absorbed based on production volume. This means that high volume, standardised products would be charged with most of the overheads and short run production with lower overheads in spite of the fact that short run production causes more set-ups, re-tooling, production planning and thereby generates more support overhead costs. Thus, traditional volume related overhead absorption tends to *overcost* products made in *long runs* and *undercost* products made in *short runs*.

ABC seeks to overcome this problem by relating support overheads to products, not by production volume, but by a number of specific factors known as *cost drivers*. A cost driver is an activity which causes cost. Table 3.1 shows some typical cost drivers and the costs which the activity influences (or drives).

Examples of cost drivers	*Typical costs influenced or 'driven' by cost driver*
Number of production runs	Inspection, production planning & scheduling, set-up, tooling
Number of despatches	Despatch department, invoicing etc
Number of purchase orders	Purchasing department, stock-holding etc
Number of engineering changes	Technical department, production planning, stock-holding etc

ABC seeks to deal with the fact that many overhead costs vary not with the *volume* of items produced but with the *range* of the items, i.e. the complexity of the production processes. Using ABC a product cost consists of its direct costs plus a share of overheads related to the number of cost driver units the production causes.

Figure 3.1 contrasts traditional volume based product costing and costing based on activity usage.

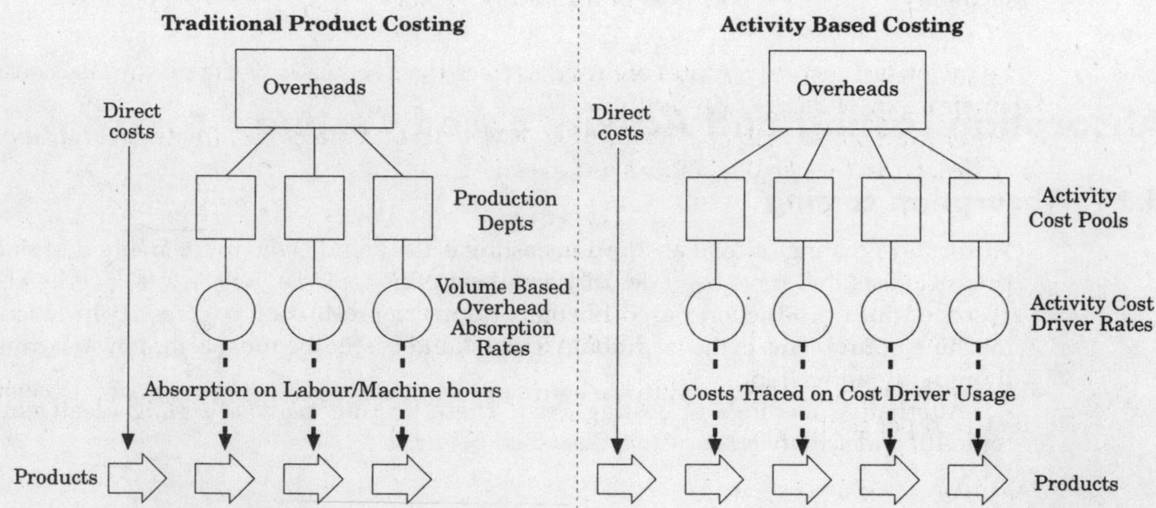

Figure 3.1

It will be seen from the diagrams that there are considerable similarities between the two systems. In both systems, direct costs go straight to the product and overheads are charged or 'traced' to the product using a two stage process. It is in the second stage that differences arise.

In a traditional system overheads are charged to products using at the most two absorption bases (labour hours and/or machine hours). On the other hand, ABC systems use many drivers as absorption bases (e.g. number of set-ups, number of orders, number of despatches and so on). Because of this, ABC cost driver rates should produce more realistic product costs, especially where support overheads are high.

Example of cost driver calculation and use

A firm using ABC has separated its main support activities into cost pools and has selected appropriate cost drivers thus:

Cost pool	*Cost driver*
Set-up	No of set-ups
Quality control	No of inspections
Material procurement	No of orders
Engineering design	No of design drawings
Machinery	No of machine hours

Budgeted overheads and cost driver volumes

Cost pool	Budgeted overheads £'000	Cost driver	Budgeted volume	Cost driver rates
Set-up	110	No of set-ups	4,500	$\frac{£110,000}{4,500}$ = £24.4 per set-up
Quality control	185	No of inspections	7,000	$\frac{£185,000}{7,000}$ = £26.4 per inspection
Material procurement	420	No of orders	385	$\frac{£420,000}{385}$ = £1,091 per order
Eng. design	292	No of drawings	550	$\frac{£292,000}{550}$ = £531 per drawing
Machinery	360	No of MC hours	100,000	$\frac{£360,000}{100,000}$ = £3.6 per hour

The calculated cost driver rates are used to trace the overheads to the products according to their usage of the cost drivers.

For example a batch of 3,500 Part No AX2950 had a direct cost (material and labour) of £155,250 and usage of activities as follows.

213 set-ups
391 inspections
23 purchase orders
17 engineering drawings
3,810 machine hours

What overheads will be traced to the batch and what is the production cost of the batch in total and per unit?

Solution

Batch Production Cost – 3,500 Part No Ax2950

	£	£
Direct costs		155,250
Plus overheads:		
213 set-ups @ £24.4	5,197	
391 inspections @ £26.4	10,322	
23 orders @ £1,091	25,093	
17 drawings @ £531	9,027	
3,810 MC hours @ £3.6	13,716	63,355
	Total batch cost	218,605

Unit cost = $\frac{£218,605}{3,500}$ = **£62.46 each**

The principles of ABC are equally applicable to service industries and the technique has been used successfully in hospitals, banks and elsewhere.

Key point summary

- Overhead absorption shares the overheads over production.
- Overhead absorption rates for a cost centre are calculated thus

$$\text{OAR} = \frac{\text{Estimated overhead}}{\text{estimated units of absorption base}}$$

- Overhead absorption based on labour or machine hours is generally preferred.
- If absorbed overheads are more than actual overheads there is over-absorption; if less, then there is under-absorption.
- The under or over absorption calculation is needed to bring absorbed overheads in line with actual overheads.
- Non-production overheads are usually absorbed either as a percentage of production cost or sales value.
- Depreciation is the decline in value of an asset and is an important part of overheads.
- Important depreciation methods include: straight line, reducing balance, and production unit.
- Activity based costing relates support overheads, not to production volume, but to cost drivers, i.e. activities which cause cost.

Need more detail or want to pursue a topic further?

Overheads	See *Costing*, T Lucey, DP Publications.
Activity Based Costing	See *Management Accounting*, T Lucey, DP Publications; Professional Accounting Journals e.g. *Management Accounting*, *Accountancy* etc. for articles.

Costing methods: job, batch, contract and process costing

Costing methods are introduced and the key features of order costing and continuous costing are explained. Job, batch and contract costing are described and exemplified. Process costing, equivalent units and joint products are described.

Contents

Job, batch and contract costing

Scenario A Job and batch costing

After spending his first month at Precision Tool, Alan returned to Group Headquarters to find out what he had to do next.

In discussion with John Wellington, the Group Management Accountant, Alan explained that although he felt he now had a good grasp of CMA basics, as applied to a Jobbing firm, he wanted to contrast the methods he had seen with those used by other manufacturers.

John thought this an excellent idea and explained that although the methods used to cost production had to be tailored to suit the type of production, certain principles were universal. These included the two way coding of expenditure, cost analysis into direct and indirect costs and so on. John explained that the major sub-division of costing methods was into Order Costing and Continuous Costing. Order Costing was used where the work consisted of separate jobs or contracts which generally were different from one another. On the other hand continuous costing was used to find the average cost for a number of identical cost units.

Alan recognised that the Job Costing system he had seen at Precision Tool was an example of Order Costing and asked John if there were other types of Order Costing. John explained that there was also Batch Costing and Contract Costing.

As an example of Batch Costing he showed Alan some figures he was looking at from Mordern Engineering, one of the group of companies. This company made control panels to customers' specifications in quantities ranging from 50 to several thousand. Mordern had just completed an order for 300 control panels for a Local Authority and the following costs had been recorded.

Batch No. 948 for 300 Control Panels

	£
Materials	
Steel	847
Components	2,948
Printed circuits	1,400
Labour	
Fabrication	985
Assembly	1,703
Testing	770
Overheads	
Fabrication	2,810
Assembly	4,600
Testing	950
General admin.	3,840

Quick answer questions

1. How does Batch Costing differ from Job Costing?
2. What is the Prime Cost and Total Cost of Batch No. 948?
3. What is the cost per control panel and the profit per panel if the selling price is £95 each?

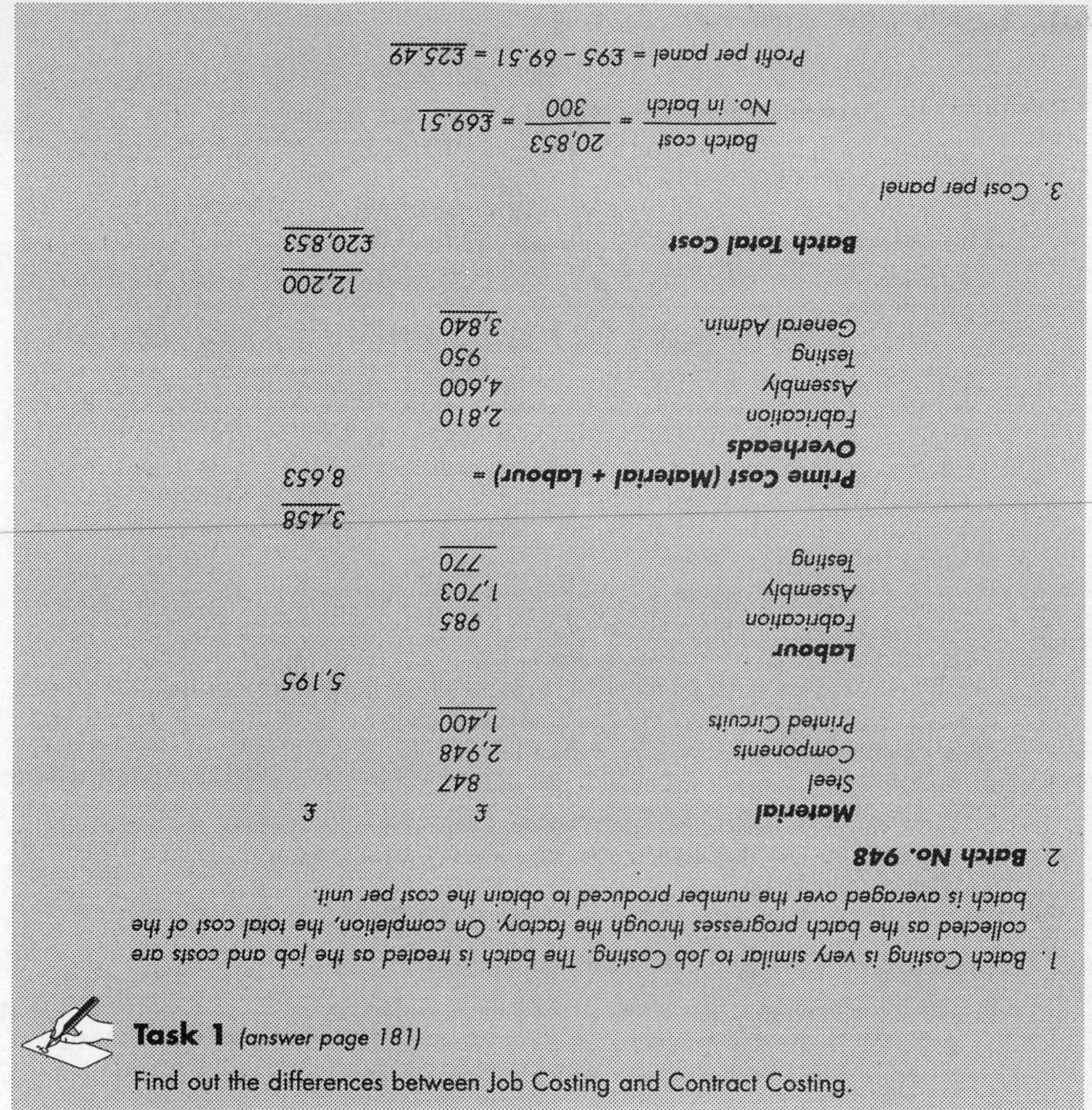

Task 1 *(answer page 181)*

Find out the differences between Job Costing and Contract Costing.

4.1 Costing methods introduced

It is important that the method of costing suits the way goods are manufactured or services provided. What suits a refrigerator manufacturer is unlikely to suit an oil refinery or a local authority or vice versa.

There are two broad categories of costing methods; *order costing* and *continuous costing*.

Order costing is used where the work consists of separate jobs or contracts which generally are different from one another. This type of costing would typically be used by contractors, builders, jobbing engineers, accountancy firms, garages and so on. The cost unit is the job or contract and the costing system shows the profit or loss on individual jobs or contracts.

Continuous costing seeks to find the average cost per unit during a period for a number of identical cost units. The key feature is the presence of a continuous series of processes or operations producing identical or near identical products or services. Continuous costing can be used in any form of process industry, for example, oil refining, food and drink manufacture, mining and so on. It can also be applied to suitable service industries, for example, the provision of meals, hamburgers and so on in fast food outlets.

These categories and their main sub-divisions are shown in figure 4.1.

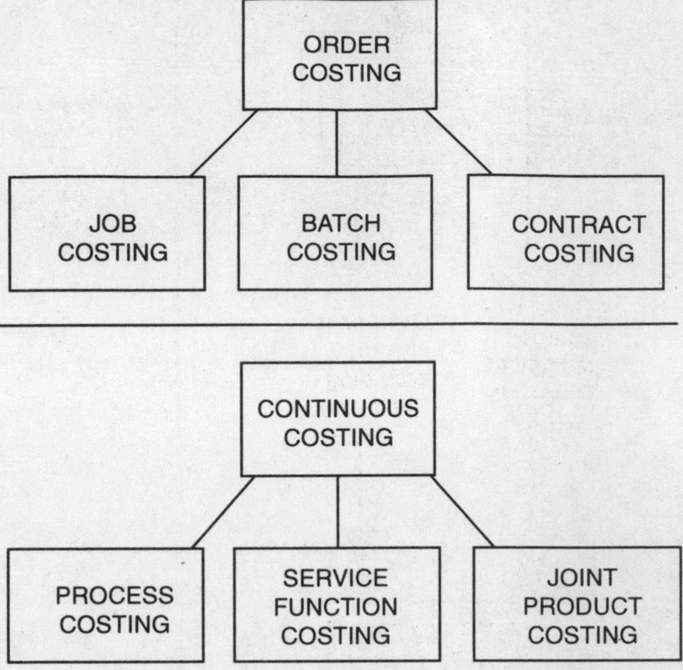

Figure 4.1 Categories of costing methods

Order costing is dealt with in detail first and then continuous costing, but first a key difference in the way that the cost elements (material, labour and overheads) are dealt with, must be understood.

4.2 Cost elements in order and continuous costing

Using continuous costing *all* costs, i.e. labour, materials and overheads, are charged to a cost centre then the total is divided equally amongst the cost units produced. This simple, one stage procedure is possible because identical cost units are being produced.

This differs from order costing where only direct materials and labour can be charged directly to the cost unit. Overheads must be charged first to cost centres then spread over the cost units by the absorption process.

This procedure is necessary because the cost units (i.e. jobs, batches and contracts) are all different. Accordingly the individual amounts of materials and labour in the jobs and the varying times spent producing them must be reflected in their cost.

This difference is summarised in figure 4.2.

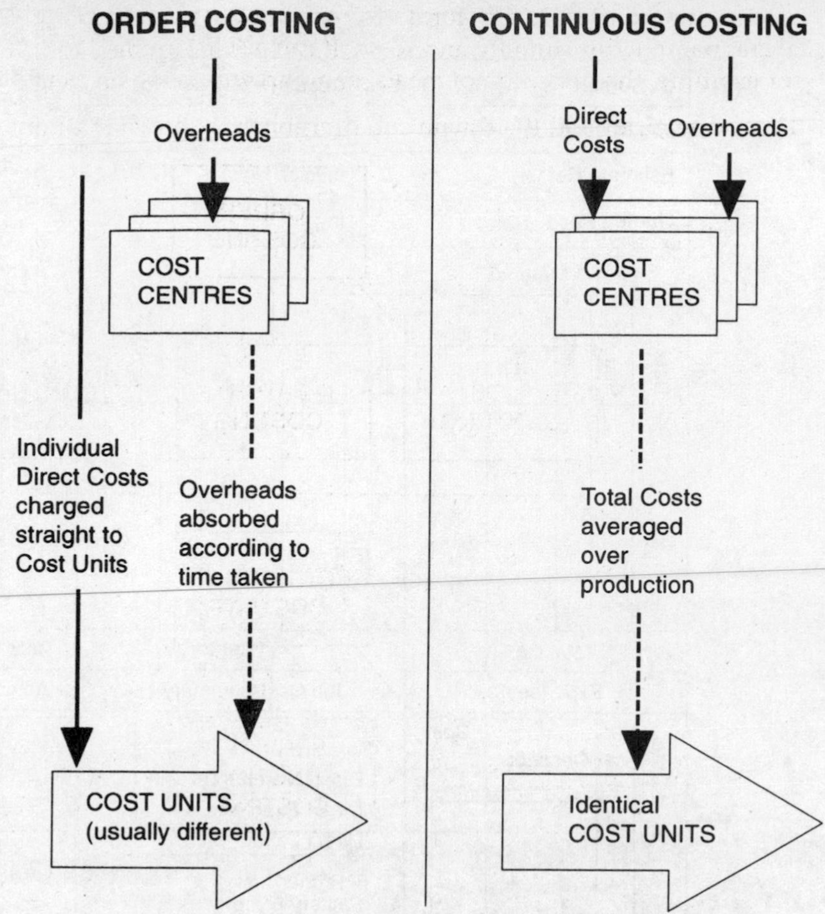

Figure 4.2 Order and continuous costing compared

Order costing can be sub-divided into job costing, batch costing and contract costing.

4.3 Job costing

The main objective is to charge all costs incurred to the particular job. This is done by creating a job card (or equivalent entry on a computer file) for every job; each of which is given its own number.

The following information is recorded on the job card:

- Actual labour times and grades/rates of pay
- Actual issues of material, with quantities and prices
- Actual time spent in each production cost centre
- Actual direct expenses incurred, e.g. special tool equipment hire
- Absorbed production overhead (this is calculated by using the labour or machine hours times the appropriate overhead absorption rate)

When a job is finished its job card is completed by adding to production cost an appropriate amount of general overheads (e.g. selling, administration, finance and so on). This gives total cost which enables the profit or loss on the job to be calculated.

An example of a job card is shown in figure 4.3.

JOB COST CARD		Job No.
Customer	Customer's Order No.	Start Date
Job Description		Delivery Date
Estimate Ref.	Invoice No.	
Quoted Price	Invoice Price	Despatch Note No.

Material						Labour							Overheads			
Date	Req. No.	Quantity	Price	Cost £	Cost p	Labour Anal.Ref.	Cost Centre	Hours	Rate	Bonus	Cost £	Cost p	M/c Hours	OAR	Cost £	Cost p
Total C/F						Total C/F							Total C/F			

Expenses					Job Cost Summary	Actual £	Actual p	Estimate £	Estimate p
Date	Ref	Descript.	Cost £	Cost p					
					Direct Material B/F				
					Direct Expenses B/F				
					Direct Labour B/F				
					= Prime Cost Factory Overheads B/F				
					= Factory Cost Selling & Admin. Overheads % on Factory Cost				
					= Total Cost				
					Invoice Price				
					Job Profit/Loss				

Comments

Job Cost Card Completed by ....

Figure 4.3 Typical job cost card

4.4 Batch costing

This is a form of costing used where a quantity of identical articles is manufactured in a batch. In general the procedures for costing batches are very similar to those for costing jobs. The batch would be treated as a job during manufacture and the costs collected as described above. On completion of the batch the cost per unit would be calculated by dividing the total batch cost by the number of good units produced. Batch costing is common in the footwear, clothing, engineering and similar industries.

Example 1 – Job/batch costing

An order for 150 brackets at £45 was received and was manufactured as job no. 875. Job no. 875 passed through three cost centres; blanking, assembly and finishing whose overheads absorption bases and rates were:

Blanking	– machine hour basis OAR	–	£20 per hour
Assembly	– labour hour basis OAR	–	£9 per hour
Finishing	– labour hour basis OAR	–	£12 per hour.

The following production costs and data were recorded:

Direct materials	£630		
Labour	80 hours	blanking at	£5.50 per hour
	140 hours	assembly at	£4.00 per hour
	60 hours	finishing at	£4.50 per hour.

40 machine hours were recorded in blanking and general administration overheads are absorbed at 10% of total product cost.

Calculate the total cost of the batch, the unit total cost and the profit per unit.

Solution

Total cost job no. 875

		£	£
Direct material			630
Direct labour			
Blanking	80 × £5.50	440	
Assembly	140 × £4.00	560	
Finishing	60 × £4.50	270	
			1,270
Prime cost			1,900
Production overhead absorption			
Blanking	40 × £20	800	
	140 × £9	1,260	
	60 × £12	720	
			2,780
Production cost			4,680
+ general overheads (10% × 4,680)			468
Total cost			5,148

$$\text{Cost per unit} = \frac{£5,148}{150} = \mathbf{£34.32}$$

Profit per unit = £45 – 34.32 = **£10.68.**

4.5 Contract costing

Contract costing has many similarities to job costing and is generally used for work which is:

(a) Of relatively long duration (usually longer than a year)

(b) Site based

(c) Frequently of a constructional nature, e.g. bridges, road building and so on.

Because of the self contained nature of most site operations, many costs normally classed as indirect can be considered as direct and charged straight to the contract. Examples include; power usage, site telephones, transportation, supervisory salaries and so on.

Cost control is a problem on many contracts because of their scale and the size of sites. Difficulties include; wastage, pilferage, vandalism, problems of labour control and so on. Good on-site management can help to reduce these problems but there are no perfect solutions.

As with job/batch costing the objective of contract costing is to find the final profit or loss on the completed contract. However, because many contracts last for several years it becomes necessary to consider interim profits and losses as the contract progresses, rather than wait until completion for the final result. This is explained below.

4.6 Interim results on uncompleted contracts

Because of the scale and duration of many contracts it would be misleading if the firm ignored interim assessments of the profits or losses and stock valuations for contracts which are uncompleted at the year end.

The recommendations governing interim assessments are complex and detailed but the main principles are given below:

(a) If it is estimated that an overall contract profit will be made, taking into account costs already incurred and expected future costs to completion, then it is correct to take credit in the current period for a reasonable proportion of the expected total profit.

(b) It a loss is expected for the contract as a whole then this should be provided *in full* in the current period's accounts.

The effect of the above points is that a conservative view is always taken. This is entirely reasonable given the unexpected difficulties which can occur in contract work. Examples include; adverse weather, ground problems, material shortages, labour difficulties and so on. There are several methods of deciding what is a 'reasonable proportion' of total profits and a common way is to obtain an architect's valuation of the work done to date. However, whatever method is used it is important that interim profits are not overstated.

An example follows which illustrates the above principles.

Example 2 – Profit/loss on uncompleted contracts

Apex Developments had two contracts in progress at their financial year end as follows:

	Contract no. 83	**Contract no. 77**
	£'000s	**£'000s**
Contract value	250	186
Costs incurred to date	65	140
Estimated additional costs to final completion	130	55
Architect's value of completed stages	78	150
Cost of completed stages	63	140

What profits or losses, if any, would be included in the current year's accounts in respect of the two contracts?

Solution

Contract no. 83

	£'000s	£'000s
Contract value		250
less costs to date	65	
Estimated costs to completion	130	
		195
Estimated total contract profit		55

As it is estimated that the contract will give an overall profit it is correct to take a reasonable proportion into account in the current period thus:

	£'000s
Architect's value of stages completed	78
less costs of completed stages	63
Profit for current period	15

Thus £15,000 profit from contract no. 83 would be included in the firm's results for the year.

Contract no. 77

	£'000s	£'000s
Contract value		186
less costs to date	140	
Estimated costs to completion	55	
		195
Estimated contract loss		(9)

As an overall loss of £9,000 is expected *all* of this would be taken into account in the current period.

Note that it is the estimated total contract result (in this case, a loss) which determined what is taken into account in the current period not the notional surplus of £10,000 between the architect's valuation and costs incurred (i.e. £150,000 – £140,000)

4.7 Balance sheet entries for uncompleted contracts

A balance sheet can be simply described as a statement of an organisation's assets and liabilities, i.e. what it *owns* and what it *owes*. All the various activities of the organisation result in assets and/or liabilities, including the transactions relating to uncompleted contracts. These transactions include expenditure on the numerous costs (labour, materials and so on) and also the periodic receipt of money from the client when agreed stages are completed; for example, foundations complete, first floor reached and so on. These interim payments are known as *progress payments* and are a normal feature of contract work.

The main principles concerning assets and/or liabilities arising from uncompleted contracts are:

(a) The stock valuation for an uncompleted contract (usually known as work-in-progress or WIP) is the total costs incurred less any costs used in interim profit calculations less foreseeable losses (if any) and payments on account.

(b) Debtors (i.e. someone who owes you money; an asset) arise if progress payments received are less than the agreed sales value of the completed stages.

(c) Creditors (i.e. someone you owe money to: a liability) arise if progress payments are greater than the agreed sales values of completed stages after allowing for any WIP value.

Scenario B **Process costing**

John Wellington thought it was now time Alan gained some experience of continuous costing so he sent Alan to one of the largest Group companies, System Building Products (SBP)

During his initial discussions with Brian Tanner, SBP's Chief Accountant, Alan discovered that the Company manufactured various standardised building products such as rainwater and drainage pipes, building blocks, tiles and so on. Products were made continuously on various production lines using a series of sequential processes. Because of this the method of costing used was known as *process costing*.

Alan realised that this was all very different from Precision Tool where the jobs were unique and were costed accordingly. Brian explained that the major difference between Job and Process Costing was that, in process costing, *all* costs (material, labour and overheads) were gathered by cost centre and then averaged over the number of identical cost units passing through the cost centre. The cost of the output of one cost centre formed the material input to the next process. He explained that process losses were a factor that had to be considered. If losses were at standard levels they were termed *normal process losses* and if they were above or below expectation they were called *abnormal losses* or *abnormal gains*. Normal losses were part of the cost of good production. To illustrate these he showed Alan some data from his records of the plastic mixing process in which a 15% loss was considered normal. The scrap plastic could be sold at 30p per kilo.

Period 1

Input	Good output
Material – 12,500 kgs at £1 kg	10,625 kgs
Labour & Overheads – £3,250	

Period 2

Input	Good output
Material – 14,000 kgs at £1.1 kg	11,600 kgs
Labour & Overheads – £6,200	

Period 3

Input	Good output
Material – 8,700 kgs at £1.05 kg	7,550 kgs
Labour & Overheads – £2,950	

Quick answer questions

1. Why is it reasonable to average all costs (material, labour and overheads) over production at SBP yet not possible at Precision Tool?
2. How many kilograms of scrap were there in Periods 1, 2 and 3?
3. Calculate whether losses in the three periods were; as expected or above or below expectations.

1. All costs can be averaged over production in SBP because identical products are made. In job costing as at Precision Tool, jobs are individual and different and so incur differing material, labour and overhead costs so averaging is not possible.

2.

	Input	-	Output	=	Scrap
Period 1	12,500	-	10,625	=	1,875 kgs
Period 2	14,000	-	11,600	=	2,400 kgs
Period 3	8,700	-	7,550	=	1,150 kgs

3. $\frac{\text{Scrap}}{\text{Input}}$ = % Loss

Period 1 $\frac{1,875}{12,500}$ = 15% i.e. Normal loss

Period 2 $\frac{2,400}{14,000}$ = 17.14% i.e. Greater than normal = Abnormal loss of 2.14%

Period 3 $\frac{1,150}{8,700}$ = 13.22% i.e. Less than normal = Abnormal gain of 1.78%

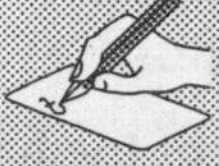

Task 2 *(answer page 181)*

Calculate the cost of good production per kilo for Periods 1, 2 and 3 from the data in Scenario B.

Continuous costing

Continuous costing is used where identical or near identical cost units are produced. All costs can thus be averaged over production, greatly simplifying the costing and recording systems required. There are three sub-divisions of continuous costing; service costing, process costing and joint product costing, all of which are dealt with in this Topic.

4.8 Service costing

Service costing is concerned with the costs of *services* provided, not items of production. The services may be for external sale, eg. public road, rail and air transport, hotel accommodation, restaurants, power generation and so on. Alternatively, the services may be those provided within an organisation. Examples include; canteen facilities, libraries, stores and so on. The costing of internal services is necessary where the organisation uses an internal pricing system and also as a way of providing information to management about comparative costs and efficiency.

Cost units for service costing

A particular difficulty is to define a cost unit that represents a suitable measure of the service provided. Frequently, a composite cost unit is considered to be the most useful. For example, a hotel may use 'occupied bed-night' as an appropriate unit for cost ascertainment and cost control.

Typical cost units used in service costing are shown below:

Service	Possible cost units
Hospitals	Patient-days, number of operations
Transport	Tonne-miles, Passenger-miles, miles travelled
Electricity	Kilowatt-hours
Colleges	Full time equivalent student.

Whatever unit is used the cost per unit is found thus:

$$\text{Cost per service unit} = \frac{\text{Total costs per period}}{\text{No. of service units supplied in the period}}$$

4.9 Process costing

This method of costing is used where a series of sequential processes produce identical units.

Process costing normally has the following characteristics:

(a) Accumulation of all costs (material, labour and overheads) by process cost centre.

(b) Accurate recording of units and part units produced, and costs incurred by each process.

(c) Averaging the total costs of a process over the total production of that process.

(d) Charging the cost of output of one process as the raw materials input cost of the following process.

Process costing is widely used in industries such as: food manufacture, chemical and drug manufacture, oil refining and so on.

The basis of all process costing systems is shown in Figure 4.4.

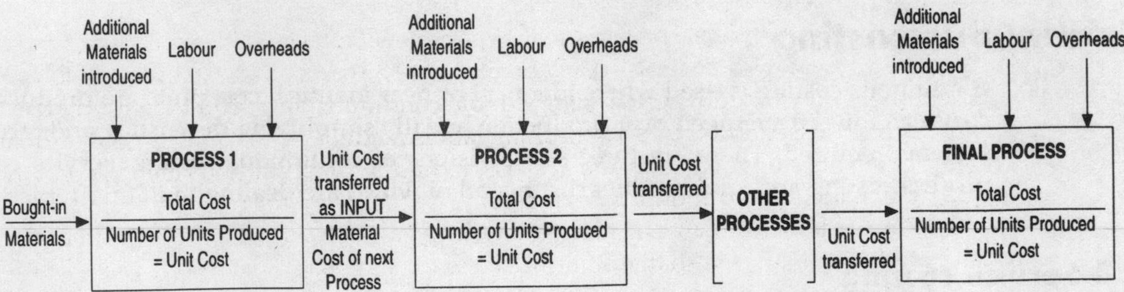

Figure 4.4 Process costing outline

4.10 Process losses

In many process industries the quantity, weight or volume of the process *output* will be less than the quantity, weight or volume of materials *input*. This loss is due to various reasons including, evaporation, swarf, breakage, testing and so on.

If the losses are at standard levels they are termed *normal process losses.* If they are above or below expectations they are known as *abnormal process losses or gains.* It is necessary to find out whether there are normal or abnormal losses or abnormal gains because the costing treatment varies according to the category.

4.11 Normal process losses

These are unavoidable losses arising from the nature of the prodution process so it is logical that the cost of these inevitable losses is included as part of the cost of good production. If any money can be recouped from the sale of the wastage this helps to reduce total costs.

Example 3 – Normal process losses

A chemical process has a normal wastage of 10% which can be sold as scrap at £8 per tonne. In a period the following data were recorded:

Input material 260 tonnes at £45 per tonne, Labour and overheads £5,450

What is the cost per tonne of good production assuming that losses were at normal levels?

Solution

	Tonnes	**£**	
Input material	260	11,700	
Labour & overheads		5,450	
	260	17,150	
Less normal loss	26	208	(income from scrap sales)
= Net good production	234	16,942	

$$\therefore \text{ cost per tonne of good production} = \frac{£16,942}{234} = \mathbf{£72.40}$$

4.12 Abnormal process losses or gains

Abnormal losses are those which are above the level expected. They cannot be foreseen and are due to factors such as; plant breakdowns, inefficient working and so on. Conversely there may be unexpectedly favourable conditions and actual losses may be lower than 'normal' losses and thus an abnormal gain is made. The cost effects of abnormal losses and gains are excluded from the Process account which will thus contain only normal costs (which include normal process losses).

Abnormal losses or gains are costed on the same basis as good production and so, like good production, carry a share of normal losses.

Example 4 – Abnormal process loss

Assume the same data as Example 3 except that actual good production is 229 tonnes. Calculate the abnormal loss and show the cost calculations for the process.

Solution

Abnormal loss = Actual Loss – Normal Loss
= (260 – 229) – (10% of 260)
= 31 – 26
= **5 tonnes**

Cost calculations for process

	Tonnes	£	
Input material	260	11,700	
Labour & overheads		5,450	
	260	17,150	
less normal loss	26	208	
less abnormal loss	5	362	*Note 1*
= Net good production	**229**	**16,580**	*Note 2*

Note 1

The 5 tonnes abnormal loss is costed at the net cost of good production, £72.40 per tonne, ie. 5 × £72.40 = £362.

The 5 tonnes of abnormal loss can also be sold as scrap for £8 per tonne so that the net cost of the abnormal loss is £322 (£362 – 40). This will be charged to the firm's profit and loss account.

Note 2

The net output of the process is 229 tonnes at £72.40, ie. £16,580. This becomes the material input to the next process. The effect of the above is that only normal costs remain in the process account even though losses are greater than normal.

Example 5 – Abnormal process gain

Assume the same data as Example 3 except that actual good production is 236 tonnes. Calculate the abnormal gain and shown the cost calculations for the process.

Solution

Abnormal gain = Normal Loss – Actual Loss
= (10% of 260) – (260 – 236)
= 26 – 24
= **2 tonnes**

Cost calculations for process

	Tonnes	£	
Input material	260	11,700	
Labour & overheads		5,450	
Abnormal gain	2	145	*Note 1*
	262	17,295	
less Normal loss	26	208	
= Net good production	**236**	**17,087**	*Note 2*

Note 1

The 2 tonnes of abnormal gain are costed at the net cost of good production £72.40, ie. 2 × £72.40 = £145 (rounded).

Because of the 2 tonnes abnormal gain there were only 24 tonnes of scrap (instead of the 'normal' 26 tonnes) available for sale. Thus the benefit of £145 from the abnormal gain must be reduced by £16 (2 × £8), the amount of scrap sales lost, before the firm's Profit and Loss account is credited.

Note 2

The net output of the process is 236 tonnes at £72.40, ie. £17,087 (rounded). This becomes the material input to the next process. As previously, only normal costs remain in the process account even though losses are less than normal.

Scenario C Equivalent units in process costing

Alan saw that, in some ways, Process Costing was simpler than Job Costing and asked Brian if there were any other complications. Brian said a recurring one was to allow for the work-in-progress (WIP) at the end of each period in the product cost calculations. Obviously at the end of a period some units may be only partly complete and in order to spread the process costs fairly over all production (both fully and partly complete) it is necessary to make an assessment of the work content of the WIP. In this way the process costs would be spread over the total equivalent production.

For example, assume that production in a period was 4,000 fully complete units and 300 partly complete and it was estimated that the partly complete units were 80% complete. The total equivalent production would be:

4,000 + 80% of 300 = 4,240 equivalent units.

The total costs would be divided by 4,240 to obtain the cost per unit. Brian explained that it was sometimes necessary to consider the degree of completion of the individual cost elements of the WIP, i.e. the material, labour and overheads, rather than just the cost units as a whole.

A further problem with costing process manufacture, Brian explained, was when a process produced two or more different products simultaneously. These were known as joint products. An example at SBP was the stone treatment process which, simultaneously, produced aggregate used in the manufacture of building blocks and enriched slurry used in tile manufacture. The point at which the joint products become identifiable was known as the 'split-off point' and the main costing problem was to share out the process costs over the joint products. Brian explained that there were two possible methods: the physical unit method and the sales value method. He stressed that neither was more accurate or more correct than the other; both were merely conventions. SBP used the physical unit method which simply meant that costs were shared in proportion to the weight (or numbers) of output.

Brian showed Alan the results of the Stone Treatment Process for the last period:

Total process costs	£26,500
Output	3,850 tonnes of aggregate
	6,750 tonnes of enriched slurry

Quick answer questions

1. It is pointed out in the Scenario that the equivalent units in the WIP must be included in the calculation of product cost per unit. In what circumstances do you think the WIP could be ignored?
2. Why do you think that it is not possible to say which of the joint cost apportionment methods is more correct that the other?
3. What are the product costs of aggregate and enriched slurry using the physical unit method of apportionment.

1. The WIP could be ignored in the product cost calculations if; (a) it was of an insignificant amount and (b) it was constant from period to period.
2. If a common process produces two or more joint products it is not possible to find out what actual share of the common costs each product should bear. All that is possible is to use an arbitrary system or convention to share the common costs between the joint products.
3. Total output = 3,850 + 6,750 = 10,600 tonnes

$$\therefore \text{ cost per tonne} = \frac{26{,}500}{10{,}600} = £2.5 \text{ per tonne}$$

Note that even though the products are different they are deemed to have the same unit costs This means that costs of £9,625 (i.e. £2.5 × 3,850) will be transferred to the Building Block process and £16,875 (i.e. £2.5 × 6,750) to Tile manufacture representing input material costs.

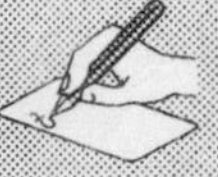

Task 3 *(answer page 181)*

What would be the joint cost apportionment of the 3850 tonnes of aggregate and 6750 tonnes of slurry if their selling prices were £4 per tonne and £2 respectively and the sales value method of apportionment was used?

4.13 Equivalent units in process costing

At the end of a period it is quite normal for there to be some units which are only partly complete. It is clear that some of the process costs are attributable to these units as well as to those that have been fully completed. In order to spread total process costs fairly over both part finished and fully complete units it is necessary to calculate the number of equivalent units contained in the partly finished units. The number of equivalent units is the number of equivalent fully complete units which the partly complete units (i.e. the WIP) represent.

For example, assume that production was 3,400 complete units and 800 partly complete units. The partly complete units were deemed to be 75% complete.

$$\begin{aligned} \text{Total equivalent production} &= \text{Completed units + equivalent units in WIP} \\ &= 3{,}400 + \tfrac{3}{4}(800) \\ &= 3{,}400 + 600 \\ &= \mathbf{4{,}000} \end{aligned}$$

The total costs for the period would then be spread over the total equivalent production.

$$\text{i.e. cost per unit} = \frac{\text{Total costs}}{\text{Total equivalent production in units}}$$

Equivalent units and cost elements

On occasions, an overall estimate of completion, as described above, is not feasible or desirable and it becomes necessary to consider the percentage completion of the individual cost elements; material, labour and overheads. The same principles are used but each cost element is treated separately and then the individual element costs per unit are added to give the cost of a complete unit. An example follows:

Example 6 – Equivalent units and cost elements

In a period production and cost data were:

Total costs	Material	£12,555
	Labour	£9,208
	Overheads	£6,460
		£28,223

Production was 2,800 complete units and 300 partly complete. The degree of completion of the cost elements of the 300 WIP was as follows:

Materials	80% complete
Labour	60% complete
Overheads	50% complete

Calculate the total equivalent production, cost per complete unit and value of the WIP.

Solution

Cost element	**Equivalent units in WIP**				**Fully complete units**		**Total equivalent production**	**Total costs £**	**Cost per unit £**
Material	300 × 80%	=	240	+	2,800	=	3,040	12,555	4.13
Labour	300 × 60%	=	180	+	2,800	=	2,980	9,208	3.09
Overheads	300 × 50%	=	150	+	2,800	=	2,950	6,460	2.19
								£28,223	£9.41

Value of completed production = 2,800 × £9.41 = £26,348.

∴ Value of WIP = £28,223 – 26,348 = **£1,875**

The value of the WIP can be checked by multiplying each element's cost per unit by the number of equivalent units in the WIP, thus:

Cost element	**Equivalent units in WIP**	**Cost per unit £**	**Value of WIP £**
Material	240	4.13	991
Labour	180	3.09	556
Overheads	150	2.19	328
			£1,875

Remember: Total cost = cost of completed units + cost of WIP.

4.14 Joint products defined

A joint product is the term used when two or more products arise simultaneously during processing. Joint products each have a significant sales value in relation to each other and occur in numerous industries, for example; oil refining (where diesel fuel, petrol, paraffin, lubricants and other joint products arise), mining (different metal ores arise from the crushing process) and so on.

4.15 Joint product costing

Because joint products arise from the nature of the production process it follows that none of the products can be produced separately. The products become separately identifiable at a point known as the 'split off point'. Up to the split-off point all costs incurred are joint costs; after the split-off point, costs can be identified with individual products and are known as 'subsequent' or 'additional processing costs'. This is shown in Figure 4.5.

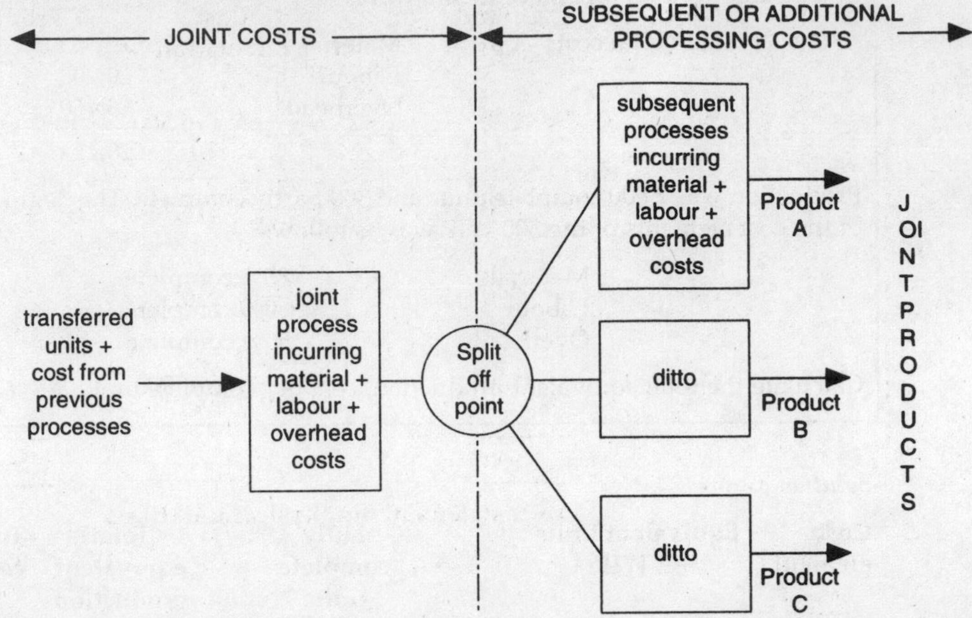

Figure 4.5 Joint product costing

Because subsequent processing costs are readily identifiable with a specific product they do not pose any particular costing problem. For product costing purposes the major problem in joint-product costing is how to divide up the joint costs, ie. those prior to the split-off point, among the joint products in an acceptable manner.

4.16 Dividing up joint costs

The two most common methods of dividing up joint costs are:

(a) *The physical unit method*

The joint costs are shared between the joint products in proportion to the physical weight or volume of the production.

(b) *The sales value method*

The joint costs are shared between the joint products in proportion value of the products. Both methods are illustrated in the following example.

Example 7 – Joint costs

Four joint products, A, B, C and D arise from a process. Total joint costs are £16,500 and outputs, selling prices and sales values are as follows:

A 200kgs sold at £20 kg giving a sales value of £4,000
B 300kgs sold at £14 kg giving a sales value of £4,200
C 500kgs sold at £18 kg giving a sales value of £9,000
D 100kgs sold at £30 kg giving a sales value of £3,000.

Divide up the joint costs and calculate the profit percentage using

(a) The physical unit method and

(b) The sales value method

Solution

Physical unit method

Product	**Output kgs**	**Cost calculation**	**Product cost £**
A	200	$\frac{200}{1,100} \times £16,500$	= 3,000
B	300	$\frac{300}{1,100} \times £16,500$	= 4,500
C	500	$\frac{500}{1,100} \times £16,500$	= 7,500
D	100	$\frac{100}{1,100} \times £16,500$	= 1,500
	1,100		£16,500

Profit statement on physical unit basis

	A	**B**	**C**	**D**	**Total**
	£	£	£	£	£
Sales value	4,000	4,200	9,000	3,000	20,200
less Apportioned costs	3,000	4,500	7,500	1,500	16,500
Profit (loss)	1,000	(300)	1,500	1,500	3,700
Profit (loss) percentage	25%	(7%)	16.7%	50%	18.3%

(The Profit/Loss percentage is calculated in relation to sales, eg. A = $\frac{£1,000}{£4,000}$ = 25%)

Sales value method

Product	**Sales value £**	**Cost calculation**	**Product costs £**
A	4,000	$\frac{4,000}{20,200} \times £16,500$	3,267
B	4,200	$\frac{4,200}{20,200} \times £16,500$	3,431
C	9,000	$\frac{9,000}{20,200} \times £16,500$	7,351
D	3,000	$\frac{3,000}{20,200} \times £16,500$	2,451
	£20,200		16,500

Profit statement on sales value basis

	A	**B**	**C**	**D**	**Total**
	£	£	£	£	£
Sales value	4,000	4,200	9,000	3,000	20,200
less Apportioned costs	3,267	3,431	7,351	2,451	16,500
Profit	733	769	1,649	549	3,700
Profit percentage	18.3%	18.3%	18.3%	18.3%	18.3%

Notes:

(a) It will be seen that the sales value basis produces the same profit percentage for each product unlike the physical unit method where varying profits (or losses) result.

(b) Neither of the two methods is more correct than the other. They are merely two different methods or conventions which produce different results from each other.

(c) The apportioned costs, by either method, can be used for Stock Valuation or for profit calculations but they are not a suitable basis for decision making. This latter point is developed later in the book.

4.17 By-product

Joint products are the main required output of a process but on occasions there are other, small value, incidental products. These are known as *by-products*. For example, in the timber trade, sawdust, bark, off-cuts would be classed as by-products as they arise during processing and have a low value in relation to the main products such as planks, joists and so on.

Any income received from the by-products is deducted from the total process cost before the joint costs are divided amongst the joint products.

Key point summary

- The costing method used must suit the method of manufacture or service provision.
- There are two broad categories of costing methods: order costing and continuous costing.
- Order costing generally deals with dissimilar cost units; continuous costing is used where similar cost units are produced.
- Using continuous costing all costs are averaged over units whereas with order costing a more individual method is necessary.
- Using job costing, individual costs are recorded on the job card to find the profit or loss on the job.
- Batch costing uses similar principles to job costing. The final cost is averaged over the number of good units in the batch.
- Contract costing is typically used for site based work of relatively long duration.
- Where a profit is expected on the contract as a whole a conservative proportion can be taken at interim year ends.
- Where an overall loss is expected this would be provided for in full at the interim stage.
- Balance sheet entries (assets and/or liabilities) arise from uncompleted contracts for WIP valuations and debtors or creditors.
- Service costing can be used either for services provided for sale or for internal services.
- A problem is defining a suitable cost unit and composite units are often used.
- Process costing is used where a series of processes produce identical units.
- All costs are collected by the process cost centre and averaged over the units produced.

- Normal process loss is the expected loss. Where losses differ from those expected, abnormal losses or gains may arise.
- Equivalent units are the number of fully complete units that are equivalent to the partly finished units.
- Joint products arise when two or more main products are produced simultaneously.
- Joint costs may be spread either on the physical unit basis or by the sales value method.
- Apportioned joint costs are used for stock valuations and profit calculations. They are not appropriate for decision making.
- By-products are low value outputs, which arise incidentally during processing.

Need more detail or want to pursue a topic further?

Job, batch and contract costing

Service, process and joint product costing See *Costing*, T. Lucey, DP Publications.

Developing knowledge and skills

You have now dealt with the first four units, and should have a good grasp of the basics of Cost Analysis and Cost Ascertainment.

At this stage, you will find it useful to consolidate and develop your knowledge by attempting some or all of the questions, cases and assignments you will find in Part 1 of Section II. As this is your first reference to Section II you are advised to read the Section II introduction before attempting any of the questions in the Section.

Section II starts on page 191.

Part 2

Planning and control

Change of emphasis

Topics 1 to 4 dealt with cost analysis and cost ascertainment which is largely concerned with the detailed analysis and recording of past events. Important though this is, management also need information about the future particularly to assist them to plan and to control. This means that the emphasis of the CMA System must change so that management are provided with relevant information. This important aspect of CMA is dealt with in this part.

Planning, control and cost behaviour

Planning and control are introduced and the reasons for studying cost behaviour explained. Fixed, variable and semi-variable costs are defined and two methods of analysing semi-variable costs are described.

Contents

What is meant by planning and control?

5.1 Planning and control

Before considering how accounting information can assist management to plan and to control it is useful to examine, in outline, what is meant by planning and control. Planning and control are closely related management tasks and, in practice, are effectively inseparable.

Planning is the managerial process of deciding in advance *what* is to be done and *how* it is to be done. Planning is done on both a formal and informal basis and the planning process uses information of various types from internal and external sources.

Planning can cover the short term and the long term and the planning process can be summarised as

Aims and Means:

Aims These are the goals or results or objectives which should be achieved. These should be stated in some measurable way rather than by vague generalisations.

Means This is the selection of specific actions and activities to achieve the stated objectives. (Note that the activities also include control activities).

Control is an important management task, especially for middle and lower management, and can be defined as the process of ensuring that operations proceed according to plan.

Remember, planning must precede control for it is meaningless to consider any form of control activity without a clear idea of what is to be achieved, ie. the target or plan. In organisations, control is exercised mainly by the use of information in the form of *feedback loops*.

Control, especially at the lower levels of management can be summarised as:

Measure actual results, **compare** results with the plan, **adjust** operations if necessary.

5.2 Long term and short term planning

Long term planning (sometimes known as strategic or corporate planning) involves senior management and is a wide ranging process which uses judgement, information and forecasts from many sources, especially those external to the organisation. Long term planning covers periods from, say, two or three years and upwards, depending on the nature of the business. The details of long term planning are outside the scope of this book but it has been mentioned to emphasise that organisations need to have the discipline and framework of a long term plan so that short term planning can take place.

Short term planning is normally taken to be that dealing with the year ahead. Within this time period one particular accounting technique, that of *budgeting*, is probably the most widely used short term planning and control technique. Budgeting, with its associated technique of budgetary control, is dealt with in detail in Topic 6 but it is first necessary to consider the problems of cost behaviour for these lie at the heart of the budgeting process.

Scenario A Cost behaviour

After Alan had come to grips with Process Costing, Brian Tanner thought it was time he started to consider the other major aspect of CMA; providing information about the future. He explained to Alan that what he had learnt to date, such as cost analysis, product costing and so on dealt with the recording and analysis of *past* events. Clearly, this was essential, but for planning and decision-making the CMA system had also to provide information about the future.

Brian explained that a primary requirement was the need to understand how costs are likely to behave in the future. For example, would costs increase (and by how much) if a second shift was worked? What costs would increase, and by how much, if a production line was converted from a largely manual process to an automatic one? and many, many other similar questions. Brian explained that it was often essential to understand how costs behaved when activity changed. Did a cost remain the same when sales or production increased or decreased or did it vary more or less proportionately?

Considerable guidance on a cost's likely future behaviour could be obtained from studying its past behaviour and, as an example, Brian showed Alan some data on past costs and production for the Dressing Department.

Dressing Department – Past costs

	Period 1	Period 2
Production level	8500 units	9000 units
	£	£
Rates	15,000	15,000
Salaries	43,500	43,500
Material	25,500	27,000
Wages	27,000	28,000
Power	11,000	11,500

Quick answer questions

1. Sales and production are given as examples of measures of 'activity'. Can you think of any other examples of the way activity might be measured?
2. What do you think a cost is called that remains the same when activity changes?, and one that varies proportionately?
3. What types of costs are Rates, Salaries and Materials as shown by the recorded cost levels?

1. The measure of activity chosen should be that which is most appropriate for the department or problem being considered. It could be sales or production as mentioned, it could be a number of hours worked, or miles travelled, or tonnage output, or number of meals served, or number of patient visits; whatever most appropriately measures the activity being studied.

2. A cost that remains the same when activity changes is a fixed cost. One that varies in direct proportion is a variable cost. Some costs vary with activity but not proportionately and these are known as semi-fixed or semi-variable or mixed costs.

3. Rates – fixed cost (because it remains unchanged)
Salaries – fixed cost (because it remains unchanged)
Materials – because the cost alters when activity changes it has a variable element. Without more analysis we cannot tell at this stage whether it is wholly variable or semi-variable.

Task 1 *(answer page 182)*

(a) Estimate what you think the costs of the Dressing Department would be if the production level was 9750 units.

(b) State what assumptions you have used in answering (a).

Cost behaviour

5.3 Why study cost behaviour?

In the forthcoming period more orders may be received, production may increase (or decrease), there may be variations in inflation, shift working may be contemplated, there may be industrial disputes and innumerable other changes could occur. All of these changes will affect the costs of an organisation to a greater or lesser degree. Consequently, management require accurate information from the accounting system about the likely behaviour of costs so that they can make better plans and take more informed decisions.

5.4 Cost behaviour and changes in activity

Although not the only factors, changes in the *level of activity* are major influences on costs. The level of activity is a measure of the amount of work and is expressed in many ways, eg. hours worked, output produced, sales, number of invoices typed, number of enquiries handled and so on.

Alternative terms for level of activity include; volume, throughput and capacity. The behaviour of costs in relation to changes in the level of activity is so important that it forms the basis of the accounting definitions of fixed and variable costs.

5.5 Fixed and variable costs

A *fixed cost* is a cost which tends to remain the same even though the activity level changes. A fixed cost is usually related to time and alternatively may be called a *period cost*. An example of a fixed cost is rates. Once the amount of rates is known, the amount is fixed for the year ahead and remains the same regardless of whether sales, output or any other measure of activity changes.

In contrast, a *variable cost* is one that tends to follow changes in the level of activity. When activity increases, variable costs also increase; when it decreases variable costs also decreases. Direct material is an example of a variable cost; when more units are produced, direct material costs increase in proportion.

Fixed and variable costs are shown in Figure 5.1.

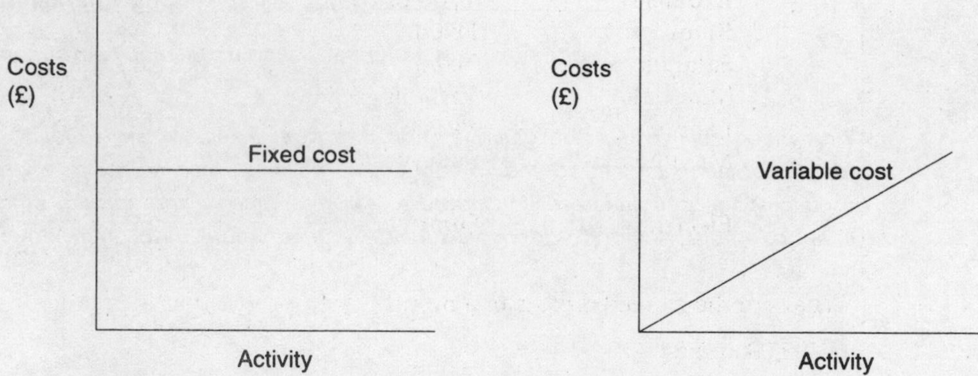

Figure 5.1 Fixed and variable costs

Note that the diagrams and the definitions given above only apply in the short term and, in the case of the variable costs, assume a direct or linear relationship between cost and activity. For example, if activity increases by 20% then variable costs also increase by 20%. In the longer term, conditions and cost relationships do change and a variable cost which is assumed to behave linearly is not always an accurate representation.

Nevertheless, unless there are clear indications to the contrary, students are advised to assume that a cost described as fixed will remain the same when activity changes and that a variable cost will vary linearly, i.e. in direct proportion with activity changes.

Examples of fixed costs are; rent, rates, most types of insurance, salaries, depreciation and so on.

Examples of costs which are frequently variable in nature are; raw materials, royalties, sales commissions, carriage and packing charges and so on. Note that in many examination questions, direct wages are assumed to be variable although, in practice, wages tend not to vary directly with output.

5.6 Semi-variable costs

These are costs which have both fixed and variable elements and thus are only partly affected by changes in activity. A typical example would be telephone costs containing a fixed element, the standing charge, and a variable element, the cost of calls made.

These type of costs may alternatively be called *semi-fixed* or *mixed costs* and can be shown graphically, as in Figure 5.2.

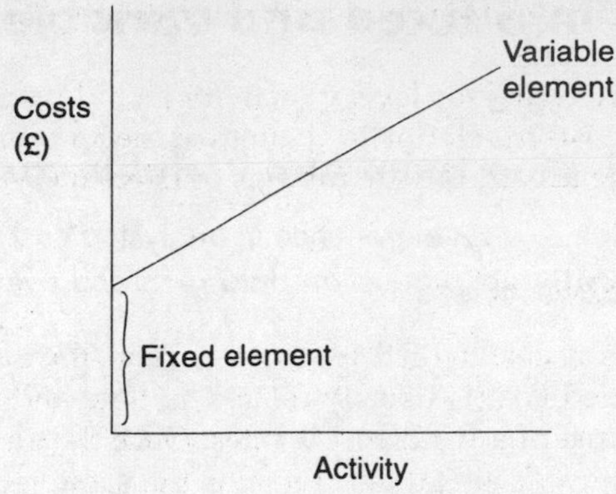

Figure 5.2 Semi-variable cost

Example 1 – Fixed, variable and semi-variable costs

Analysis of a department's costs has produced the following data:

Expense	Type of cost	Cost characteristics
Rates	Fixed	£1,650 per month
Salaries	Fixed	£7,800 per month
Materials	Variable	£2 per unit
Labour	Variable	£18.50 per 10 units
Maintenance	Semi-variable	£1,600 per month plus £35 per 100 units
Electricity	Semi-variable	£150 per month plus £12 per 100 units

What are the expected costs in a month when production is planned for

(a) 2,000 units

(b) 2,400 units

Solution

Expense		2,000 units		2,400 units
		£		£
Rates		1,650		1,650
Salaries		7,800		7,800
Materials	(2,000 × £2)	4,000	(2,400 × £2)	4,800
Labour	(200 × £18.50)	3,700	(240 × £18.50)	4,440
Maintenance	(£1,600 + 20 × £35)	2,300	(1,600 + 24 × £35)	2,440
Electricity	(£150 + 20 × £12)	390	(150 + 24 × £12)	438
Cost estimates:		£19,840		£21,568

5.7 Classifying costs

By studying records of past cost variations against activity it is possible to classify a cost as fixed or variable or semi-variable according to its behaviour. In general, pure fixed costs, ie. those that remain unchanged, and pure variable costs, ie. those that change in direct proportion to activity changes, pose few problems. It is semi-variable costs which cause most difficulties as their fixed and variable elements need to be estimated before cost predictions can be made. In practice, most costs are semi-variable in nature so finding the cost characteristics is a recurring problem.

Analysing costs into fixed and variable

Scenario B Finding fixed and variable costs

In order for Alan to gain experience in analysing cost behaviour Brian provided him with the following cost and production data recorded over several recent periods:

	Period					
	1	2	3	4	5	6
Production (units)	9,850	10,700	10,200	11,450	11,000	11,500
Expenditure	£	£	£	£	£	£
Wages	31,250	34,300	33,650	35,800	33,950	36,720
Telephone	7,100	7,250	6,980	7,475	7,050	7,550
Materials	30,500	31,900	30,750	34,400	33,200	34,150

Brian explained that the objectives were; to identify what types of costs the three examples were, and then to express the cost in a simple expression that could be used for forecasting. He explained that this could be done either, graphically by plotting the expenditure against production or, arithmetically using the difference between the highest and lowest values for each cost item.

Quick answer questions

1. Can you decide, by inspection only, what types of costs are the three examples?
2. List the High/Low values for each cost item.
3. Find the range of expenditure for each cost item.

1. Because each of the costs vary with changes in activity, expressed as production units, it can be seen that none is a fixed cost.
Accordingly they are either variable or semi-variable costs.
However some calculation or graph plotting is necessary to decide whether they are wholly variable or semi-variable.

2. and 3.

Cost Item	High	Low	Range (High-Low)
	£	£	£
Wages	36,720	31,250	5,470
Telephone	7,550	6,980	570
Material	34,400	30,500	3,900

Task 2 *(answer page 182)*

(a) Plot each cost item on a scattergraph and estimate the Fixed and Variable elements.

(b) Calculate the Fixed and Variable elements using the High/Low method.

(c) Contrast the results of (a) & (b) and comment on any differences.

(d) What problems are there in forecasting cost behaviour?

5.8 Finding the fixed and variable elements

In Example 1 the fixed and variable components of the semi-variable costs were given but in practice these have to be estimated and there are a number of ways this can be done. Some of the methods use statistical techniques outside the scope of this book but two useful approaches; the scattergraph and the high/low method, are described below.

5.9 High/low method

This is a simple approximate technique which uses the highest and lowest values contained in a set of data and, arithmetically or graphically, finds the rate of cost change and hence the variable costs. The variable costs are then used to estimate the fixed element of the costs.

Example 2

High/low method

Records have been kept of maintenance expenditure at various activity levels, expressed in machine hours

Machine hours	Costs (£)
502	2,591
471	2,208 *
563	2,411
542	2,316
593	2,405
494	2,280
601	2,663 *
585	2,602
567	2,398
480	2,300

* It will be seen that the high/low cost points are

471 hours at a cost of £2,208
601 hours at a cost of £2,663

This is a range of 130 hours (601–471) and £455 (£2,663–2,208).

From this the rate of cost change, i.e. the variable element of cost, can be found thus:

$$\frac{£455}{130} = \textbf{£3.5 per hour}$$

From this rate of variable cost the fixed cost can be deduced:

Cost at 471 hours	=	£2,208
less variable element		
(471 × £3.5)		£1,648
∴ Fixed costs		**£560**

Maintenance costs are semi-variable and can be summarised as containing a fixed element of £560 plus a variable element of £3.50 for every machine hour worked.

(The above values could also be found by plotting the hours and costs on a graph).

The high/low method only produces approximate results and if the extreme values are unrepresentative the calculated variable and fixed costs will be inaccurate.

5.10 Scattergraph

This is a simple method where past data of costs and activity are plotted on a graph and then, by judgment, a line is drawn representing the average cost level. This line is known as the 'line of best fit'.

The data in Example 2, costs against machine hours, have been plotted on Figure 5.3, together with a possible line of best fit.

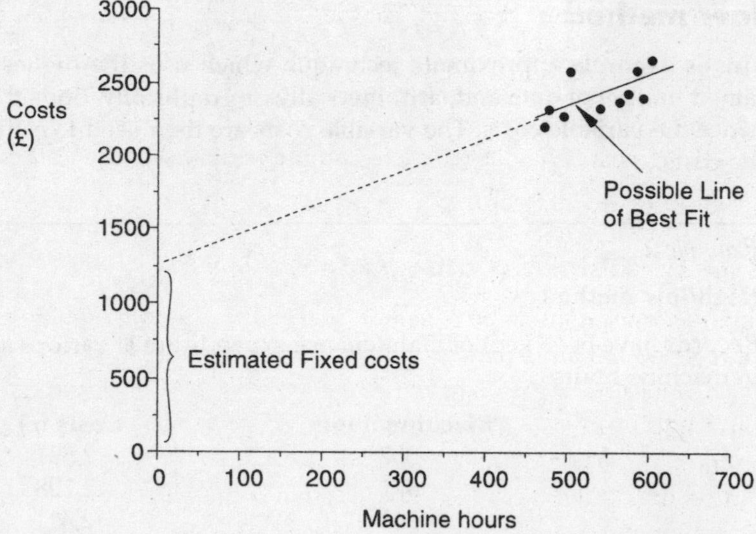

Figure 5.3 Scattergraph of costs and hours

Notes on Figure 5.3

(a) Each cost and activity has been plotted individually.

(b) Using judgement, a line of best fit has been drawn. It is a solid line within the known values and, where it has been extended, it is shown as a dotted line. As judgements will, of course, vary between persons so will the lines of best fit.

(c) Based on the graph the fixed cost estimate is £1,250 and the variable cost is represented by the slope of the line. At zero activity the cost is £1,250 and at 600 hours the cost is £2,650.

$$\text{Variable costs per hour} = \frac{£2{,}650 - 1{,}250}{600} = £2.33.$$

(d) Using the high/low technique maintenance costs were calculated as £560 fixed plus £3.5 per hour variable. Using a scattergraph with the line of best fit shown costs were estimated at £1,250 fixed and £2.33 per hour variable. These estimates differ but this is not surprising and, in practice, further investigation and analysis would take place to improve accuracy.

(e) Instead of using estimation, the line of best fit can be found using the statistical technique of *least squares*. This process is sometimes known as *regression analysis*.

5.11 Problems in forecasting cost behaviour

Although estimates of future costs are often required, there are many problems in making forecasts of cost behaviour (and with any other type of forecasting). Typical of these are the following:

(a) Conditions may change in the future. Many forecasting methods make an analysis of past patterns and behaviour and prepare a forecast for the future based on the past patterns. This may be satisfactory if present trends continue but unsatisfactory if conditions change, as is all too likely.

(b) The typical assumption used in accounting is that all variable costs vary according to the same factor, i.e. the level of activity. This is too simplistic in practice as different costs vary in response to different factors. One cost may vary with machine hours, one with orders received, another according to the number of set-ups and so on.

(c) Costs do not necessarily behave linearly, although this is the typical accounting assumption. Costs may behave in a *curvi-linear* fashion, they may change in *steps*, they may alter at different rates when activity is rising to when it is falling and so on. In short, cost behaviour is more complex than normally assumed.

Scenario C Planning and control

Alan recognised the importance of being able to make reliable estimates of future costs but realised there were many problems. Brian had already told him that future cost estimates were one of the items of CMA information used in planning and control but Alan was not too sure exactly what was meant by planning and control!

Brian explained planning is the vital management task of deciding in advance *what* is to be done, and *how* it is to be done. It was carried out by all levels of management, though naturally the type of planning and the information requirements differed between the various levels. As an example of top level planning he told Alan about a recent exercise where the Board of Directors examined plans to enter the Glazed Tile market which was a new field for SBP. This required information on many, many factors, much of which was long-term and concerned external conditions. In contrast he showed Alan information he had just supplied to one of the Production Supervisors about plans to alter the Building block production line. Much of the information related to internal, short-term factors such as cost changes, capacities, times and so on.

Brian explained that, once a plan was put into effect, it was necessary to have a control process to check whether actual operations were in accordance with the plan. If not, it was necessary to make adjustments to bring operations into line with the plan. This could be summarised as: *measure: compare,* and *adjust* if necessary.

Quick answer questions

1. Apart from financial considerations, what other factors do you think the Board might have to consider about the top level planning example given?
2. Why do you think that internal factors are more important for planning by lower level management?
3. Can you think of an organisational example of the control process?

1. *Typical of the other factors that the Board might consider in deciding whether to enter the Glazed Tile market would be; size/growth of market, competition, likely market share, production capacity required, skills and personnel requirements, impact on existing products and so on.*

   Note how many of these relate to external conditions. This is typical of top level planning.

2. *In general, planning by lower-level is shorter term and works within the framework set by top-management. Operational management seek to maximise the efficiency and use of existing resources. Accordingly they will be interested in lowering costs, improving quality, reducing waste and so on. External factors are, of course, still important but less so than internal ones.*

3. *Numerous examples are possible. A typical one is cost control. A department would have a targeted level of expenditure set (this is known as a budget), actual expenditure is recorded and, if expenditure is above the budget, action is taken to bring expenditure in line with the budget, perhaps by reducing staff or in some other way.*

Task 3 *(answer page 183)*

Part of formal top-level planning is known as SWOT analysis.

Find out what this is and how it is used.

Key point summary

- Planning is deciding what is to be done and how it is to be done, i.e. Aims and Means.
- Control ensures that operations proceed according to plan.
- All changes in the future will cause cost variations.
- A fixed cost is one that does not alter when activity changes.
- A variable cost is one that tends to follow changes in activity. Linearity is usually assumed.
- A semi-variable cost contains both fixed and variable elements.
- The high/low method finds the variable and fixed elements of a cost using the extreme values.
- A scattergraph is formed by plotting costs against activity.
- A line of best fit is the assumed average cost level from which the fixed and variable elements can be found.

Need more detail or want to pursue a topic further?

Planning and control	See *Management Information Systems*, T Lucey, DP Publications.
Cost behaviour	See *Costing*, T Lucey, DP Publications.
Forecasting methods	See *Quantitative Techniques*, T Lucey, D.P Publications

Budgeting

Budgeting and its benefits are introduced and fixed and variable budgets are defined. Budgetary control and budget variances are described and exemplified.

Contents

What is budgeting?

Scenario A Budgeting

Alan's next task at SBP was a difficult one. Brian Tanner explained that a new manager for the Maintenance Department was to start the following week. Unfortunately, he had no experience of budgeting and budgetary control so Brian wanted Alan to brief him about what budgeting was, what it tried to achieve and what was necessary to ensure it worked.

This assignment caused Alan a few problems as he had only a hazy idea himself. He set to work and after some background reading and discussions with existing managers he felt a little happier. He discovered that budgeting was a short-term planning tool with budgets for the year ahead separated into months for control purposes. An agreed plan was made and the expenditures necessary to achieve the plan were estimated. This became the manager's budget for which he was responsible. Progress against budget was monitored monthly by comparing actual expenditure against budgeted expenditure and showing the differences, which Alan found were called variances.

Alan discovered that some budgets had to be meshed with others and this was an important co-ordinating mechanism which avoided gross mis-matches. As an example, he was shown the following partly complete working paper used in developing the Production Budget. From this Alan could see that the Production Budget was directly connected to Budgeted Sales and Budgeted Stock.

(In '000s units)

	Period 1	Period 2	Period 3
Opening Stock	440	?	?
Required Production	?	?	?
Budgeted Sales	2100	2300	2650
Budgeted Closing Stock	750	650	400

He asks Bill Jones, one of the budget holders, what he thought he gained from the budgeting system. Bill said he found it motivating to have a clear target and felt happier that he was involved in drawing up his Department's plans. He also felt it saved some time because he was able to concentrate on the relatively few things not going to plan, as shown by the variances, rather than having to give the same attention to all items.

Quick answer questions

1. Do you think that budget holders should be part of the team that determines their budgets?
2. Do you think that budgeting is purely an accounting technique or are there human factors to be considered?
3. Can you think of a good name for the technique Bill Jones mentions of being able to concentrate on the few items not going to plan?

1. It is of paramount importance that budget holders are involved with development of their own budgets. Budgets must be acceptable to the managers and they will not be acceptable if they are imposed without consultation.

2. There are many vital human factors associated with budgeting e.g. motivation, co-operation, team work and so on. If budgeting is perceived as merely a technical, policing process it will not be successful.

3. The technique is called 'Management by Exception' and budgeting is an excellent example of the technique in practice.

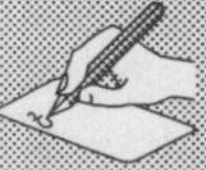

Task 1 *(answer page 183)*

(a) Calculate the budgeted production in Periods 1, 2 and 3 in the partly complete working paper shown in Scenario A.

(b) What is the Master Budget and how do the individual budgets contribute to it?

(c) What is a 'Limiting Factor'?

6.1 Budgets and budgeting introduced

Budgeting is a short-term planning and control technique which is widely used in industry, commerce and government. The budgeting process produces budgets for the forthcoming accounting period, usually a year sub-divided into months. A budget is a financial and/or quantitative expression of a plan of action. Thus a plan is made, for example, produce 10,000 units, then a budget is devised showing the types and amounts of expenditure necessary to produce 10,000 units.

Ideally, budgeting should take place within the framework of a long term plan.

6.2 Benefits of budgeting

These can be summarised as follows:

- *Co-ordination*

  Budgets are prepared for all the departments and functions (i.e. sales, purchasing etc.) of the organisation. Each budget dovetails and inter-relates to other budgets thus helping to ensure the co-ordination of activities throughout the organisation.

- *Communication*

  Budgeting is an important way of communicating the organisations policies and objectives between the levels of management. Each manager who has responsibility for fulfilling a part of the overall plan is involved in budgeting thus communication up and down and across the management structure is improved.

- *Management by exception*

  Budgeting makes it necessary to clarify the responsibilities of each manager who has a budget. This together, with an agreed budget, makes possible management by exception i.e. where a subordinate is given a clearly defined role with the authority to carry out the tasks required. When activities are not proceeding to plan (as expressed in the budget) the variations are reported to a higher level. Thus higher management need only concentrate on exceptions to the plan.

- *Control*

  The process of comparing actual results with the budget and reporting variations, known as budgetary control, help to control expenditure and imposes a financial discipline on the organisation.

- *Motivation*

  The involvement of lower and middle management in budgeting and the resulting establishment of clear targets has been found to be a motivating factor. People respond positively when their opinions are sought and they know where the firm is going. Budgeting, and a related technique known as Standard Costing which is dealt with in Topic 9 are known in America as *responsibility accounting*. This is an appropriate name because it focuses attention on a key aspect of the techniques whereby a named manager is given the responsibility for a task together with the necessary funds to fulfil that task.

The benefits of budgeting do not automatically arise, they have to be worked for. If the manager responsible for a budget does not participate in budget preparation most benefits will not be achieved. Imposed budgets and unwilling managers make a bad system.

6.3 Limiting factor

During the budgeting process it will become apparent that there is a factor which limits the activities of the organisation. This is known as a *limiting factor* and its effect on all budgets must be carefully assessed. In a normal commercial company the typical limiting factor is sales demand i.e. the company cannot profitably sell all it could produce or supply. This means that it is usual to commence budgeting with the sales budget so that all other budgets reflect the influence of the limiting factor. If sales were the limiting factor and the sales budget was for, say, 12,500 units it would clearly be essential that the Production Budget reflected this, after allowing for any stocks.

Of course, the limiting factor need not be sales. It might be lack of finance or space, lack of machine time or of skilled labour and so on. At any time there will be a limiting factor otherwise the firm could expand infinitely, but from time to time the limiting factor might change.

Note: The limiting factor can also be called the *key factor* or the *principal budget factor*.

6.4 Preparing budgets

The preparation of budgets may take weeks or months and in many organisations budgeting is done on a rolling basis, i.e. budgeting is a regular, continuous activity. A *budget committee* is formed, usually serviced by the Management Accountant, consisting of people from various parts of the organisation. The committee's task is to oversee the preparation and administration of the budget and to improve planning and control within the organisation.

It is usual for a *budget manual* to be issued. This manual does not contain the current budgets but sets out such matters as:

- ❐ What budgets should be prepared and who is responsible for each budget
- ❐ Details of how to prepare the budgets, including a budget timetable
- ❐ An outline of the inter-relationships between the budgets
- ❐ Samples of forms used in budgeting, and so on.

All budgets produced must be co-ordinated with each other and contribute towards the final summary budget known as the *Master Budget*. This comprises the budgeting operating statement and balance sheet of the organisation. (An operating statement is akin to a Profit and Loss account and shows the results for a period and a balance sheet shows the assets and liabilities at the end of the period).

The budget preparation process is summarised in Figure 6.1.

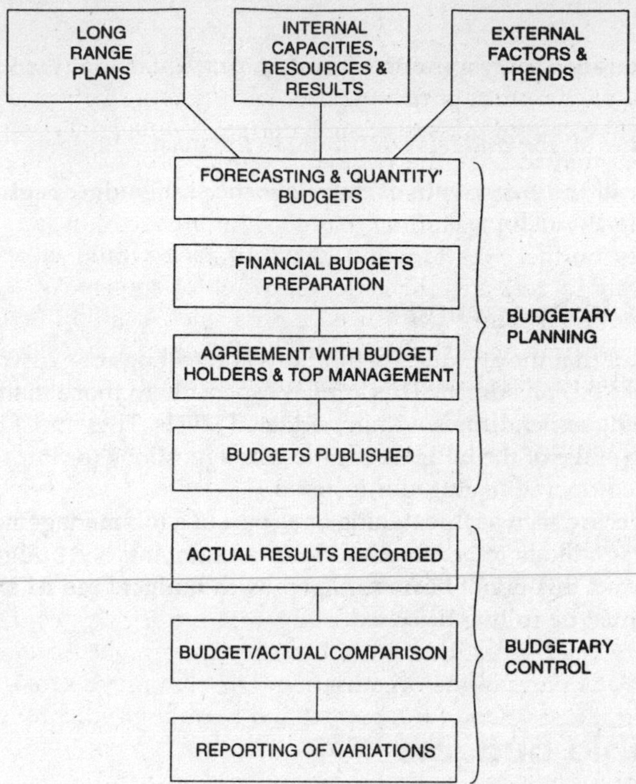

Figure 6.1 Outline of budgeting

6.5 Budget inter-relationships

A key objective of budgeting is to ensure that activities, departments and functions are co-ordinated with each other. Thus it is vital to consider how the budgets influence and inter-act with each other. The budget relationships within each organisation will be unique to that particular organisation and it is always necessary to consider the linkages between budgets as well as the contents of individual budgets.

As an example, the major budgets and their interrelationships for a typical manufacturing company are shown in Figure 6.2

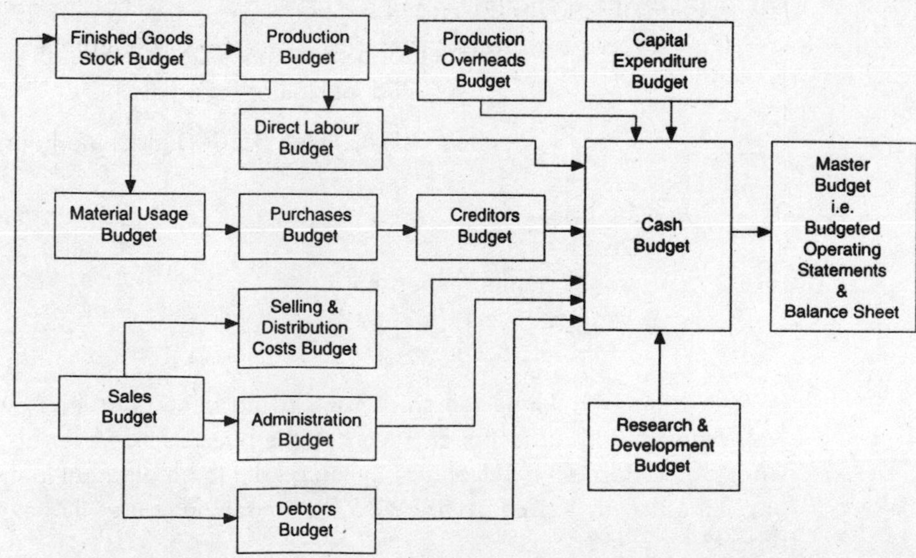

Figure 6.2 Typical budgets and relationships in a manufacturing company

Notes on Figure 6.2

(a) The diagram is only a summary and, in practice, there would be many more budgets especially for control purposes.

(b) Note how all the budgets contribute to the master budget.

(c) Because of the importance of cash flow, the cash budget is given special attention and is dealt with in Topic 8.

6.6 Human factors in budgeting

It is important that the attitudes, aspirations and feelings of everyone associated with budgeting should be considered. This applies especially to those managers who are responsible for keeping expenditures within budgeted levels. They must be encouraged to participate in each stage of the budgeting process, suggestions for improvement should be welcomed and co-operative attitudes fostered.

If budgets are seen as threatening or as part of a top management policing system then the system is unlikely to be effective. Some accountants see budgeting purely as a technical exercise but this is not how managers with budgets see it. Their human reactions to budgeting must be fully considered.

Fixed and flexible budgets

Scenario B Developing a useful budget

After explaining the principles and objectives of budgeting to Ron Hall, the new Maintenance Manager, Alan was asked to work with Ron and SBP's Budget Committee in developing the Maintenance Budget.

Alan discovered that the key measure of activity influencing the maintenance budget was the number of machine hours planned for the production departments. Alan found that 35,000 machine hours were planned for the next period; No. 8.

Based on this planning figure and close analysis of cost records, the following outline budget was prepared:

Budget for Maintenance Dept. Period 8.
Budget Holder – Ron Hall

Planned activity level: 35,000 machine hours

	£
Salaries	9,600
Rates	2,850
Other admin. expenses	7,500
Wages	18,250
Materials & Parts	9,100

In discussion with Alan, Ron said that, having been consulted over the budget setting, he was prepared to accept and work to the budget. However he was concerned about what would happen if actual activity turned out to be different to that planned. For example, if the activity turned out to be 36,000 machine hours what expenditure levels would be set?

Alan recognised this as a cost behaviour problem and realised he would have to do some further analysis of the budgeted costs. After doing this he found the following cost characteristics:

Cost	Type	Fixed content
Salaries	fixed	£9,600
Rates	fixed	£2,850
Admin. exp.	semi-variable	£2,250
Wages	semi-variable	£9,500
Materials	variable	–

Quick answer questions

1. The budgeted cost levels were set for a single activity level of 35,000 hours. What type of budget do you think this is called?
2. Why is the type of budget in 1. unsuitable for control purposes?
3. What is the vital characteristic of a budget that is suitable for control purposes?

1. A budget set for one activity level and which cannot be adjusted is known as a fixed budget.

2. A fixed budget can be useful for planning purposes. However, as it shows only the cost levels for one activity level without any adjustment possibility, it is not suitable for control purposes. It will be remembered that control is the process of comparing actual results to expected results. In practice, it is extremely unlikely that actual activity will be the same as planned activity so that the budgeted costs specified for the planned activity level will not be a realistic yardstick against which to compare actual costs.

What is required is the following comparison:

Budget costs for actual activity : Actual costs for actual activity

3. The vital characteristic is the ability to be able to adjust or flex the budgeted costs to suit the actual activity levels. This means that each cost must be analysed into types (fixed, variable and semi-variable) and their behaviour patterns (i.e. by how much they will vary) established.

The type of budget that includes this cost analysis and is thus capable of being adjusted is known as a flexible budget. It is the only type suitable for control purposes.

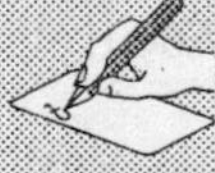

Task 2 *(answer page 183)*

(a) Work out the cost behavioural characteristics of the 5 budgeted costs in Scenario B.

(b) Prepare a suitable budget for the Maintenance Dept. for an activity level of 36,000 hours.

6.7 Fixed budgets

A fixed budget is one prepared to suit one given level of volume or activity. It is a single budget which cannot be adjusted to suit any other level of activity. The main use of fixed budgets is at the preliminary planning stage. Because of the rigidity of fixed budgets most budgets in practice are flexible budgets.

6.8 Flexible budgets

A *flexible budget* is one designed so that the permitted cost levels can be adjusted to suit the level of activity actually attained. This is done by recognising the existence of fixed, variable and semi-variable costs so that the budget may be 'flexed' or adjusted to correspond with actual activity. The basis of flexing a budget is an understanding of cost behaviour, described in Topic 5.

Flexible budgets are useful for planning and are essential elements of the control part of budgeting, known as budgetary control, for the following reasons:

- All budgets are based on estimates so actual volumes of sales and production cannot be expected to conform exactly to the estimates in the fixed budget.
- To provide useful control information, *actual costs* for the actual activity level should be compared with the *expected costs* for that level of activity, i.e. the flexible budget.

In summary:

Actual Costs for **Actual Activity**

should be compared with

Budgeted Costs for **Actual Activity.**

It is meaningless to compare actual costs levels for the production of, say, 8,000 units with a budget for the production of 7,000 units. Like must be compared with like.

The following example illustrates the main principles of flexible budgeting.

Example 1

Uni-product Limited make a single product and has an average monthly production of 12,000 units, although production varies widely. The necessary cost analysis has been done and the following budget has been prepared.

Cost budget for average production of 12,000 units

Cost	Cost behaviour	Budget £
Direct labour	Variable (£2 per unit)	24,000
Direct material	Variable (£3.5 per unit)	42,000
Production overheads	Semi-variable (£10,000 fixed + £2 per unit)	34,000
Admin. overheads	Fixed	27,000
	Total budgeted cost	£127,000

(a) Prepare budgets for 10,000 and 14,000 units

(b) In a month, actual production was 12,800 units and actual costs were

	£
Labour	£28,200
Material	£43,500
Production overheads	£34,800
Admin. overheads	£27,300

Find the cost variations from budget.

Solution

(a) The budget as given needs to be flexed to produce cost budgets for 10,000 and 14,000 units, having regard to the types of cost and their behaviour.

	Flexed budget for 10,000 units	**Original budget 12,000 units**	**Flexed budget for 14,000 units**
	£	**£**	**£**
Labour (£2 per unit)	20,000	24,000	28,000
Material (£3.5 per unit)	35,000	42,000	49,000
Production overheads (£10,000 + £2 per unit)	30,000	34,000	38,000
Admin. overheads	27,000	27,000	27,000
Total	£112,000	£127,000	£142,000

(b) As previously stated, actual costs for a given production level must be compared with a budget for that level. In this case a budget for 12,800 units must be prepared by the usual flexible budgeting procedure.

Cost	**Flexed budget for 12,800 units**	**Actual costs for 12,800 units**	**Cost differences**
	£	**£**	**£**
Labour	25,600	28,200	– 2,600
Materials	44,800	43,500	+ 1,300
Production overheads	35,600	34,800	+ 800
Admin. overheads	27,000	27,300	– 300
Total	£133,000	£133,800	– 800

Notes

(a) The cost differences are called *variances.*

(b) A negative variance indicates an overspend compared with budget, a positive variance an underspend.

(c) Although the budget and actual totals are quite close, this masks substantial variances, especially for labour and material. These would be investigated.

(d) Comparison of the actual costs for 12,800 units with the original budget for 12,000 units would have been meaningless. The budget had to be flexed first.

(e) The accuracy of a flexed budget is entirely dependent on the accuracy of the original cost behaviour analysis.

6.9 Flexible budgeting and contribution

It will be apparent by now that the underlying principle of flexible budgeting is the separation of costs into fixed and variable. This separation makes it possible to present budgets and results in a way that shows more information to management. Instead of just showing a final profit figure, the amount of *contribution* can also be shown.

Contribution is calculated thus:

Sales *less* variable costs = Contribution

Fixed costs are then deducted from the contribution to arrive at the final profit. The separation of fixed and variable costs in the collection, recording and presentation of information is known as *marginal costing*.

This is illustrated below:

Example 2

Assume that the units in Example 1 are sold at £11 each. Re-present the flexed budget for 14,000 units using the marginal costing approach showing contribution and profit, and contrast this with the total cost method.

Solution

Flexed budget for 14,000 units using the marginal cost approach

	£	£
Sales (14,000 × £11)		154,000
Less **variable costs**		
Labour	28,000	
Materials	49,000	
Variable production overheads (14,000 × £2)	28,000	
	105,000	105,000
	= Contribution	49,000
Less **fixed costs**		
Fixed production overheads	10,000	
Admin. overheads	27,000	
	37,000	37,000
	= Profit	£12,000

Flexed budget for 14,000 units using the total cost approach

	£	£
Sales		154,000
Less **costs**		
Labour	28,000	
Materials	49,000	
Production overheads	38,000	
Admin. overheads	27,000	
	142,000	142,000
	= Profit	£12,000

Notes

(a) The marginal cost approach separates out the fixed and variable costs whereas the total cost method does not. Naturally, both methods give the same final profit.

(b) The marginal cost method enables the amount of contribution to be calculated. This can be very useful to management. Contribution and Marginal Costing are explored in more detail in Topic 9.

Because of the extra information provided it is usual for flexible budgets to be presented in marginal cost form.

Using budgets for control

Scenario C Budgetary control

After studying budget preparation and the problems of devising flexible budgets, Alan now turned his attention to the control aspect of budgeting; known as Budgetary Control. He found that soon after the period ends, a Budgetary Control report was prepared showing for each expenditure item, the Budgeted Cost (flexed to actual activity), the Actual Cost and the Variances. These were shown both for the period and the year-to-date (YTD). SBP used a Standard Budgetary Control form shown in Figure 6.3.

Alan found that not all variances were investigated, only those deemed to be significant. A rule of thumb used was that any variance greater than ±5% of budget was investigated. As an exercise he was asked to calculate whether any of the variances for Period 8 for the Maintenance Department were significant.

Standardised Building Products Ltd
Budgetary Control Report No.

Budget centre -- Date prepared ------------------------------
Budget holder -- Budgeted activity level --------------------
Report relationship: Up ------------------------------ Actual activity level ------------------------
Down ----------------------------
Accounting period -------------------------------------

Budgeted item		Current period			Year to date			Trend of variance	Significant (yes/no)	Comments
code	description	budget	actual	variance	budget	actual	variance			

Figure 6.3

The Actual results were:

Activity level: 36,300 hours

Actual expenditure:

Salaries	£9,885
Rates	£2,850
Admin. expenses	£8,157
Wages	£18,020
Materials	£9,816

Alan realised that he must base the budget on the data from Scenarios A and B.

Quick answer questions

1. Why does the Budgetary Control Form show the Report Relationships; Up and Down?
2. Why do you think that both the Current Period and YTD figures are shown?
3. Why do you think significant variances are investigated? What is this an example of?

1. Budgets of various departments are related to one another so that it is important to show these links. Also, senior budget holders who may be responsible for several junior budgets need copies of these so that they can monitor operations.

2. Budgetary Control reports are usually prepared each month. However a month is a relatively short time and short-term fluctuations may occur and distort the picture. Thus, YTD figures enable a longer-term view and also show the cumulative progress towards meeting annual budgets.

3. Except by coincidence actual results will always differ from budget. Not every minor fluctuation should be investigated as it would be a waste of time. Only those that are a reasonable size should be examined to see the reason for the discrepancy between the plan, expressed in the budget, and actual results.
This is an example of 'Management by Exception'.

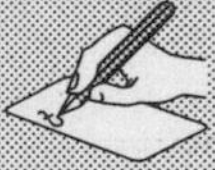

Task 3 *(answer page 183)*

(a) Calculate the variances from budget of the actual results, for an activity level of 36,300 hours.

(b) Calculate what variances, if any, are significant.

(c) Comment on the variances calculated.

(d) What cost items should be included in a Budgetary Control report?

6.10 Budgetary control

This is the process of comparing actual costs with budgeted costs on a regular basis, usually monthly. Variances are calculated and reports, showing budget, actual and variances (if any), are produced for every manager responsible for a budget and, in summary form, for higher management. In order to show realistic cost allowances, flexible budgeting must be used.

The aim of budgetary control is to highlight variations from the plan so that corrective action can be taken to bring operations back into line with the plan or, if circumstances have changed drastically, to make adjustments to the plan.

6.11 Controllable and non-controllable costs

Budgetary control reports for a manager should show only those cost items for which he is accountable and which are under his control. These are known as *controllable costs*.

Costs over which the manager has no control are known as *non-controllable* and would not normally appear on a manager's budgetary control report. It is important to note that *all* costs are controllable by someone in the organisation and part of the development of a proper budgeting system is the detailed clarification of responsibilities for all levels of management. A proper budgetary control system forms a hierarchy of control. Each level of reporting should be inter-related with the levels which are above and below the one concerned. In this way each manager is kept informed of his own performance and of the progress of budget holders junior to him for whom he is responsible.

Remember, the primary objective of budgetary control is not merely the production of regular reports. The purpose of the reports is to serve as a trigger for corrective action to put right any problems shown up.

6.12 Budgetary control reports

A budgetary control report is an important part of the control process. Its purpose is to initiate effective action so its design, content and timing must be carefully considered.

The key items which should be shown are:

(a) The budgeted costs and revenues for the period and year to date (YTD)

(b) The actual costs and revenues for the period and YTD

(c) The variances between (a) and (b) together with the trends in the variances

(d) An indication of whether the variance is of sufficient size to be considered significant.

Budgetary control reports are often very detailed and show the above items for each of the costs for which the manager is responsible. A typical budgetary control report is shown in Figure 6.4. The budgeted figures would be found using a flexible budget.

BUDGETARY CONTROL REPORT NO

BUDGET CENTRE ____________ DATE PREPARED ____________

BUDGET HOLDER ____________ BUDGETED ACTIVITY LEVEL ____________

REPORT RELATIONSHIP UP ________ DOWN ________ ACTUAL ACTIVITY LEVEL ____________

ACCOUNTING PERIOD ____________

BUDGETED ITEM		CURRENT PERIOD			YEAR TO DATE			TREND OF VARIANCE	SIGNIFICANT? (Yes/No)	COMMENTS
CODE	DESCRIPTION	BUDGET	ACTUAL	VARIANCE	BUDGET	ACTUAL	VARIANCE			

Figure 6.4 Typical budgetary control report

It will be apparent that variances are important figures and the following example illustrates the development of a flexible budget and the resulting variance calculations.

Example 3

Flexible budgets have been prepared for two output levels as follows:

Production and sales (units)	5,000	7,000
	£	£
Sales revenue (£6 per unit)	30,000	42,000
Direct materials	7,500	10,500
Direct labour	5,000	7,000
Maintenance	2,500	3,000
Depreciation	3,000	3,000
Total costs	18,000	23,500
Profit	12,000	18,500

Actual production and sales were 6,200 units and actual revenues and costs were

	£
Sales Revenue	37,820
Direct Materials	9,300
Direct Labour	7,440
Variable maintenance costs	1,600
Fixed maintenance costs	1,400
Depreciation	3,000
Total costs	22,740
Profit	15,080

Prepare a flexible budget for 6,200 units and show all variances indicating which variances are significant. In this instance a variance is significant if it is greater than ±5% of budget. A marginal cost format is required.

Solution

First it is necessary to find the types of cost and their behaviour patterns. This can be done quite easily when it is realised that the cost differences between the two budgets (at 5,000 and 7,000 units) are caused by variable cost changes only; the fixed costs remaining unchanged. The table below shows the calculations for the cost changes arising from a change of 2,000 units, i.e. 7,000 – 5,000.

	Budgeted cost 5,000 units	Budgeted cost 7,000 units	Cost difference	Difference ÷ 2,000 = Variable element per unit	Type of cost	See note
	£	£	£	£		
Materials	7,500	10,500	3,000	1.5	Fully variable	
Labour	5,000	7,000	2,000	1	Fully variable	1
Maintenance	2,500	3,000	500	0.25	Semi-variable (25p unit variable + £1,250)	2
Depreciation	3,000	3,000	–	–	Fixed	3

Note 1

Both materials and labour are fully variable, because if the variable element per unit is multiplied by either output level, the total equals the budgeted cost at the given output, e.g. Materials: 5,000 × £1.5 = £7,500 i.e. the budgeted cost.

Note 2

A similar calculation to Note 1 shows that there is a fixed element in the total maintenance cost, i.e. £2,500 – 5,000 × 0.25 = £1,250 i.e. the fixed element.

Note 3

As there is no change in the budgeted cost at the two output levels it is wholly fixed.

The derived cost characteristics can now be used in the normal way to produce a flexed budget for 6,200 units against which the actual costs and revenues can be compared and the variances calculated.

	Flexed budget for 6,200 units	**Actual results for 6,200 units**	**Variances**
	£	£	£
Sales (£6 per unit)	37,200	37,820	+ 620
Less variable costs			
Materials (£1.5 per unit)	9,300	9,300	0
Labour (£1 per unit)	6,200	7,440	– 1240 *
Var. maintenance (25p per unit)	1,550	1,600	– 50
Total variable costs	17,050	18,340	
= Contribution	20,150	19,480	
Less fixed costs			
Maintenance	1,250	1,400	– 150*
Depreciation	3,000	3,000	
Total fixed	4,250	4,400	
Profit	15,900	15,080	– 820

* Significant variances

The labour variance is $\left(\frac{1,240}{6,200} \times 100\%\right)$ = 20% over budget

The fixed maintenance cost variance is $\left(\frac{150}{1,250} \times 100\%\right)$ = 12% over budget

Note that even though the sales variance is much larger (£620) it is only 2% approximately different from budget and is therefore not deemed significant in this case.

The reasons for the significant variances would be investigated so that appropriate action can be taken to cure the problems, if possible.

Note: It should be apparent that the accuracy of the budget, and the consequent variances, is entirely dependent on the accuracy of the original cost analysis into fixed, semi-fixed and variable costs.

Key point summary

- ❐ Budgeting is a short-term planning and control technique which works within the framework of longer term plans.
- ❐ A budget is a financial expression of a plan.
- ❐ The benefits of budgeting include; co-ordination, communication, exception management, control and motivation.
- ❐ A limiting factor is something which limits the activities of the organisation.
- ❐ A budget committee is responsible for preparing and administering the budgeting system.
- ❐ A master budget comprises a budgeted operating statement and balance sheet.
- ❐ It is essential to consider the linkages and inter-relationships between budgets.
- ❐ The human factors in budgeting are all important.
- ❐ A flexible budget is one designed so that the permitted cost levels can be adjusted to suit the actual activity.
- ❐ The basis of flexible budgeting is an understanding of cost behaviour.
- ❐ Flexible budgets are essential for control purposes.
- ❐ To prepare flexible budgets, costs must be separated into variable, semi-variable and fixed.
- ❐ Cost differences between budget and actual are known as variances.
- ❐ Contribution is sales minus variable cost.
- ❐ Marginal costing is where fixed and variable costs are separated in the collection, recording, and presentation of information.
- ❐ A key part of budgetary control is the regular production of reports related to responsibilities, showing budget, actual and variance for each cost.

Need more detail or want to pursue a topic further?

Accounting and human aspects of budgeting	See *Management Accounting*, T Lucey, DP Publications.
Control principles	See *Management Information Systems* by T Lucey, DP Publications.

Topic 7

Budget relationships and cash budgeting

The relationship between functional budgets is illustrated and cash budgets are defined and exemplified. The distinction between profits and cash flows is explained and the way they can be reconciled is described.

Contents

Budget relationships

Scenario A Co-ordination in budgeting

Now that Alan had a good grasp of the detail of budgeting, Brian thought it was time that he found out how the individual budgets meshed together. Brian explained that a key element of budget preparation was to co-ordinate, or mesh together, the budgets of the various departments and activities. For example, there would be little point in planning for an increase in the Production Budget if there was not a corresponding increase in the Raw Materials Purchase Budget and the other budgets affected by an increase in production.

Brian showed Alan his Summary Budget Relationships Chart (see Figure 7.1) which was an overview of the key connections in SBP's budgeting system. Brian pointed out that this did not show all the individual departmental budgets in the company but merely convenient summaries. For example the total Administration Budget shown in the chart was a summary of 4 departmental budgets, i.e. Personnel, Finance, Data Processing and Planning.

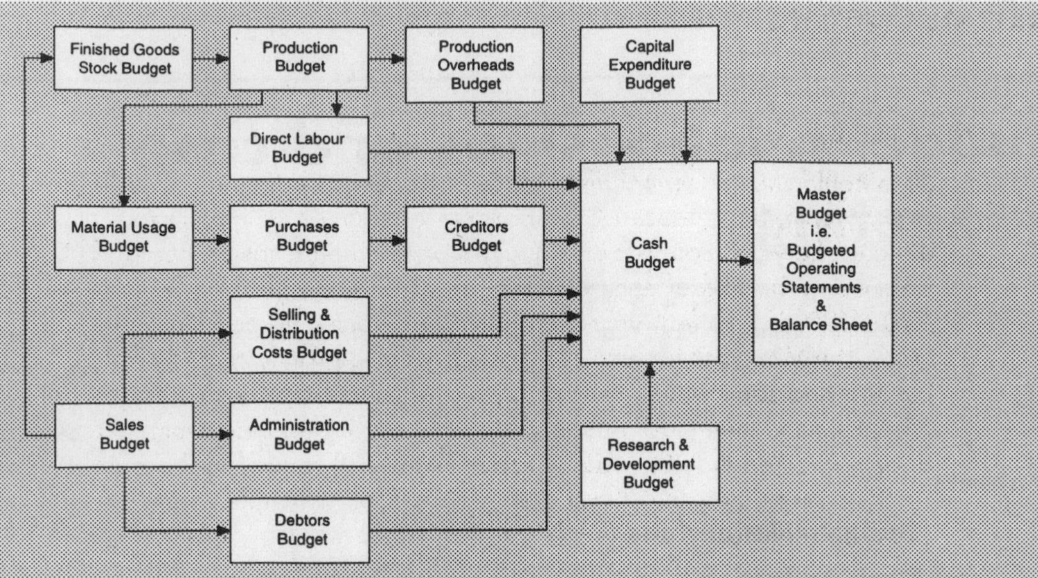

Figure 7.1 – Summary of main budget relationships, SBP Ltd

Quick answer questions

1. Which budget do you think is the first to be prepared in a normal trading organisation?
2. Why are all the budgets linked to the Cash Budget?
3. Why do you think that the Capital Expenditure and R & D budgets are not shown connected to the Production and Sales budgets?

1. Normally the Sales Budget. The budgeted sales then determine the production, after allowing for stocks.

2. Because all budgets affect the amount of cash the firm requires. The monitoring of the cash position, via the cash budget, is vital for all organisations.

3. Capital Expenditure and R & D Budgets are policy budgets which are not directly related to current activity levels. For example, the R & D budget might be increased even if sales were falling.

Cash budgeting

Scenario B Cash budgets

Alan could see the central importance of the Cash Budget to SBP. Brian explained that, every month, he produced Cash Budgets for each of the next three months. In this way the cash flow position was continually monitored on a rolling basis. The projected cash balance at the end of each month was compared with SBP's agreed overdraft limit of £100,000. If it looked as if SBP would go over its agreed limit Brian informed Barry Hope, the Managing Director, so that Barry could take corrective action in time, perhaps by delaying some expenditure or by making an arrangement with the bank. Normally SBP produced their Cash Budgets using a spread-sheet programme on the computer but Brian explained that this was for convenience and speed, not because of complexity.

Brian explained that Cash Budgets were, in principle, quite straightforward and could be represented by the following outline:

Cash Budget outline

	Opening Cash Balance for period
+	Cash Receipts in period
=	Total Cash available
–	Cash Payments in period
=	Closing Cash Balance at end of period

Naturally in the actual Cash Budget there was more detail and numerous preliminary calculations were required. Typical of these were estimates of the cash inflows expected from debtors, the cash outflows for purchases and wages and so on.

Brian showed Alan the outline figures estimated for the month of July.

Expected cash position at the end of June £32,600 overdraft.

July's estimated cash receipts and payments were £868,750 and £890,800 respectively

Quick answer questions

1. What is the cash balance at the beginning of July?
2. What is the expected cash balance at the end of July?
3. What do you think are the main sources of cash receipts for SBP?

1. *July's opening cash balance is June's closing balance, i.e. £32,600 overdraft.*
2. *Expected cash balance end of July.*

Opening balance	£32,600 (minus)
add Receipts	£868,750
= Total cash available in month	£836,150
less Payments	£890,800
= Closing balance	£54,650 overdraft

(This becomes the opening balance for August)

3. *The Main sources of cash receipts for SBP include:*

Receipts from Cash Sales
Receipts from Debtors (i.e. credit sales)
Any loans received
Any fixed assets sold
Proceeds of any share issues
Tax Rebates

(For most companies the first two items produce the largest receipts in a normal month)

Task 1 *(answer page 183)*

The £868,750 cash receipts for July consisted entirely of July's cash sales and receipts from debtors, i.e. resulting from credit sales in earlier months.

On average debtors pay according to the following pattern.

60%	in month following sale
30%	in second month after sale
8%	in third month after sale

Credit sales in previous periods were:

April	May	June
£810,000	£695,000	£918,000

(a) Calculate July's cash sales.

(b) Explain why the debtors' payments total 98% rather than 100%

7.1 What is a cash budget?

A cash budget is a detailed statement of the expected receipts and payments of cash during the next year. The annual cash budget is divided into shorter time periods (or control periods); quarterly, monthly or even weekly to suit the requirements of the organisation.

The cash budget is one of the most important budgets and receives close attention in every organisation. It is vital that there is always sufficient cash to pay wages and salaries, buy materials and so on. The cash budget shows the expected cash position for each of the periods ahead. This enables the organisation to assess whether operations can continue as planned, whether they need to be curtailed, whether there is the need to approach the bank for a loan and so on.

It is important to realise that the cash flow for a period does not equal the profit for a period. This means it is quite possible for a profitable company to have a shortage of cash. This is explained later in the Topic after cash budgets have been dealt with.

7.2 Contents of cash budgets

A cash budget must include every type of cash outflow and cash receipt. In addition to the *amounts*, the *timings* of all receipts and payments must be forecast.

Examples of typical receipts and payments follow:

Typical receipts include:	*Typical payments include:*
❐ Cash sales	❐ Cash purchases
❐ Receipts from debtors (i.e. arising from credit sales)	❐ Payments to creditors for stock and material purchases on credit
❐ Sales of fixed assets	❐ Wage, salary and bonus payments
❐ Receipts of interest or dividends	❐ Payments for overhead and expense items
❐ Issue of new shares	❐ Purchase of fixed assets
❐ Any other fees, royalty or incomes	❐ Payments of dividends, interest and tax.

Note:

A fixed asset is an asset bought for use within the business. For example, a greengrocer might buy a van to make deliveries. This would be a fixed asset as opposed to the purchase of, say, cabbages for re-sale which are termed *current assets*. Expenditure on fixed assets is known as *capital expenditure*.

The format of a typical cash budget is shown in Figure 7.2.

CASH BUDGET

	Period 1	Period 2	Period 3	Period 4
Receipts:	£ £	£	£	
OPENING CASH BALANCE b/f	ZZZ	AAA	BBB	CCC
+ Receipts from Debtors + Sales of Capital Items + Any Loans Received + Proceeds from Share Issues + Any other Cash Receipts				
= TOTAL CASH AVAILABLE				
Payments: - Payments to Creditors - Wages and Salaries - Loan Repayments - Capital Expenditure - Dividends an d Taxation - Any other payments				
= TOTAL CASH PAYMENTS				
= CLOSING CASH BALANCE c/f	AAA	BBB	CCC	

Figure 7.2 Format for a cash budget

Notes

(a) The closing balance for one period becomes the opening balance for the next period.

(b) It is always necessary to know the opening cash balance.

Scenario C Preparing a cash budget

The following day Alan was taken aback by Brian's request that he should prepare SBP's cash budget for August by himself. Brian passed over his working papers and Alan set to work.

Alan found the following information in the papers:

SBP Cash budget

	July £
Opening balance	32,600 o/d
Cash sales	100,810
Cash from debtors	767,940
Sales of fixed assets	–
Loans received/share issues	–
Tax rebates	–
Any other receipts	–
= Total cash available	836,150
Payments for materials	212,000
Wages & salaries	503,200
Overheads	92,900
Fixed asset purchases	25,000
Loan repayments	5,000
Tax/dividend payments	52,700
Any other payments	–
= Total payments	890,800
Closing balance =	54,650 o/d

July's Credit Sales were £820,000 and August's Cash Sales were estimated to be £75,000.

August's wages and salaries were estimated to be 2% down on July's whilst material payments were down by 5%. August's total overheads were estimated to be £115,000, including £17,500 for depreciation. Fixed asset purchases were planned to be £165,000. There were no planned loan repayments or receipts and no tax transactions were planned.

Quick answer questions

1. Apart from SBP's management who else is likely to be interested in their Cash Budgets?
2. What amount will be received from Debtors in August assuming a normal pattern of receipts?

1. SBP's bankers. Banks normally require firms to which they loan money to prepare regular cash budgets so that the cash position is monitored in a comprehensive way. However regardless of whether or not a firm owes money, their cash flow position must be monitored.

2. Based on the payment experiences given receipts from debtors should be:

		Cash receipts
		£
From	May's sales = 8% × £695,000 =	55,600
	June's sales = 30% × £918,000 =	275,400
	July's sales = 60% × £820,000 =	492,000
		£823,000

Task 2 *(answer page 184)*

(a) Prepare SBP's Cash Budget for August and compare the closing balance with their overdraft limit of £100,000.

(b) What action would you recommend?

(c) Why do you think that the profit for a period is not the same as the cash flow for a period?

7.3 Cash budget example

Example 1 – Cash budget

The opening cash balance, on 1st June, is £25,000. Budgeted sales, all on credit, are as follows:

	£
May	65,000
June	95,000
July	105,000
August	85,000

Analysis of records shows that debtors settle according to the following patterns:

70% in the month of sale

25% the month following

(The balance being bad debts, i.e. the cash is never received)

All purchases are for cash and budgeted purchases are:

	£
June	65,000
July	80,000
August	55,000

Wages are £8,000 per month and overheads are £17,000 per month (including £4,000 depreciation) settled monthly. Tax of £20,500 has to be paid in July and the organisation will receive a loan repayment of £12,500 in August.

Prepare cash budgets for June, July and August.

Solution

Workings:

The cash receipts from sales are

	June cash receipts
From May Sales (65,000 × 25%)	£16,250
From June sales (95,000 × 70%)	66,500
	82,750

	July cash receipts
From June sales (95,000 × 25%)	£23,750
From July sales (105,000 × 70%)	73,500
	97,250

	August cash receipts
From July sales (105,000 × 25%)	26,250
From August sales (85,000 × 70%)	59,500
	85,750

Cash budget

	June	July	August
	£	£	£
Opening balance	25,000	21,750	– 2,500
+ Receipts from sales	82,750	97,250	85,750
+ Loan repayment			12,500
= Total cash available	107,750	119,000	95,750
– Purchases	65,000	80,000	55,000
– Wages	8,000	8,000	8,000
– Overheads (less depreciation)	13,000	13,000	13,000
– Tax		20,500	
= Total payments	86,000	121,500	76,000
Closing balance	21,750	– 2,500	19,750

Notes

(a) Depreciation is an accounting expense but is not a cash flow. Accordingly, only those overheads which create a cash flow should appear in the budget, i.e. Total Overheads, £17,000 less depreciation of £4,000 = £13,000 cash flow.

(b) The budget shows that planned activities result in a cash deficiency of £2,500 in July. The organisation thus has advance notice of this problem and has time to take action. This may be to obtain their bank's agreement to run an overdraft for the month or to delay some expenditure for a month or so.

(c) It is normal to have to make various preliminary calculations, as in this example, before the finalised cash budget can be prepared.

7.4 Profits and cash flows

As previously stated, profit for a period does not equal the cash flow for that period, except by coincidence. Profit (or loss) is found by using a number of accounting rules or conventions. The profit or loss is calculated in an account called the Profit and Loss Account (P & L account) which, in summary form, is shown overleaf:

Profit and loss account for period

	Sales
Less	Cost of sales
=	Gross profit (or loss)
Less	Expenses
=	Net profit (or loss)

Sales, cost of sales, and expenses in a period are not the same as cash receipts and payments for a variety of reasons, including:

- Most sales and purchases are made on credit. A sale is included in the P & L account when the invoice is sent to the customer but the cash may not be received until a later period. Credit purchases create a similar problem over timing.
- Some expenses in the P & L account are not cash costs but are costs derived from accounting conventions, e.g. depreciation, loss or profit on sale of fixed assets and so on.
- Some types of cash income or cash payments may not appear in the P & L account, e.g. proceeds from a new issue of shares or a loan, payment of dividends and so on.
- Changes in working capital (e.g. stocks, creditors, debtors and cash balance) affect cash flow but not the P & L account.
- Purchases of fixed assets affect the P & L account only indirectly (through depreciation) but have immediate and often substantial cash flow effects.

7.5 Example of Profit: Cash flow reconciliation

Example 2

Motor Spares Limited supply parts and tools to garages. Goods are sold at cost plus 25%.

	Budgeted sales	Labour costs	Expenses
	£	£	£
August	85,000	5,000	7,500
September	110,000	6,000	8,500
October	180,000	8,500	11,000
November	130,000	8,000	10,500

Goods for resale and expenses are bought on credit and creditors are paid the following month. The expenses include a monthly depreciation charge of £3,000. Labour is paid monthly. It is company policy to have sufficient stock in hand at the end of each month to meet sales demand in the next half month.

40% of the sales are for cash and 60% on credit. Cash from credit sales is received the next month.

The company is buying a new delivery van in October for £15,000 cash and has to pay tax of £8,500 in September. The opening cash balance at 1st September is £30,000.

Required:

(a) Profit and Loss accounts for September and October, and in total.

(b) Cash budgets for September and October.

(c) Reconcile the profit and cash flow for September and October.

Solution

(a)

Profit and loss accounts

	September	October	Total	
	£	£	£	
Sales	110,000	180,000	290,000	
less cost of sales	88,000	144,000	232,000	*Note 1*
= Gross profit	22,000	36,000	58,000	
less labour	6,000	8,500	14,500	
expenses	8,500	11,000	19,500	*Note 2*
= Net profit	7,500	16,500	24,000	

Note 1:

As stated, the selling price is cost + 25%.

This means that the cost of sales is 80% of sales value.

e.g. September sales = £110,000.

Cost of sales = £110,000 × 80% = **£88,000.**

(If the mark up was cost + $33\frac{1}{3}$ % the cost of sales would be 75% of sales value. If the mark up was cost + 50%, the cost of sales would be $66\frac{2}{3}$ % of sales value and so on).

Note 2:

For the P & L accounts, the expenses must include the depreciation charge.

(b) Workings for cash budget.

September cash receipts from credit sales

	£
From August sales (85,000 × .6)	51,000
From September sales (110,000 × .4)	44,000
	95,000

October cash receipts from credit sales

	£
From September sales (110,000 × .6)	66,000
From October sales (180,000 × .4)	72,000
	138,000

Purchases

The goods required for the budgeted sales can be found by taking, as previously explained, 80% of the sales value, i.e.

	Sales × 80%	= Required purchases
August	£85,000 × 80%	= £68,000
September	£110,000 × 80%	= £88,000
October	£180,000 × 80%	= £144,000
November	£130,000 × 80%	= £104,000

Each month, because of their stock policy, the firm buys 50% of the goods required for the current month's sales plus the goods required for 50% of the next month's sales. All purchases are on credit, settled a month in arrears.

The cash payments arising from purchases can be summarised thus:

		September cash flows i.e. August's purchases	October cash flows i.e. September's purchases
		£	£
For August sales	(50% × 68,000)	34,000	
For September sales	(50% × 88,000)	44,000	44,000
For October sales	(50% × 144,000)		72,000
		78,000	116,000

Expenses

Expenses less depreciation, which is not a cash cost, are paid a month in arrears.

September cash flow = August expenses – depreciation
= 7,500 – 3,000
= **4,500**

October cash flow = September expenses – depreciation
= 8,500 – 3,000
= **5,500**

Cash budget

	September	October
	£	£
Opening balance	30,000	28,000
+ receipts from sales	95,000	138,000
Total cash available	125,000	166,000
– Purchases	78,000	116,000
– Expenses (less depreciation)	4,500	5,500
– Labour	6,000	8,500
– Tax	8,500	
– Van		15,000
Total cash payments	97,000	145,000
= Closing balance	28,000	21,000

Thus the net cash flow effect over the two months is a *reduction* of £9,000 in the cash balance, from £30,000 to £21,000.

This should be contrasted with the profit for the period of £24,000 from part (a) on page 102.

The cash, profit and working capital changes are now reconciled.

Profit and cash flow reconciliation for September and October

	£	£
Profit for period		24,000
+ adjustment for item not causing cash flow		
Depreciation (2 × £3,000)		6,000
Total source of funds		30,000
Funds used for van purchase	15,000	
Taxation	8,500	23,500
Net surplus of funds		6,500

Accounted for by changes in working capital

See note	£
1. Stocks: increase of	8,000
2. Debtors: increase of	57,000
3. Creditors: increase of	(49,500)
4. Cash: decrease of	(9,000)
= *Net increase in working capital*	6,500

Note 1	£
Stocks at 1st Sept. (August's forward purchases)	44,000
Stocks at 31st October. *	52,000
= Stock increase	8,000

* Stocks at 31st October are October's forward purchases, i.e. 50% × £104,000 = £52,000.

Note 2	£
Debtors at 1st Sept. (60% of August sales)	51,000
Debtors at 31st Oct. (60% of October sales)	108,000
= *Increase in debtors*	57,000

Note 3	£	£
Creditors at 1st Sept.		
– Expenses (August's less depreciation)	4,500	
– Purchases (from part (b))	78,000	82,500
Creditors at 31st Oct.		
– Expenses (October's less depreciation)	8,000	
– Purchases (from part (b))	124,000	132,000
= *Increase in creditors*		49,500

Note that an increase in creditors *reduces* the working capital.

Note 4

This is the net decrease in cash, i.e. £30,000 – 21,000 = £9,000.

Key point summary

- A cash budget is a summary of the expected receipts and payments of cash.
- Both the amounts and timings of cash flows must be estimated.
- The closing cash balance of one period becomes the opening balance of the next.
- Profits (or losses) are found from the Profit and Loss Account (P & L account).
- Gross Profit is the difference between Sales and Cost of Sales. Net Profit is Gross Profit less expenses.
- Profit is derived using rules and conventions. Normally it does not equal the cash flow.
- Profit for the period can be reconciled to the cash movement for the period, having regard to working capital changes.

Need more detail or want to pursue a topic further?

Fixed and current assets and profit and loss accounts	See *Foundation Accounting*, AH Millichamp, DP Publications.
Cash budgets	See *Management Accounting*, T Lucey, DP Publications.

Standard costing

The principles of standard costing are described and the objectives of variance analysis explained. Labour, materials and overhead variances are exemplified.

Contents

What is standard costing?

Scenario A Standard costing

During Alan's time at SPB he had heard several references to Standard Costing and had found that it was used in SPB's loft window production line where double glazed window units for loft conversion were made in large quantities. He was not sure what Standard Costing was, so he asked Brian.

Brian explained that Standard Costing was a system where a target cost, called a standard cost, was calculated for a product, based on defined methods, efficient working practices and good material use i.e. good but not perfect conditions. After production the actual costs (for labour, materials and overheads) were compared with the

Standard Cost and any differences, called variances, analysed to find the causes of the difference. This might be because labour was paid above or below standard rates and/or the operatives worked above or below standard efficiency and/or more or less material was used than planned and so on. Thus, inefficiencies, or possible ways to improve efficiency, were highlighted by the variance analysis so that management could take action. John emphasised the detailed nature of Standard Costing and as an example showed Alan the Standard Cost Summary of the material and labour content of the T200 Loft Light.

Abstract from Standard Cost of 1 T200 'Loft Light'

	£	£
Materials		
Wood Grade XX3		
5 kgs @ £1.80 kg	9.00	
Glass – 1.72 sq. metres @ £5 sq. metre	8.60	
Hinges – 2 × £1.1	2.20	
Sealing Strip – 6.4 metres @ 40p metre	2.56	
Total material		22.36
Labour		
Machining & Glass Cutting		
1.2 hours @ £5.60	6.72	
Assembly – 1.8 hours @ £4.75	8.55	
		15.27

Quick answer questions

1. What type of production is best suited to Standard Costing?
2. Why do you think it is not good practice to use the previous periods average cost as the Standard Cost for the next period?
3. What is the Standard Prime Cost of one T200 'Loft Light'?

1. *Large quantity repetitive production of standardised items. Standard Costing would be quite unsuitable for, say, a jobbing manufacturer such as Precision Tool (visited by Alan previously). There, jobs were different, quantities low and there was no repetition.*
2. *The previous period's actual average cost may contain inefficiencies, bad practice or special problems. The objective of a Standard Cost is to provide a tough, but realistic, target. Consequently it is based on good, but not perfect, performance levels.*
3. *Standard Prime Cost = Standard Materials + Standard Labour*
   = £22.36 + 15.27 = £37.63

8.1 Standard cost defined

A standard cost is the planned cost for a unit of production. It is prepared in advance and it is an estimate of what production costs are expected to be having regard to:

(a) Expected prices of labour, materials and expenses

(b) Expected labour times and amounts of material usage

(c) Expected overhead costs and level of activity (i.e. as the budget)

A standard cost is *not* an average of past costs; it is a target cost for a future period taking into account what conditions are expected to be like.

8.2 Standard costing

Standard costing is a system of accounting based on standard costs. Standard costs are prepared, actual costs are recorded and the differences (i.e. variances) between actual and standard are analysed in order to help management control operations. It will be seen that standard costing and budgetary control are based on similar principles but they differ in scope. Budgets are concerned with totals; they lay down cost limits for functions, departments and the organisation as a whole. In contrast standards are a unit concept. They are more detailed and apply to particular products, to individual operations or processes. Standard costing is best suited to repetitive manufacturing processes.

8.3 The standard cost card

After detailed technical studies, analyses of rates and prices, and so on, standard costs are prepared and recorded on a standard cost card or on a computer file. It is common practice for the standard cost card to include only factory costs although a full standard costing system would include, administration and marketing overheads and selling prices.

An example of a standard cost card follows.

Standard cost card – Product XY 596

	£	£
Direct materials		
Material A – 10.5kg @ £6.5 per kg	68.25	
Material B – 3.2kg @ £37.8 per kg	120.96	189.21
Direct labour		
Grade K – 22 hrs @ £4.5 per hour	99.00	
Grade L – 14 hrs @ £5.75 per hour	80.50	179.50
Standard prime cost		368.71
Variable production overheads*		
36 hours @ £1.5 per hour		54.00
Standard variable production cost		422.71
Fixed production overheads*		
36 hours @ £8.00 per hour		288.00
Standard total production cost		£710.71

* Both variable and fixed production overheads are absorbed on total labour hours, i.e. 22 + 14 = 36. The overhead absorption rates of £1.5 and £8 are found from the budgeted overheads for the period.

8.4 Problems in standard costing

Standard costing is a detailed process with a number of possible problems, including:

(a) Difficulties of forecasting rates of pay, material prices, inflation.

(b) Problems of deciding what efficiency levels will apply, what material qualities will be used, and so on.

(c) Changes in prices, rates, methods and other factors which make the standard cost less appropriate.

(d) Possible behavioural problems, e.g. resentment, antagonism to system, fear of being blamed and so on.

8.5 Advantages of standard costing

If standard costing is properly used for the right type of application there can be a number of advantages including:

(a) Useful control information is provided by the standard: actual comparison and the resulting analysis of variances.

(b) The technical analysis necessary to set standards may lead to better methods, greater efficiency and lower costs.

(c) Cost consciousness is stimulated.

(d) The variances enable 'management by exception' to be practised.

(e) Standard cost simplify record keeping and stock valuation because standards are used throughout the system.

(f) Motivation may be increased because of the existence of clear targets.

Variance: meaning and calculation

Scenario B Variance analysis

Alan quickly grasped the idea of Standard Costing but wanted to know more about how the differences between Actual costs and Standard costs, known as variances, were calculated.

Brian explained that the principle behind virtually all variance calculations could be expressed quite simply as follows:

Actual costs for *Actual* output

is compared with

Standard costs for *Actual* output

Any difference is known as a variance. If actual expenditure is *greater than* standard then there is an *adverse variance*; if actual expenditure is *less than* standard there is a *favourable variance.*

As an example of variance calculations Brian showed Alan the actual results for the last period for T200 Loft Light production in which 1,800 units were produced.

Actual results – 1,800 T200 units produced

Material used	
Wood: 9,160 kgs at a cost of	£16,300
Glass: 2,975 sq. metres at a cost of	£14,875
Hinges: 3,604 at a cost of	£3,964
Strip: 11,900 metres at a cost of	£4,723
= Total material cost	£39,862
Wages paid	
Machining: 2,210 hours at a cost of	£12,155
Assembly: 3,100 hours at a cost of	£15,880
= Total labour cost	£28,035

The Standard Costs for material and labour were given in Scenario A.

Quick answer questions

1. What is the Total Materials Variance for the period, i.e. the difference between what the materials actually cost and what should have been the materials cost for 1,800 units?
2. What is the Total Labour Variance for the period?
3. Do you think the two Total Variances you have calculated are of much value for control purposes?

1. Total Materials Variance = Actual material cost for production of 1,800 units − standard material cost for 1,800 units
= £39,862 − (1,800 × £22.36 [from A])
= £39,862—£40,248
= £386 Favourable i.e. Actual costs are £386 lower than standard

2. Total Labour Variance = Actual labour costs − standard labour costs for 1,800 units.
= £28,035 − (1,800 × £15.27 [from A])
= £28,035 − £27,486
= £549 Adverse i.e. Actual costs are £549 higher than standard.

3. The two total variances are not of great value for control purposes because they are not detailed enough. For example was the £549 overspend on labour due to machining or assembly? Was it due to working less efficiently or paying too much? To answer these questions, more detail is required.

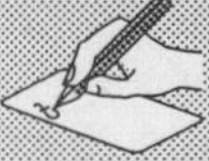

Task 1 *(answer page 184)*

(a) Calculate the Materials Price and Usage Variances for the period in as much detail as possible.

(b) Similarly calculate the Labour Rate and Efficiency Variances.

(c) Explain what each of the variances means.

8.6 Variance analysis

A variance is the difference between standard cost and actual cost. Variance analysis subdivides the difference between total standard cost and total actual cost into the detailed differences (relating to material, labour, overheads and so on) which make up the total difference.

The purpose of variance analysis is to provide practical pointers to the causes of off-standard performance so that management can improve operations and increase efficiency. The only criterion for the calculation of a variance is usefulness; if it is not useful for management purposes, it should not be produced. Ideally, variances should be in sufficient detail so that responsibility for a specific variance can be assigned to a particular individual, although this ideal is not always achievable in practice.

8.7 Relationship of variances

Variances are related to each other and Figure 8.1 shows some typical cost variances which are generally found useful. However it should be emphasised that many other variances exist and the chart only shows variances relating to product costs and does not cover variances for administration overheads nor for sales.

The chart should be studied carefully together with the following notes.

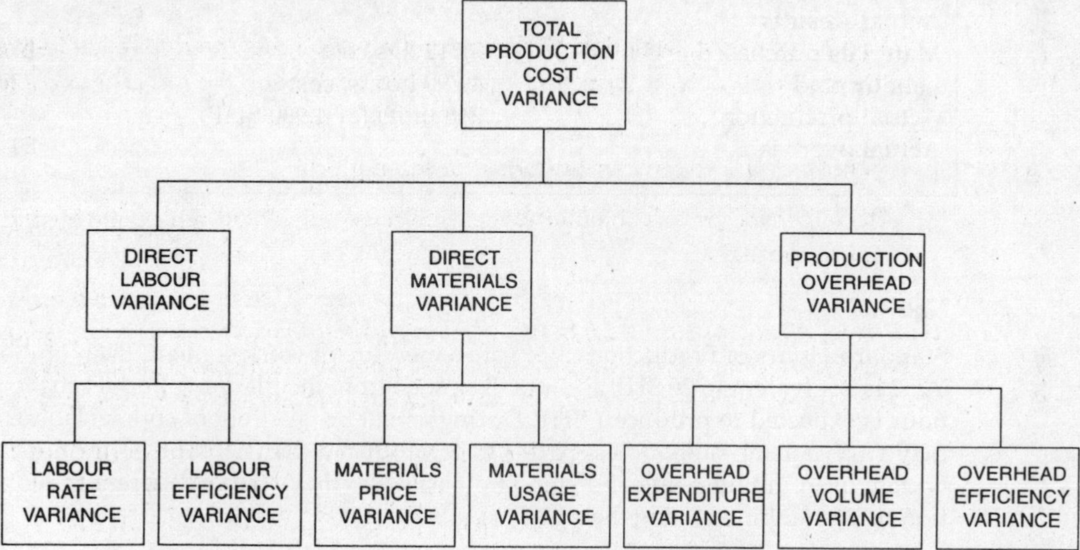

Figure 8.1 Typical cost variances and relationships

Notes on figure 8.1

(a) Each variance shown is described and exemplified in the following paragraphs.

(b) The chart is arithmetically consistent, i.e. the linked variances equals the senior variance shown.

(c) In general, variances show the differences due to *price* or *rate* and the differences due to *usage*. As examples, the Direct Material variance can be sub-divided into a Price Variance and a Usage Variance; the Direct Labour Variance into a Rate Variance and an Efficiency Variance and so on.

8.8 The variances described

In the following paragraphs each variance shown in Figure 8.1 is explained and a formula provided to together with a worked example.

The worked examples are all based on the following details for Part No. Y252 and the budget and actual results.

Standard cost card (extract)		
Standard production cost per unit	Part No. Y252	
		£
Direct materials	15kgs @ £3.50 kg	52.50
Direct labour	20 hrs. @ £6	120.00
Standard prime cost		172.50
Budget for period (extract)		
		£
Production fixed overheads		25,530
Production variable overheads		18,630
Budgeted labour hours		4,600
Budgeted standard hours of production (SHP)		4,600
Actual Results		
Materials purchased and used	3,712 kgs cost	£12,620
Labour paid	4,790 hours, cost	£29,524
Actual production	248 units (or 4,960 SHP)	
Actual overheads		£44,600

Figure 8.2 Data for examples

Note:

Standard Hours of Production (SHP) are a measure of work content. Each unit of Part No. Y252 is equivalent to 20 SHP and it will be seen from the planning budget that each labour hour is expected to produce 1 SHP. During actual production, of course, labour efficiency may vary causing more or less SHP's to be produced than actual labour hours. SHP's are widely used in budgeting and standard costing as they enable different types of production to be combined using their SHP's.

8.9 Principles of variance calculations

Before considering the individual variances it is worthwhile emphasising some general principles:

(a) Price variances are always extracted first. Thereafter the standard price is used for all calculations. Depending on the type of cost, Price Variances may be called Rate or Expenditure variances.

(b) The basis of virtually all variances is the following comparison:

Actual cost of actual quantity is compared with the **standard cost of actual quantity**.

(c) As previously mentioned under budgeting, a *minus* variance is where the actual price/usage is *greater than* standard and a *plus* variance is where the actual price/usage is *less than* standard. (Alternative names are *adverse* and *favourable* variances, usually abbreviated to *adv* and *fav*).

(d) As with budgeting, if a variance is sufficiently large it would be thoroughly investigated so that management can take appropriate action.

Remember variances are the triggers for actions not an end in themselves.

8.10 Labour variances

The three labour variances can be defined thus:

- *Direct labour variance*

  the difference between actual labour cost and the standard labour cost of the production achieved.

  This variance can be sub-divided into the Rate Variance (i.e. the *price* variance) and the Efficiency Variance (i.e. the *usage* variance).

- *Direct labour rate variance*

  the difference between actual and standard hour rate for the total hours worked.

- *Direct labour efficiency variance*

  the difference between the actual hours worked and the standard hours for the actual production achieved, valued at the standard labour rate.

Formulae

Labour total variance:

(Standard labour hours produced × standard rate) – (Actual hours × Actual rate)

Labour rate variance:

(Standard rate – Actual rate) × Actual hours *or*

(Standard rate x Actual hours) – (Actual rate × Actual hours)

Labour efficiency variance:

(Standard hours produced – Actual hours) × Standard rate

Notes:

Rate + Efficiency Variances = Total Variances

and

(Actual hours × Actual Rate) = Actual wages paid.

Example 1

Calculate the labour variances for the data in Figure 8.2 and interpret

Solution

Rate variance

(Standard rate × Actual hours) – (Actual rate × Actual hours)

= (£6 × 4,790) – £29,524
= £28,740 – £29,524
= £784 ADV

Efficiency variance

(SHP – Actual hours) × Standard Rate

= (4,960 – 4,790) × £6
= **£1,020** FAV

Rate + Efficiency = Total variance
= – 784 + 1,020
= **£236** FAV

Proof of total variance

(SHP × Standard rate) – (Actual hours × Actual rate)

= (4,960 × £6) – £29,524
= £29,760 – 29,524
= **£236** FAV

Interpretation

Rate variance

Payments above standard rate have caused costs to be £784 over standard. This may be due to paying the right grade of worker above standard rates or using a higher grade of worker than planned.

Efficiency

During 4,790 actual hours 4,960 standard hours were produced. An obvious gain in efficiency resulting in a large favourable variance. Because both variances are large they would be investigated in order to find the reason for paying above standard rates and if possible to be able to capitalise on the efficient production methods used.

8.11 Material variances

The material variances can be defined thus:

- *Direct materials variance*

  The difference between the standard material cost for the actual production and the actual cost.

  The total variance can be sub-divided as follows:

- *Direct materials price variance*

  The difference between the standard price and actual purchase price for the actual quantity of material.

  (Note that this variance can be calculated at the time of purchase or the time of usage. As price variations are deemed to be the responsibility of the buyer, calculation at the time of purchase is more usual).

- *Direct materials usage variance*

  The difference between the actual quantity used and the standard quantity for the actual production achieved, valued at standard price.

Formulae

Materials total variance:

(Standard quantity × Standard price) – (Actual quantity × actual price)

Materials price variance:

(Standard price – Actual price) × Actual quantity *or*

(Standard price × Actual quantity) – (Actual price × Actual quantity)

Materials usage variance:

(Standard quantity for actual production – Actual quantity) × Standard price

Notes:

Price + Usage variances = Total variance

(Actual quantity × Actual price) = Purchase cost

Example 2

Calculate the material variances for the data in Figure 8.2 and interpret.

Solution

Price variance

(Standard price × Actual quantity) – (Actual price × Actual quantity)
(£3.50 × 3,712) – £12,620 = £12,992 – 12,620
= **£372** FAV

Usage variance

(Standard quantity for Actual production – Actual quantity) × Standard price
= ((248 × 15) – 3,712) × £3.50
= (3,720 – 3,712) × £3.50
= **£28** FAV

Price + Usage = Total variance
£372 + 28 = **£400** FAV

Proof of total variance

(Standard quantity × Standard price) – (Actual quantity × Actual price)
((248 × 15) × £3.50) – £12,620 = £13,020 – 12,620
= **£400** FAV

Interpretation

There is a large favourable Price variance of £372 which should be investigated. Price variances arise from paying higher or lower prices than standard, gaining or losing quantity discounts or buying a different quality of material.

Usage variances arise from greater or lower yields or rates of scrap than planned, or gains or losses arising from non-standard material. In this case the variance is very small in relation to material expenditure so it would appear that usage is very much as planned.

Not all variances are investigated – only those deemed significant are worth pursuing in depth.

Overhead variances

Scenario C Overhead variances

Alan saw that there could be numerous advantages in identifying detailed material and labour variances but realised that considerable administrative work was needed to make the system work well. He wondered whether variance analysis could also be applied to the other major element of costs, overheads, and decided to ask Brian for guidance.

Brian explained that variance analysis could certainly be applied to overheads although the process was somewhat more involved because of the way that overheads were absorbed into production. One problem was that departmental overheads had to be absorbed fairly by all products passing through the department so that there had to be a way of combining different types of production unit. Brian explained that the way this was done was to measure the work content of products in terms of Standard Hours Produced (SHP) and to use the SHP's as the basis of overhead absorption. For example the Loft Light department manufactured, in varying proportions, three sizes of loft windows, the T200, T400 and T600. These had work contents, expressed in SHP's, as follows:

T200:	3 SHP per unit
T400:	4.2 SHP per unit
T600:	5.6 SHP per unit

As an example of the use of SHP's and of overhead variance calculations Brian showed Alan the following budget and actual details for the Loft Light department.

Overhead budget for period – Loft Light Department

Fixed overheads	£32,550
Variable overheads	13,950
Budgeted labour hours	9,300
Budgeted standard hours of production (SHP)	9,300

Actual for period

Actual production:
- 1,800 units of T200
- 400 units of T400
- 460 units of T600

Actual overheads	£48,500
Actual labour hours	9,450

Quick answer questions

1. It will be seen that the budgeted labour hours and budgeted SHP's are the same. What do you understand from this?
2. Calculate the budgeted total overhead absorption rate for the Loft Light department.
3. How many SHP's were actually produced in the period?
4. Was actual activity more or less than budget?

1. This shows the normal planning assumption, i.e. 1 SHP is produced in 1 labour hour. During actual production, labour efficiency is likely to vary causing more or less SHP's to be produced than actual labour hours.

$$\text{Budgeted Total OAR} = \frac{\text{Budgeted Total Overheads}}{\text{Budgeted Absorption base (SHP's in this case)}}$$

$$= \frac{£32,550 + 13,950}{9,300}$$

£5 per SHP

3. Actual SHP's produced = Production × SHP content

(1,800 × 3) + (400 × 4.2) + (460 × 5.6)

∴ Actual production = 9,656 SHP's

4. Actual activity was 356 SHP's (9,656 – 9,300) greater than budget.

Task 2 *(answer page 185)*

(a) Calculate the following overhead variances based on the data in Scenario 8.3: overhead expenditure, overhead volume, and overhead efficiency.

(b) Reconcile these three variances to the Overhead Total Variances.

(c) Explain what the variances mean.

8.12 Overhead variances

It will be recalled that overheads are absorbed into production by using predetermined Overhead Absorption Rates (OAR) calculated from the budget. Overheads can be absorbed using production units or labour hours but when standard costing is used, absorption based on the standard hours of production (SHP) is most commonly used. Thus:

Total overheads absorbed = OAR × SHP

The overhead variances can be defined thus:

- *Production overhead total variance*:

  The difference between the standard overhead for actual production and the actual overheads.

The total variance can be sub-divided as follows:

- *Overhead expenditure variance*:

  The difference between budgeted and actual expenditure

- *Overhead volume variance*:

  The difference between standard overheads for actual hours and the flexed budget for actual hours

  (This variance measures the fixed overhead difference between absorbing overheads using a total OAR and flexing a budget).

- *Overhead efficiency variance*:

  The difference between the standard overheads for production achieved (measured in SHP) and the standard overheads for the actual hours taken (measured in labour hours).

  (This variance measures the overhead effects of working above or below standard efficiency).

Formulae

Total overhead variance:

SHP × OAR – Actual overheads

Overhead expenditure variance:

Actual total overhead – Budgeted total overheads

Overhead volume variance:

Budgeted total overheads – Actual hours × OAR

Overhead efficiency variance:

(SHP – actual hours) × OAR.

Notes:

Expenditure + volume + efficiency variances = Total variance. Budgeted total overheads are found by *flexing* the budget using the actual hours worked.

Example 3

Calculate the overhead variances for the data in Figure 8.2 and interpret.

Solution

It is necessary first to calculate the OAR from the budgeted figures.

Total budgeted overheads = Fixed + variable
= £25,530 + 18,630
= £44,160

Budgeted labour hours and SHP = 4,600

$$\text{OAR} = \frac{£44{,}160}{4{,}600} = £9.6 \text{ per hour.}$$

Overhead expenditure variance

(actual overheads – budgeted overheads)

£44,600 – 44,929.50 = **£329.50 FAV**

Note: The budgeted overheads is found by the usual process of flexing a budget, i.e.

Fixed overheads + Actual hours × Variable OAR

$$= £25{,}530 + \left(4{,}790 \times \frac{£18{,}630}{4{,}600}\right)$$

= £44,929.50.

Overhead volume variance

Budgeted total overheads – Actual hours × OAR
= £44,929.50 – (4,790 × £9.6)
= £44,929.50 – 45,984
= **£1,054.50 FAV**

Overhead efficiency variance

(SHP – Actual hours) × OAR
(4,960 – 4,790) × £9.6 = **£1,632 FAV**

Expenditure + volume + efficiency = Total variance
= £329.50 + 1,054.50 + 1,632
= **£3,016 FAV**

Proof:

Total overhead variance

(SHP × OAR) – Actual overheads
(4,960 × £9.6) – £44,600 = £47,616 – 44,600
= **£3,016 FAV**

Interpretation

Overhead variances are somewhat more complex than material and labour variances, mainly because of the conventions of overhead absorption.

The expenditure variance shows the difference between actual overheads and the budgeted allowance. In this example, actual spending is £329.50 less than the allowance when 4,790 hours are worked.

When activity is greater or less than budget, the volume variance shows the under or over recovery of the fixed element of the OAR. When activity is greater than budget (as in this example) there is over-recovery of fixed overheads resulting in a favourable variance. When activity is less than budget, an adverse variance will result. An alternative way of calculating the volume variance which demonstrates this point is:

(Actual hours – Budgeted hours) × Fixed OAR

$$= (4{,}790 - 4{,}600) \times \frac{£25{,}530}{4{,}600}$$

= 190 × £5.55 = **£1,054.50 FAV**

The efficiency variance shows the overhead effect of working above or below standard efficiency. In this example, 4,960 standard hours were produced in 4,790 actual labour hours which is above standard efficiency results in a favourable variance of £1,632.

Example 4

In conclusion, calculate the Total Production Cost Variance and reconcile with the material, labour and overhead variances already calculated.

Solution

The Total Production Cost Variance is the difference between the Actual cost of Actual Production and the Standard cost of Actual Production.

Standard cost, 1 unit Y252

	£
(from figure 8.2) Prime Cost	172.50
+ overheads 20 hours × £9.6	192.00
= Standard total cost per unit	364.50

Total variance = Actual costs – Standard cost of production
= £(12,620 + 29,524 + 44,600) – 248 × £364.50
= £86,744 – £90,396 = **£3,652 FAV**

i.e. actual costs were lower than standard.

Proof: Labour variance + Material variance + Overhead variance
= Total variance
= £236 + 400 + 3,016 = **£3,652 FAV**.

8.13 Extensions of variance analysis

This topic has introduced variance analysis but it must be realised that many more variances could be produced, if thought useful.

More detailed material, labour and overhead variances could be calculated plus those for sales. However, all variances follow a similar pattern so it is essential that the basics as covered in this topic are thoroughly understood.

Key point summary

- A standard cost is a target cost for a future period. It is not an average of past costs.
- Standard cosing is an important control technique best suited to repetitive manufacturing operations.
- Detailed standards for each product are recorded on a standard cost card.
- Problems in standard costing include: forecasting difficulties, changes in prices and methods, and possible behavioural difficulties.
- The advantages of standard costing include: cost control, simplification of record keeping, enhanced motivation.
- Variance analysis sub-divides the total difference between actual and standard into differences relating to material, labour and overheads.
- Price variances are always calculated first; thereafter standard price is used.
- The basis of virtually all variances is the following comparison: *Actual* cost of *Actual quantity* c.f. *Standard* cost of *Actual quantity*.
- A total variance can be sub-divided into a variance for, Price, Rate or Expenditure and a variance for Efficiency and Usage.
- The variances which should be calculated are those which are useful to management.

Need more detail or want to pursue a topic further?

Standard costing variance analysis	See *Management Accounting*, T. Lucey, DP Publications.

Developing knowledge and skills

Having dealt with the units covering Planning and Control, you are now in a position to tackle Part 2 of Section II.

As previously you will find it useful to deal with the Multiple Choice Questions (MCQ's) first. These range across the area of Planning and Control and will help to pin-point your weaknesses (if any). If you cannot understand any of the MCQ's, work through the relevant part of Section I again, and the additional references if required.

Part 2 of Section II starts on page 211.

Part 3

Decision making and performance appraisal

Introduction

This part outlines the ways to analyse short and long-term decision making and emphasises the key financial information required to assist management to make better decisions. As decision making relates to the future, risk and uncertainty are ever present and some ways of incorporating the effects of uncertainty into the analysis are covered.

It concludes with coverage of the ways accounting assists with performance appraisal.

Decision making and marginal costing

Decision making is explained and relevant costs and revenues defined. The principles of and use of marginal costing for short-run decision making is explained. Finally, the use of marginal costing for the routine accounting system is covered.

Contents

Background to decision making

Scenario A Decision making

It was the end of Alan's period at SBP so he thanked Brian for all his assistance and patience. Alan felt he had learned a lot about management accounting although he realised that there was still much he didn't known.

Alan spent his first day back at Group HQ discussing what he had learned with John Wellington who was quite impressed. John thought it was now time Alan turned his attention to the way management accounting information helped management to make decisions. He explained that management continually had to make choices between alternatives and needed information on which to base their decisions. He emphasised that although financial considerations were usually important in a decision, many other factors had also to be considered. These might include; personal characteristics, consumer preferences, political influences, social and marketing factors, communication implications and so on.

Alan was puzzled about what financial information a manager needed to make decisions and asked John about this. John explained that the key requirement was *relevance*, that is, the information must be specific to the decision being considered. He explained that as all decision making concerned the future, relevant information must relate to the future. Also, relevant information was concerned with differences between the alternatives. If, say, a cost was common to all alternatives then it was not relevant; it was the differences that were important. John explained that, for convenience, decisions could be sub-divided into those concerned with the short-term (say within the next year) and longer-term ones dealing with several years. He thought that Alan should first concentrate on information for short-term decision making.

John explained that it was not always obvious which were relevant costs and incomes for a particular decision and showed Alan some examples he had dealt with recently.

(a) An enquiry had been received for a product which required two types of material; steel and plastic.

Steel: Used regularly for various products. The present enquiry needs 2,000 kgs and there is 27,000 kgs in stock bought at £3.50 per kg. The current replacement cost is £3.80 kg.

Plastic: The enquiry requires 800 kgs and there is 1,200 kgs in stock bought at £8 kg. The current replacement price is £9 kg. This material is not used on any other product and the current stock could be sold at £7.50 kg.

(b) The Group rents a small office building for £800 per week and because there is no immediate use for the building, sub-lets it for £1,000 per week.

Quick answer questions

1. What is decision making?
2. What are the key features of relevant costs and incomes for decision making?
3. Are financial factors the only ones to be considered in making decisions?

1. Decision making is choosing between alternatives. It always concerns the future as we clearly cannot alter what has already happened.

2. Relevant costs and incomes are: future costs and incomes; and differential costs and incomes, i.e. those that will alter as a result of the decision.

3. No. Depending on the particular decision, numerous other factors may need to be considered e.g. psychological, social, environmental, political etc.

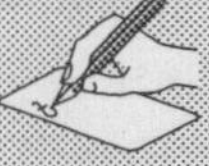

Task 1 *(answer page 185)*

(a) What are the relevant costs of steel and plastic for use in preparing the quotation in response to the enquiry? (Example a).

(b) In Example b the Group is considering using the rented offices for their own purposes. What is the appropriate rental cost to use in this decision?

(c) What general rules govern the identification of relevant costs?

9.1 What is decision making?

Decision making means making a choice between alternatives in pursuit of an objective. Decision making relates to the future; nothing can be done now that will alter the past. As the future cannot be known with certainty, decision making must cope with the effects of uncertainty.

The emphasis of this book is on decision making by managers in organisations; what may be termed rational decision making. Although many other factors are involved in these types of decision (for example personal, psychological, and social considerations) quantitative and financial information plays a crucial part, especially that relating to costs and revenues. It is vital however that the information supplied is relevant for the decision being considered. What is relevant information is dealt with later in the chapter.

In summary, decision making:

- means making choices between future, uncertain alternatives.
- needs clear objectives to be specified.
- needs relevant information.

9.2 The decision process

The decision process can be sub-divided into stages although in practice the divisions between the stages may be blurred. The stages are:

(a) *Definition of objectives*

The objectives should be specific and quantified wherever possible; eg. maximise profit or contribution, minimise cost, reduce delivery and so on.

(b) *Consider possible alternatives*

The various ways that the objective(s) can be achieved should be listed. Ideally, all possible options should be included.

(c) *Evaluate alternatives*

The financial and quantitative implications of each of the alternatives should be compared. It is at this stage that the 'relevant' information mentioned earlier would be used, especially that relating to the costs and revenues of each alternative. In addition, the risk and uncertainties of the options should be assessed, if possible.

(d) *Choose the best option*

Having regard to the analysis outlined above and the specified objectives the best option(s) is chosen. This may be the one that produces the maximum profit or contribution or one that is the best compromise between profit and risk. In practice of course, decision making is rarely as clear cut as indicated. There are competing claims for limited resources, there are political and personal pressures, there is risk and uncertainty and so on.

9.3 Relevant costs and revenues

The importance of relevancy has already been stressed and it is now time to consider what are relevant costs and revenues. In summary, relevant costs and revenues are:

(a) *Future costs and revenues*

Decision making is concerned with the future so it is *expected future costs and revenues* which are important to the decision maker. This means that the records of past costs and revenues contained in the accounting system are of value only in so far as they provide a guide to future values. Costs which have already been spent, known as *sunk costs*, are irrelevant for decision making. Fortunately, past cost levels are often a good guide to future levels but they cannot be accepted uncritically. It is how costs behave tomorrow that is important for decision making; not how they behaved yesterday.

(b) *Changes in costs and revenues*

Only costs and revenues which alter as a result of a decision are relevant. If a cost or revenue remains the same for all the options being considered it can be ignored; only the differences are relevant. These types of cost and revenues are known as *differential* costs and revenues. They are costs which may be avoided or revenues foregone, if the particular alternative is not adopted.

Some examples follow illustrating relevant costs.

Example 1 – Relevant cost examples

A contract has been offered which will utilise an existing machine which is suitable only for such contracts. The machine cost £40,000 four years ago and has been depreciated on a straight line basis. It has a current book value of £24,000. The machine could be sold now for £28,000 or for £22,000 after completion of the contract.

The contract uses three types of material:

	Units		Prices per unit		
Material	**In stock**	**Contract requirements**	**Purchase price of stock**	**Current buying-in price**	**Current resale price**
			£	£	£
A	1,700	1,300	4.80	5.30	5.00
B	2,400	3,600	3.75	3.30	2.50
C	1,200	400	2.20	3.10	2.40

A is in regular use within the firm. B could be sold if not used for the contract. There are no other uses for C which has been deemed to be obsolete.

What are the relevant costs to use in the contract decision for the machine and the three materials?

Solution

Machine costs.
The original purchase price is a sunk cost and is not relevant.
The depreciation details given relate to accounting conventions and are not relevant.
The relevant cost is the reduction in resale value over the contract life, i.e.

£28,000 – 22,000 = **£6,000**

Materials

Material A

Although there is sufficient in stock, the use of 1,300 units for the contract would necessitate the need for replenishment at the current buying in price.

Relevant cost = 1,300 × £5.30 = **£6,890**

Material B

If the contract was not accepted, 2,400 units of B could be sold at £2.50 per unit. The balance of 1,200 required would need to be bought at the current buying in price.

Relevant cost = 2,400 × £2.50 =	£6,000
+ 1,200 × £3.30 =	£3,960
	£9,960

Material C

If 400 units were used on the contract they could not be sold so the relevant cost is the current resale price of £2.40.

Relevant cost = 400 × £2.40 = **£960**

Note: It will be seen that the recorded historical cost, which is the 'cost' using normal accounting conventions is not the relevant value in any of the circumstances considered.

Example 2

A firm is considering whether to continue work on an existing contract or to terminate it now and pay an agreed penalty of £70,000 to the client. This is being considered because the penalty is less than the anticipated contract loss.

The following summary has been prepared:

	£	£
Expenditure to date		130,000
Estimated future costs to completion in 1 year's time		
Material	60,000	
Staffing	30,000	
Overheads	60,000	
		150,000
Estimated total cost		280,000
Contract value		200,000
Estimated loss on contract		£80,000

The following information is also available.

Material

Contracts have been exchanged for the purchase of the £60,000 material. This is special purpose material which has no alternative use. If not used on this contract it will incur disposal costs of £10,000.

Staffing

Two specialists are employed on the contract each at £12,500 pa. If the contract was terminated now they would each receive £7,000 redundancy pay. The other £5,000 staffing cost is the allocated cost for a supervisor who is also in charge of several other contracts.

Overheads

The £60,000 comprises £20,000 specific to the contract and £40,000 general fixed overheads allocated to the contract.

Required:

Prepare relevant financial information so that the firm can decide whether or not to abandon the contract.

Solution

Relevant benefits of continuation.

	£	Notes
Contract	200,000	
Penalty saved	70,000	1
Material disposal costs saved	10,000	2
	280,000	

Relevant costs of continuation.

	£	Notes
Staff	11,000	3
Overheads	20,000	4
	31,000	

∴ net benefit from continuation = £280,000 – 31,000 = £249,000

Contract should be continued to completion.

Notes

1. If the contract is continued the firm will not have to pay the penalty of £70,000. This is therefore a benefit of continuation.
2. Similarly, if the material is used on the contract, the £10,000 disposal costs will be saved. Note that the cost of £60,000 for the material will be incurred whether or not the contract continues so is not a relevant cost for the decision being considered.
3. The staff will cost £25,000 if the contract is continued but their redundancy pay will be saved. (£25,000 – 14,000 = £11,000).
   The £5,000 allocated cost is not relevant as the supervisor will continue to be paid whether or not the contract continues.
4. The £20,000 overheads specific to the contract are avoidable and therefore relevant. The allocated fixed costs are not relevant.
5. The expenditure to date of £130,000 is a sunk cost and is not relevant for the decision.
6. To prove the net benefit of £249,000 from continuation the statement below shows the opposing position, i.e. if the contract is abandoned. This naturally produces a cost of £249,000.

	£
Benefits from abandonment	
Staff salary savings	25,000
Overhead savings	20,000
Total savings	45,000
Costs of abandonment	£
Penalty	70,000
Material disposal costs	10,000
Redundancy payments	14,000
Loss of contract value	200,000
Total costs	294,000

∴ cost of abandonment: + 45,000 – 294,000 = **– £249,000.**

Examples of decision making

Scenario B A make or buy decision

Having explained to Alan the background to decision making, John thought that Alan should look at some specific decisions and their information requirements. He selected a recent example:

A make or buy decision

Morden Engineering were considering whether to manufacture or purchase a switch assembly. This would be in batches of 1,000. The buying in price was £13 and the marginal cost of manufacture was £9.50. However the switch would have to be made in the contactor department which was busy and manufacture of the switch would cause output of Control Panel ME7 to be reduced by 40 units. The Panels sell at £550 each and have a marginal cost of £410 each.

Should Morden make or buy the switch assembly?

The cost analysis provided for Morden's management was as follows:

Cost analysis : Switch assembly

Make or buy decision (batches of 1,000)

	£
Marginal cost of manufacture = £9.50 × 1,000	9,500
+ Lost contribution for Control Panels = £140 × 40	5,600
Relevant manufacturing cost	15,100
Buying-in price = £13 × 1,000	13,000

∴ Gain from buying-in; £2,100 per 1,000 batch
∴ Buy in.

John explained that in a normal make or buy decision the comparison is between the marginal cost of manufacture and the buying-in price. In this example the contribution lost from the displaced manufacture was also relevant so had to be included in the analysis.

Quick answer questions

1. What is:
   Marginal cost?
   Contribution?
2. In the example the decision was to buy-in. What would be the decision if there was spare manufacturing capacity so that no other products were displaced?
3. What is the type of costing called that distinguishes between fixed and marginal costs?

1. *Marginal cost = Variable cost, i.e. those costs which vary with activity changes.*

   Contribution = Sales – Marginal cost

2. *Where there is spare capacity the comparison is between the marginal cost of manufacture and the buying-in price. In this case, £9,500 and £13,000. Thus it would be better to manufacture rather than buy-in.*

3. *Marginal costing distinguishes between fixed and variable costs. Marginal costing principles are widely used in short-run decision making.*

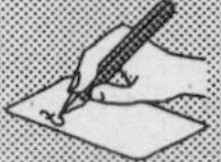

Task 2 *(answer page 186)*

(a) What type of cost is the £5,600 lost contribution from the displaced manufacture?

(b) What relevance for decision making has this type of cost?

(c) Why haven't fixed costs been included in the cost analysis shown in B?

(d) Are sunk costs relevant for decision making?

9.4 Short term and long term decision making

The principles of decision making and of relevant costs and revenues apply equally to short and long term decision making.

Short term decision making deals with problems concerning the immediate period ahead say, up to 1 year hence. Problems covering periods longer than a year would normally be classed as long term.

The major difference between the two is that for long run decisions, usually called investment decisions, the time value of money has to be considered. Investment decisions are dealt with later in the book. Short term decision making is dealt with below.

9.5 Short-term decision making and marginal costing

Marginal costing was introduced earlier. Its key features are: the separation of costs into fixed and variable and the calculation of contribution. Contribution is: sales less variable costs.

Marginal costing is a useful technique for short-term decision making because, in the short term, fixed cost remain the same, and the only costs that alter (and thus the only ones that are relevant) are the variable costs. Accordingly, the selection of the option which maximises contribution is usually the correct decision.

Note: Variable costs can also be called *marginal costs.*

9.6 Examples of decision making using marginal costing

Several typical problems using marginal costing are illustrated below. Once the general principles are understood they can be applied in any other similar circumstances.

The steps in analysing such problems are:

(a) If necessary, separate out fixed and variable costs.

(b) Check that fixed costs are expected to stay the same.

(c) Calculate the revenue, marginal cost and contribution of each of the alternatives.

(d) Check to see if there will be a key factor which will be binding. If so, calculate the contribution per unit of the key factor.

(e) Finally, select the alternative which maximises contribution.

Example 4 – Special order decision

(Typically these decisions are required when a firm has spare capacity and is offered a special order, below normal prices, which will take up the unused capacity.)

Morning Start Limited manufacture a breakfast cereal which they sell for 50p per packet. Current output is 200,000 packets per period which represents 80% of capacity. They have the opportunity to use the surplus capacity by selling their product at 30p per packet to a supermarket chain who will sell it as an 'own label' product.

Total costs for last period were £70,000 of which £20,000 were fixed. This represented a total cost of 35p per packet.

Should the supermarket order be accepted even though the selling price is below total cost?

What other factors should be considered?

Solution

The key point is that the price of 30p offered by the supermarket should be compared with the marginal cost of production, not with total cost (assuming fixed costs do not change).

The present position is

	£	
Sales (200,000 × 50p)	100,000	
less marginal cost	50,000	(i.e. 25p per packet)
= Contribution	50,000	
less fixed cost	20,000	
= profit	30,000	

The supermarket order would produce the following extra contribution:

	£
Sales (50,000 × 30p)	15,000
less marginal cost (50,000 × 25p)	12,500
= contribution	2,500

Thus, assuming that fixed costs remain the same the profit would increase from £30,000 to £32,500 so, on the figures above, the supermarket order looks worthwhile.

However, before a final decision is made several other factors need to be considered.

(a) Will the acceptance of one order at a lower price lead other customers to demand lower prices as well?

(b) Is this particular order the most profitable wayof using the space capacity?

(c) Will the supermarket order lock up capacity which could be used for future full price business?

(d) Is it absolutely certain that fixed costs will not alter?

(e) Will sales of the product in the supermarket's 'own label' form reduce the main branded sales?

Example 5 – Dropping a product

(If a company has a range of products one of which is thought to be unprofitable it may consider dropping the 'loss-making' product. Exactly the same principles would be involved if it was a department, not a product).

A company makes three products, one of which shows a loss, and it is considering whether to drop the unprofitable product. The following statement has been prepared.

	Product A	Product B	Product C	Total
	£	£	£	£
Sales	90,000	160,000	145,000	395,000
Total costs	102,000	126,000	108,000	336,000
Profit (loss)	(12,000)	34,000	37,000	59,000

The total costs are $\frac{2}{3}$ variable $\frac{1}{3}$ fixed.

Based on the above information should Product A be dropped. What other factors should be considered?

Solution

First calculate the fixed costs for the firm as a whole and the marginal or variable costs for each Product.

	Product A	Product B	Product C	Total
	£	£	£	£
Total costs (as given)	102,000	126,000	108,000	336,000
Fixed costs $(\frac{1}{3})$	34,000	42,000	36,000	112,000
Variable costs $(\frac{2}{3})$	68,000	84,000	72,000	224,000

It is a feature of the Marginal Costing approach that Fixed Costs are not spread over the individual products or department, but kept as a single total, in this case £112,000.

The original statement can now be rearranged in Marginal Costing form.

	Product A	Product B	Product C	Total
	£	£	£	£
Sales	90,000	160,000	145,000	395,000
Less marginal costs	68,000	84,000	72,000	224,000
= contribution	22,000	76,000	73,000	171,000
			less fixed costs	112,000
			= profit	59,000

Naturally, this presentation gives the same overall profit but, in addition, the contribution of each product is shown. It will be seen that Product A provides a contribution of £22,000 which means that the Product is worthwhile.

If Product A was dropped the position would be:

	£
Contribution Product B	76,000
Contribution Product C	73,000
	149,000
less Fixed costs	112,000
Profit	£37,000

Thus dropping Product A with an apparent loss of £12,000 reduces total profit by £22,000 which is, of course, the amount of contribution lost from Product A.

Other factors which need to be considered.

(a) The assumption above was that the fixed costs were general fixed costs which would remain if Product A was dropped. If some of the fixed costs were specific to Product A and would cease if the product was dropped then this would need to be taken into account.

(b) Although Product A produces some contribution, it is at a low rate compared to the other products. Other more profitable products should be considered.

Scenario C **Limiting or key factors**

John explained to Alan that for short-run decision making the general rule was to choose the alternative which produced the maximum contribution. Normally the option was obvious but sometimes it was not so clear cut. This could happen when one of the factors in the problem was limited or constrained. For example, skilled labour or a special material might be in short supply. In these circumstances, overall contribution would be maximised when the option was chosen which produced the most contribution per unit of the limiting factor. John was working on a typical problem and showed Alan the following details:

All-Round Security Ltd is one of the Group Companies and manufactures electronic security and surveillance equipment. It makes four main systems each of which uses a number of E5986 micro-chips which, because of a labour dispute in the suppliers, are limited to 110,000 in the next period. The following cost and production data are available.

	System 1	System 2	System 3	System 4
	£	£	£	£
Selling price				
Unit	400	600	800	720
Marginal cost/unit	240	440	480	440
Maximum sales				
Demand (units)	5,000	5,000	5,000	5,000
Usage of micro-chips per unit	6	18	10	12

The Management of All Round Security Ltd wish to know what is the most appropriate mix of production for the period given that no other materials are in short-supply and there is adequate capacity to make all products up to their maximum demand.

Quick answer questions

1. Why is the supply of micro-chips a limiting factor?
2. What is the contribution per unit for each of the four systems?
3. In practice what do you think is the most common limiting factor?

1. *The total requirement for micro-chips is: (5,000 × 6) + (5,000 × 18) + (5,000 × 10) + (5,000 × 12) =* ***230,000*** *but only 110,000 are available ∴ the reduced availability of micro-chips is a limiting factor.*

2. ***Contribution calculations***

	System 1	*System 2*	*System 3*	*System 4*
	£	*£*	*£*	*£*
Sales price	*400*	*600*	*800*	*720*
less Marginal cost	*240*	*440*	*480*	*440*
= Contribution per unit	*160*	*160*	*320*	*280*

3. *The most common limiting factor is sales i.e. a firm is generally unable to sell all it can manufacture.*

Task 3 *(answer page 186)*

(a) Calculate the contribution per unit of the limiting factor for the data in C.

(b) Devise the most appropriate mix of production for All-Round Security for the period.

(c) Calculate the contribution in the period for your plan.

9.7 Key factor

Sometimes known as the limiting factor or principal budget factor. This was mentioned previously when dealing with budgeting and it will be recalled that the key factor is a binding constraint upon the organisation, i.e. the factor which prevents indefinite expansion or unlimited profits. It may be sales, availability of skilled labour, space, supplies of material or finance. Where a single key factor can be identified, then the general objective of maximising contribution can be achieved by selecting the option which *maximises the contribution per unit of the key factor.* An example follows which illustrates the principles to be used for short-run decision making where a limiting or key factor exists.

Example 6 – Key factor decision

(This is a problem where a firm has a choice between various products and there is a single binding constraint).

A company is able to produce four products and is planning its production mix for the next period. Estimated cost, sales, and production data are:

Product	L	M	N	O
	£	£	£	£
Selling price per unit	60	90	120	108
Less Variable costs				
Labour (at £6 per hour)	18	12	42	30
Material (at £3 per kg)	18	54	30	36
= Contribution per unit	24	24	48	42
Resources per unit				
Labour (hours)	3	2	7	5
Material (kgs)	6	18	10	12
Maximum demand (units)	5,000	5,000	5,000	5,000

Example 6 – continued

Based on the above information what is the most profitable production mix under the two following assumptions:

(a) If labour hours are limited to 50,000 in a period, *or*

(b) If material is limited to 110,000 kgs in a period

Solution

It will be seen that all the products show a contribution so that there is a case for their production. However, because constraints exist, the products must be ranked in order of contribution per unit of the limiting factor so that overall contribution can be maximised. Accordingly, the contribution per unit of the inputs must be calculated.

Product	L	M	N	O
	£	£	£	£
Contribution per unit	24	24	48	42
Contribution per labour hour	8	12	6.85	8.5
Contribution per kg. of material	4	1.33	4.8	3.5

When labour hours are restricted to 50,000:

To make all products to the demand limits would need (5,000 × 3) + (5,000 × 2) + (5,000 × 7) + (5,000 × 5) = 85,000 hours. As there is a limit of 50,000 hours in a period the products should be ranked in order of attractiveness judged by contribution per labour hour, i.e. M, O, L and N.

Best production plan when labour is restricted

Produce	5,000 units M using	10,000	labour hours
	5,000 units O using	25,000	labour hours
	5,000 using L using	15,000	labour hours
and no units of N			
which uses the total of		50,000	hours available

Thus if labour hours are restricted to 50,000 the maximum possible contribution is (5,000 × £24) + (5,000 × £42) + (5,000 × £24) = £450,000

No other plan will produce more total contribution when labour is limited.

When material is restricted to 110,000 kgs.

Similar reasoning produces a ranking by contribution per kg of material of N, L, O, M which will be noted is the opposite to the ranking produced if labour was the constraint.

Best production plan when material is restricted

Produce	5,000 units N using	50,000	kgs material
	5,000 units L using	30,000	kgs material
	2,500 using O using	30,000	kgs material
and no units of M			
which uses the total of		110,000	kgs material

Thus if material is restricted to 110,000 kilograms the maximum possible contribution is (5,000 × £48) + (5,000 × £24) + (2,500 × £42) = **£465,000**. No other plan will produce more contribution when material is limited.

Note: In general where no constraint is identified a reasonable decision rule is to choose the alternative which maximises contribution per £ of sales value.

Marginal costing and decision making – summary

The examples above are merely some indicative ones and marginal costing principles can be applied to many other types of short run decisions. Where fixed costs remain the same for all the alternatives being considered, and this should always be verified, then variable or marginal costs and the resulting contributions are the relevant factors.

The use of total costs, including a fixed element, can be misleading in decision making and it is usually more informative to separate fixed and variable costs and to show contribution.

9.8 Marginal costing and the routine accounting system

In addition to its use in decision making, marginal costing can also be used in the routine accounting system for calculating cost, valuing stocks and as a basis for the presentation of information. The alternative method is known as total costing (or absorption costing) and the two approaches are illustrated below.

Example 7

In a period 40,000 units of S were produced and sold. Costs and revenues were:

	£
Sales	200,000
Production costs	
variable	70,000
fixed	30,000
General overheads	
fixed	50,000

Produce operating statements using total costing and marginal costing showing the results for the period.

Solution

Operating statements

Total costing approach	**£**	**Marginal costing approach**		**£**
Sales	200,000	Sales		200,000
Less production cost of sales	100,000	*Less* marginal cost		70,000
= Gross profit	100,000	= Contribution		130,000
Less general overheads	50,000	*Less* fixed costs		
		Production	30,000	
		General	50,000	
				80,000
= Net profit	£50,000	= Net profit		£50,000

Notes

(a) The key figure in the marginal statement is the contribution of £130,000. Note that this is not the same as the gross profit in the total cost approach because the production costs of £100,000 are a combination of fixed and variable elements.

(b) In this case the statements produce the same net profit. This is because there were no stocks but where stocks exist, differences arise. This is dealt with below.

9.9 Stock valuations: marginal and total costing

Where there are stocks at the end of a period they are normally valued as follows:

Using Total Costing:

at total production cost (i.e. including both fixed and variable costs)

Using Marginal Costing:

at marginal production cost (i.e. no fixed costs are included)

The effect of these valuation methods is, that, using total costing, some of a period's fixed costs are transferred to the next period through the stock valuation. Using marginal costing *all* the fixed costs of a period are charged in that period as only variable costs are transferred in the stock valuation.

This is illustrated below.

Example 8

Assume the same data as Example 7 except that only 36,000 of the 40,000 units produced were sold, 4,000 units being carried forward to the next period.

Produce operating statements based on marginal costing and total costing principles.

Solution

Workings

Stock valuations:

Using total costing

$$\text{Cost per unit} = \frac{\text{Total production cost,}}{\text{No. of units produced}}$$

$$= \frac{£100{,}000}{40{,}000} = £2.50$$

Closing stock value = 4,000 × £2.50 = **£10,000**

Using marginal costing

$$\text{Cost per unit} = \frac{\text{Marginal production cost}}{\text{No. of units produced}}$$

$$= \frac{£70{,}000}{40{,}000} = £1.75$$

Closing stock value = 4,000 × £1.75 = **£7,000**

The statements can now be prepared.

Operating statements

Total costing		**£**	**Marginal costing**		**£**
Sales (36,000 × £5)		180,000	Sales		180,000
Less Production cost	£100,000		*Less* Marginal cost	£70,000	
– closing stock	10,000		– closing stock	7,000	
		90,000			63,000
= Gross profit		90,000	= Contribution		117,000
Less General overheads		50,000	*Less* Fixed costs		
			Production	30,000	
			General	50,000	
					80,000
= Net profit		£40,000	= Net profit		£37,000

Notes

(a) The difference in profits shown is entirely due to the difference in stock valuation.

(b) In effect, the total absorption approach transfers £3,000 of this period's fixed costs into next period and thus shows a £3,000 higher profit.

(c) All other things being equal the position would be reversed in the next period. Then, the results using the marginal costing approach would show the higher profit because they would not be carrying part of a previous period's fixed costs.

(d) Either technique could be used for routine internal reporting. However, because absorption costing is the recommended basis for external financial accounting, the total costing approach is probably more commonly used for internal purposes as well.

It must be stressed, however, that the use of marginal costing principles as an aid to *decision making is universal* and is very important.

Key point summary

- Decision making is making a choice between alternatives in pursuit of an objective.
- Decision making relates to the future, which is always uncertain.
- The decision process is: consider alternatives, evaluate alternatives, choose best option.
- Relevant costs and revenues are; future costs and revenues which change as a result of the decision.
- Sunk costs and costs which are common to all options, are irrelevant for decision making.
- Expected value is probability × value.
- Marginal costing is useful for short run decision making.
- In the short run, fixed costs are likely to remain unchanged and the relevant factors are variable (or marginal) costs and contribution
- A key factor is a binding constraint which prevents indefinite expansion or unlimited profits.
- Where a key factor exists the best decision rule is to choose the option which maximises contribution per unit of the key factor.

- ❒ Marginal costing principles can be applied to numerous decisions. Examples include; special order acceptance, dropping a product or department and so on.
- ❒ Marginal costing can also be used for the routine internal accounting system. The important differences to a total absorption system is the separation of fixed and variable costs and the calculation of contribution.
- ❒ Marginal costing values stocks at variable cost. Absorption costing values them at total production cost.

Need more detail or want to pursue a topic further?

Decision making	See *Management Information Systems*, T Lucey, DP Publications.
Marginal costing	See *Management Accounting*, T Lucey, DP Publications.

Risk and uncertainty and break-even analysis

The problems of risk and uncertainty in decision making are described and then break-even (B-E) analysis is explained. Useful B-E formulae are given and the main B-E charts are described and illustrated.

Contents

Risk and uncertainty

Scenario A Risk and uncertainty in decision making

After studying various examples of decision making, Alan saw that marginal costing principles could be useful for analysing many short-run decisions. He wondered whether there were any other general problems about decision making of which he should be aware and asked John for guidance.

John explained that an ever present problem was risk and uncertainty. As decision making related to the future we could not be certain about our estimates. Sales might be less than expected, there could be cost over-runs, there might be increased competition, tastes might change and so on. The future is always uncertain and risk is ever present. John explained that decision makers had to take risk and uncertainty into account as far as possible and the information supplied to them should also allow for uncertainty. John conceded that there were no complete answers to this problem but felt that it was essential to try to include the effects of uncertainty into the information supplied to Managers. He said that many techniques were used. Examples included; showing the High-Low values expected for the estimates of sales, costs and so on, using normal single value estimates but attaching a statement about uncertainty, commissioning market research studies to assess future demand, and the use of expected value calculations.

John explained that expected value (EV) was a simple way of incorporating people's judgements about outcomes into the analysis. The EV of an outcome was: value × probability. For example, the sales manager might forecast that there was 40% chance of £100,000 sales and 60% chance of £140,000 sales.

$$\text{EV sales} = (£100{,}000 \times 40\%) + (£140{,}000 \times 60\%) = £124{,}000$$

As an example of the use of expected values John showed Alan a problem he was currently studying for Compressed Fibres Ltd, one of the Group Companies.

Compressed Fibres make specialised insulation kits and there is uncertainty both about the level of sales and the marginal cost of the kits. The following estimates have been made.

	Units	Probability
Sales:		
Optimistic estimate	250,000	0.1
Most likely estimate	220,000	0.6
Pessimistic estimate	175,000	0.3
	£	Probability
Marginal costs/unit:		
Optimistic estimate	6.50	0.3
Most likely estimate	7.25	0.7

The kits are sold at £10 per unit

Quick answer questions

1. Why must the effects of risk and uncertainty be considered in decision making?
2. How is Expected Value calculated?
3. In the Compressed Fibres example what is the total of the probabilities for the sales estimates? What does this mean?

1. Decision making is always concerned with the future. The future cannot be forecast with certainty so the effects of uncertainty must be considered in making the decision.

2. Expected Value = Value × Probability

3. Total of probabilities for sales estimates = 0.1 + 0.6 + 0.3 = 1.0
A probability of 1 means that all the options have been included. Note also that the probabilities for the marginal cost estimates also total 1.0.

Task 1 *(answer page 186)*

(a) Using the data in A calculate the Expected Value of the contribution for the period for Compressed Fibres.

(b) What is the maximum possible contribution and what is its probability?

(c) What is the minimum contribution and what is its probability?

10.1 Risk and uncertainty in decision making

If the future was known with certainty then forecasts could be made which would be exactly achieved.

This would greatly assist decision making but life is not as simple as that. Uncertainty does exist and actual results rarely turn out exactly as anticipated.

There is no technique which enables us to forecast the future perfectly. All we can do is to help the decision maker by indicating some of the uncertainties which exist and by producing information which shows the variabilities expected. There are numerous techniques which can be used. Some use advanced mathematical and statistical methods outside the scope of this book but one commonly used technique, that of *expected value*, is described below.

10.2 Expected value

Expected value is a simple way of bringing some of the effects of uncertainty into the appraisal process. Expected value is the average value of an event which has several possible outcomes. The expected value or average is found by multiplying the value of each outcome by its probability. The probability of an outcome (probability could also be called the likelihood or chance of the outcome occurring) is based on the judgement of the people concerned.

For example, assume that it is required to forecast the sales for next month. The Sales Manager thinks that there is a 40% (or.4) chance that sales will be 10,000 units and a 60% (or .6) chance that they will be 13,000 units. What is the expected value of sales?

Expected sales value = (10,000 ×.4) + (13,000 ×.6)
= **11,800 units.**

Thus, the use of expected value enables the variabilities and their likelihoods, that is the uncertainties, to be incorporated into the information. Where several alternatives are being considered each of which has several outcomes the usual decision rules is to choose the option with the highest expected value.

Example 1 – Expected value

Three options are being considered, each of which has several possible outcomes. The values and probabilities have been estimated as follows:

Option A Outcomes		**Option B Outcomes**		**Option C Outcomes**	
Probability	**Profit £**	**Probability**	**Profit £**	**Probability**	**Profit £**
0.3	8,000	0.2	4,000	0.3	2,500
0.7	11,000	0.3	7,000	0.4	9,000
		0.4	10,000	0.3	15,000
		0.1	14,000		

Required

Calculate the expected values of the three options and recommend which should be accepted.

Solution

Expected values

Option A

(0.3 × 8,000) + (0.7 × 11,000) = **£10,100**

Option B

(0.2 × 4,000) + (0.3 × 7,000) + (0.4 × 10,000) + (0.1 × 14,000) = **£8,300**

Option C

(0.3 × 2,500) + (0.4 × 9,000) + (0.3 × 15,000) = **£8,850**

Thus, on the basis of Expected Value, Option A would be preferred and the options would be ranked ACB.

Notes:

(a) In each case it will be seen that the probabilities total 1 (or 100%). This shows that all outcomes have been included.

(b) The number of outcomes can vary as shown in the example, but a commonly encountered situation is that shown for Option C where there are three outcomes; often termed Optimistic, Most Likely and Pessimistic.

What is break-even analysis?

Scenario B **Break-even analysis**

John emphasised to Alan that the interaction of marginal and fixed costs, sales and contribution that he had been studying in connection with short-run decision making was also used in what was called Break-even analysis, alternatively called Cost/Volume/profit (CVP) analysis.

It showed, in a summary fashion, what the firm's profits would be at various activity levels, at what level of sales the firm would break-even (i.e. have neither a profit nor loss) and other similar information. John warned that there were many simplifying assumptions in CVP analysis so its findings should not be taken too literally. These assumptions include the following; that cost structures remain unchanged, that there is either a single product or a constant sales mix, there are no technology or method changes and so on. In spite of these sweeping assumptions John thought that CVP analysis could be useful especially for providing a broad overview.

John explained that CVP analysis could be carried out either by using simple formulae or by drawing charts. He showed Alan some of the main formulae as follows:

$$\text{Break-even point units} = \frac{\text{Fixed costs}}{\text{Contribution/unit}}$$

$$\text{Contribution : Sales i.e. CS ratio} = \frac{\text{Contribution/unit}}{\text{Selling price/unit}} \times 100$$

$$\text{Level of sales to achieve a target profit (units)} = \frac{\text{Fixed cost + Target profit}}{\text{Contribution/unit}}$$

John had been asked by the Group Finance Director to analyse some results for Balanced Air Ltd, a Group Company specialising in commercial air conditioning units. Summary information was as follows:

	Last period	Current period
	£m	£m
Sales	8	10
Total costs	7.75	8.75
Profit	0.25	1.25

Quick answer questions

1. Why is CVP analysis only suitable for studying short-term situations?
2. If a product sells for £1 and has a marginal cost of 60p, what is its CS ratio?
3. At break-even point:
   (a) total contribution equals sales
   (b) fixed costs equals sales
   (c) total contribution equals fixed costs
   (d) fixed costs equal marginal costs
   Which is correct?

1. Because in the long run, costs and cost structures change, methods and technology alter and other changes occur. CVP analysis assumes all these factors remain the same so is only suitable for the short-run.

2. Contribution = £1 − 60p = 40p

$\therefore$ *CS ratio* $= \frac{40p}{£1} \times 100 =$ **40%**

3. At break-even, total contribution equals fixed costs i.e. (c).

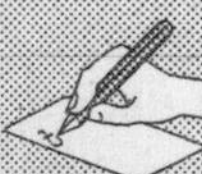

Task 2 *(answer page 186)*

1. Using Balanced Air Ltd's data calculate:
   (a) Break-even point (in units and sales value).
   (b) Sales, in units and value, to achieve £1.5m profit.
   (c) The margin of safety if the budgeted sales for next period are £10.5m.

10.3 Break-even analysis defined

This is the term given to the study of the relationships between costs, volume, contribution and profit at various levels of activity. Break-even analysis (B-E analysis) uses the principles of marginal costing and, like marginal costing, is best suited to short run problems where existing cost patterns are likely to continue. B-E analysis can be carried out using simple formulae or graphs. Both are illustrated in this Topic.

Like marginal costing, B-E analysis has a number of restrictive assumptions but it can provide useful guidance to management seeking answers to a variety of questions. For example, what profit will be made if sales are 25,000 units? How many units need to be sold to break-even (i.e. the point of neither profit nor loss)? What sales are needed to produce a profit of £75,000? and so on.

10.4 B-E Analysis by formula

Some typical B-E analysis formulae are given below and illustrated by examples.

$$\text{CS ratio} = \frac{\text{Contribution per unit}}{\text{Sales price per unit}} \%$$

(CS ratio means 'Contribution to sales' ratio)

$$\text{Break-even point (in units)} = \frac{\text{Fixed costs}}{\text{Contribution per unit}}$$

$$\text{Break-even point (sales value)} = \frac{\text{Fixed costs}}{\text{Contribution per unit}} \times \text{Sales price per unit}$$

$$\text{Level of sales to give a target profit (in units)} = \frac{\text{Fixed costs + Target profit}}{\text{Contribution per unit}}$$

$$\text{Level of sales to give a target profit (sales value)} = \frac{\text{Fixed costs + Target profit}}{\text{Contribution per unit}} \times \text{Sales price per unit}$$

Note: The above formulae assume a single product firm or one with a constant sales mix.

Example 2

A firm makes a single product which sells for £7 per unit and has a marginal cost of £4 per unit. Fixed costs are £50,000 pa.

Calculate:

(a) The CS ratio

(b) The number of units required to break-even

(c) The sales value required to break-even

(d) The number of units that need to be sold to make £31,000 profit

(e) The sales value required to make £31,000 profit.

Solution

Contribution = Sales – Marginal cost
= £7 – 4 = **£3 per unit**

(a) CS ratio = $\frac{£3}{7}$ = **0.43 or 43%**

(b) Break-even point (units) = $\frac{£50{,}000}{3}$ = **16,667 units**

(This means that when 16,667 units are sold the firm neither makes a profit nor a loss. At this level of sales the contribution exactly equals the fixed costs, i.e. 16,667 units × £3 = £50,000)

(c) Sales value to break-even = 16,667 × £7 = **£116,669**

(d) Units for £31,000 profit $= \dfrac{£50{,}000 + 31{,}000}{3}$

= **27,000 units**

(e) Sales value for £31,000 profit = 27,000 × £7

= **£189,000**

Scenario C Break-even charts

Alan asked John whether the Break-even Charts he had seen in various reports around the office were based on similar principles to those used in CVP or Break-even analysis by formula.

Exactly the same, said John. Furthermore, he explained, the charts were based on the same assumptions as CVP analysis and thus were only suitable for depicting short-run situations. John explained that there were various types of charts and they were useful for showing a broad over-view in a pictorial form. This was especially appropriate when financial information was being supplied to people without an accounting background. He explained that there were two main types of break-even chart; what was known as the *traditional break-even chart* and the *contribution break-even chart*. The main difference between the two being that in the traditional chart, fixed costs were plotted before variable costs whereas in the contribution chart variable costs were plotted first. The effect of this is that a contribution 'wedge' can be depicted on the contribution chart.

Naturally both types of chart show the same break-even point and the same profit at a given activity level.

John thought that it would be useful for Alan to prepare charts to illustrate the report he was preparing for the Group Finance Director on the results of Balanced Air Ltd, reproduced below.

	Last period	Current period
	£m	£m
Sales	8	10
Total costs	7.75	8.75
Profit	0.25	1.25

The average unit sells for £20,000.

Quick answer questions

1. What is the main purpose of preparing break-even charts?
2. What is the main difference between a traditional break-even chart and a contribution break-even chart?
3. Calculate the number of units Balance Air would have to sell to achieve their budgeted sales of £10.5m.

1. To show the interaction of costs and sales. They provide a pictorial overview of a company's position which can be useful when presenting financial information to non-accountants.
2. The main difference is the sequence of plotting fixed and variable costs. Fixed costs are plotted first in the traditional chart whereas variable costs are plotted first in contribution charts. This difference enables contribution to be shown on the latter charts.
3. $\frac{£10.5m}{£20,000}$ = **525 units.**

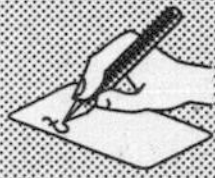

Task 3 *(answer page 187)*

(a) Using Balanced Air's data draw a traditional break-even chart showing clearly, the break-even point, margin of safety, and the profit at £10.5m sales.

(b) Draw a contribution chart for the above showing, in addition, the contribution wedge.

10.5 Graphical approach to B-E analysis

The graphical approach may be preferred when a simple overview is sufficient or when greater visual impact is required, such as in a report for management.
The basic chart is known as a *Break-Even Chart* and can be drawn in two ways. The first is known as the *traditional approach* and the other the *contribution approach*. Whatever method is used all costs must be separated into fixed and variable elements, i.e. semi-variable costs must be analysed into their components.

10.6 Traditional break-even chart

Assuming that fixed and variable costs have been separated, the chart is drawn as follows:

(a) Draw the axes

- ❐ The horizontal, showing levels of activity expressed as units of output or percentages of total capacity.
- ❐ The vertical, showing values in £'s or £'000s as appropriate, for costs and revenues.

(As with all graphs, some experimentation with the scales is usually required to produce a reasonable looking graph).

(b) Draw the cost lines

Fixed cost This is a straight line parallel to the horizontal axis at the level of the fixed cost.

Total cost This starts from the fixed cost line and is a straight line sloping upwards at an angle depending on the proportion of variable costs in total costs.

(c) Draw the revenue line

This is a straight line from the point of origin sloping upward at an angle determined by the selling price.

> *Example 3*
>
> A company makes a single product with a total capacity of 35,000 units. Cost and sales data are as follows:
>
> | | |
> |---|---|
> | Sales price | £7 per unit |
> | Marginal cost | £4 per unit |
> | Fixed costs | £50,000 |
>
> Draw a traditional break-even chart showing the profit at the expected production level of 27,000 units.

See Figure 10.1.

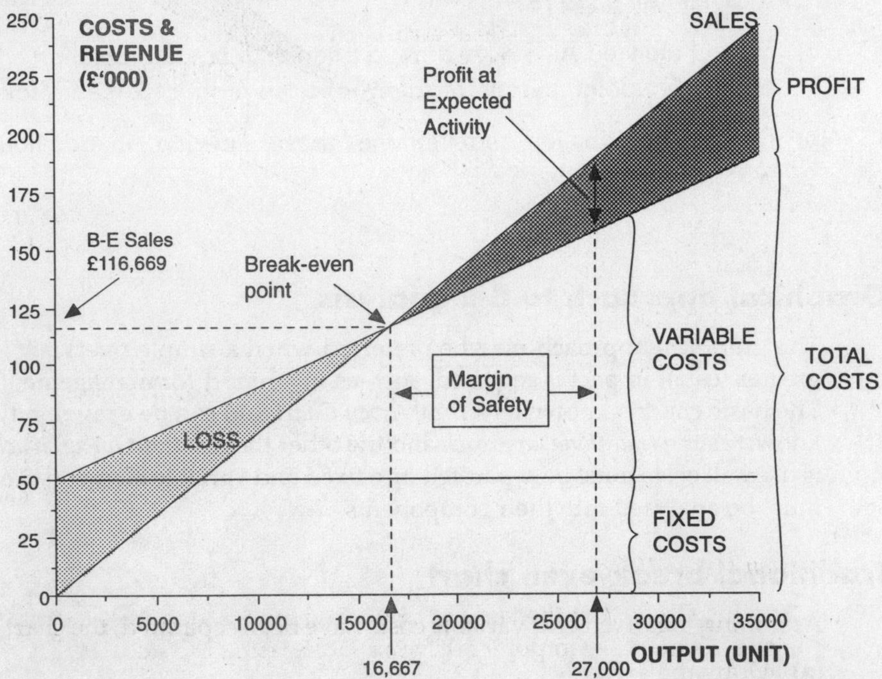

Figure 10.1 Traditional break-even chart

Notes on Figure 10.1.

(a) The *margin of safety'* shown on the graph is the term given to the difference between expected or normal production level and breakeven point. In this case, 27,000 – 16,667 units = <u>**10,333 units**</u>

(b) The graph is based on the same data used for Example 2. Compare the answers produced by using the B–E formulae and the graph.

(c) On the traditional B–E chart, plot fixed costs first *then* variable.

10.7 Contribution break-even chart

This uses the same axes and data as that for the traditional chart. The only difference is that variable costs are drawn before fixed costs. This produces a 'wedge' depicting the contribution earned at different levels.

Example 4

Repeat Example 3 except that a Contribution breakeven chart should be drawn. See Figure 10.2.

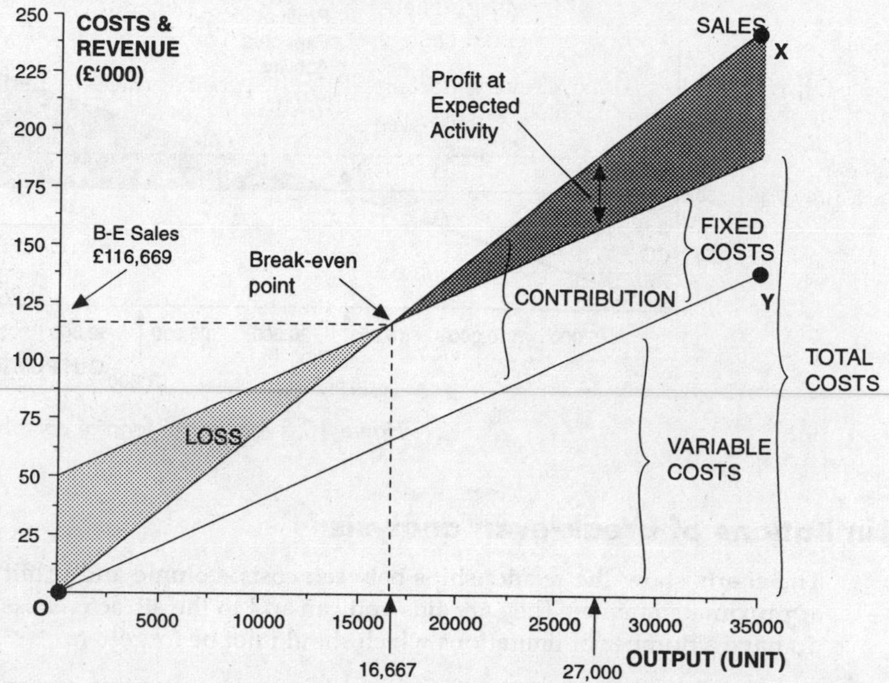

Figure 10.2 Contribution break-even chart

Notes on Figure 10.2.

(a) It will be seen that the *loss* and *profit* wedges are identical to the traditional chart and so is the break-even point and profit at the expected activity.

(b) Additional information is supplied by the *contribution* wedge (X, O, Y). This clearly shows that surplus of sales over variable cost, i.e. the contribution gradually eating into the fixed costs as activity increases. After the break-even point, the extra contribution becomes profit because all the fixed costs have been met.

(c) On the contribution B-E chart, plot variable costs first *then* fixed.

An alternative form of the contribution chart is where the contribution line (i.e. sales – variable costs) is plotted against fixed costs. This is shown in Figure 10.3. using the same data as in Examples 2, 3 & 4.

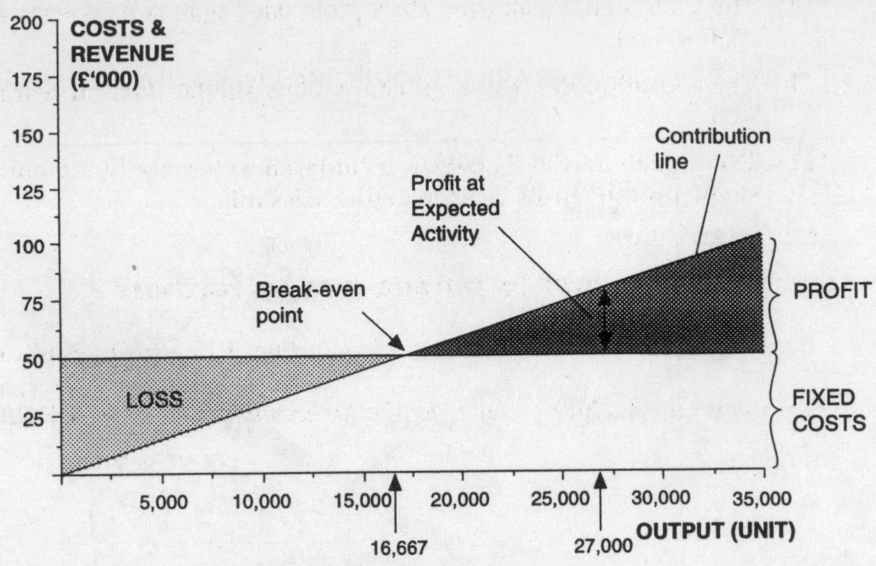

Figure 10.3 Alternative form of contribution break-even chart

10.8 Limitations of break-even analysis

The charts show the relationships between costs, volume and profit in a simplified and approximate manner. They are aids and can add to the attractiveness of a report but they do have a number of limitations which should not be forgotten.

(a) The charts are approximate guides to performance within reasonable activity ranges, say ±20% of normal activity. Outside these limits the results shown are not likely to be accurate.

(b) The simple cost patterns shown, i.e. linear variable costs and unchanging fixed costs, are unlikely to apply in practice.

(c) The charts show relationships which are essentially short-term.

(d) The charts assume either a single product firm or an unchanging sales mix; both options being somewhat unrealistic.

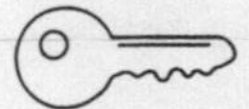

Key point summary

- Risk and Uncertainty are always present in decision making.
- Uncertainty means that multiple outcomes are possible.
- Expected value is the average value of an event which has several possible outcomes
- Expected value is probability × value.
- Break-even analysis (or cost/volume/profit analysis) considers the relationships between costs, volume, contribution and profit.
- Break-even analysis is based on the principles of marginal costing.
- The break-even point is the level of sales or output at which the firm makes neither profit nor loss.
- Various formulae are available to calculate key values such as; break-even point, level of sales to achieve a target profit and so on.

- The traditional break-even chart plots sales against total costs with fixed costs being plotted first.
- The contribution break-even charts plots similar data but variable costs are plotted first.
- The limitation of B-E analysis include; short term only, simplified cost patterns, and single product firms or unchanging sales mix.

Need more detail or want to pursue a topic further?

Break-even analysis and charts See *Costing*, T Lucey, DP Publications.

Risk and Uncertainty see *Quantitative Techniques*, T Lucey, DP Publications.

Investment appraisal

Capital expenditure decisions and the time value of money are introduced. Traditional techniques such as Accounting Rate of Return and Payback are described together with the main discounted cash flow techniques; Net Present Value and Internal Rate of Return.

Contents

Long-run decision making

Scenario A Investment appraisal

By now Alan had a good grasp of how to deal with short-term decisions but realised that he had not dealt with decisions affecting the longer-term and thought he would ask John about these.

John explained that the most important type of long-term decision making was called investment or project appraisal. Typically this meant comparing the *cost* of an investment now (say for a new machine) with the *net benefits* expected over a number of years from the investment. It was because the net benefits were spread over a number of years in the future that made this type of decision making different from short-term decision making. John explained that the real problem was that money received, or paid out, at different times in the future was not directly comparable to today's money. This was due to several factors including; risk and uncertainty, inflation and the fact that money in hand could be used productively. At the simplest it could, for example, earn interest in a bank. This meant that the value of money was related to when it was received; the earlier it was received the higher the value, the further away the lower the value. This was called, the *time value of money*.

John explained that the main methods of investment appraisal expressed all cash inflows and outflows, whenever received, in terms of their value at a common date. The common date invariably used was the present, i.e. now. This meant that the costs of a project (expressed as a present value) could be compared directly with the benefits expected (also in present values). If the benefits exceeded the costs there was said to be a positive net present value and the project would be acceptable. If the net present value (NPV) was negative (i.e. costs greater than benefits) then the project would be unacceptable.

Quick answer questions

1 Why cannot sums of money received or paid out at various dates in the future be compared directly?

2. Why is £5,000 received now worth more than £5,000 received in a year's time?

3. What is the NPV of a project which has benefits of £12,000 (present value) and costs of £9,000 (present value)?

1. Because the value of money is dependent on when it is received or paid out. Money received earlier is worth more, in present day terms, than the same sum received later.

2. £5,000 received now is worth more than £5,000 received in 1 year's time because we can use the money if we have it now, receiving it now removes uncertainty, and there might be inflation if we wait a year, so reducing the value.

3. NPV = Benefits – Costs (in PV terms)
= £12,000 – £9,000
= £3,000 positive

Normally a project with a positive NPV of £3,000 would be acceptable.

Task 1 *(answer page 187)*

(a) In the scenario John has explained to Alan that the main investment appraisal methods are based on cash inflows and outflows arising from the project. Why are cash flows used rather than profits?

(b) What are the 'traditional' methods of investment appraisal?

11.1 Long run decision making

So far the principles of short-run making have been explained but organisations also have to take decisions where a long term view is required. These are called *capital expenditure decisions* and they are dealt with by using *investment appraisal* techniques. Examples of capital expenditure decisions are; investment in a new factory, buying a new company or machine, launching a different product and so on.

There are a number of similarities between short and long-run decision making; for example the choice between alternatives, the need to consider future costs and revenues, the importance of changes in costs and revenues, the irrelevance of sunk costs and so on. However, an additional factor in long-run decision making is the need to take account of the *time value of money*. When a decision is concerned with costs and revenues arising over a number of years the sums cannot be compared directly, they must be reduced to equivalent values at a common date. This point is developed later in the chapter when discounting method are dealt with.

Numerous investment appraisal techniques are available to assist with investment decisions but, however sophisticated they all compare the *returns expected* with the *investment required*.

The techniques covered in this chapter are the so called *traditional* techniques and Discounted Cash Flow (DCF).

11.2 Traditional methods of investment appraisal

Two traditional methods are dealt with; the Accounting Rate of Return (ARR) and Payback.

Accounting Rate Of Return (ARR)

This method, also known as the Return of Capital Employed, expresses the average profits per year as a percentage of the investment required.

Example 1

Two investment projects are being considered, each with an initial investment of £50,000 and producing profits as follows:

	Estimated net profits per year	
	Project A	**Project B**
Year 1	£6,000	£8,000
2	11,000	14,000
3	9,000	8,000
4	10,000	3,000
5	4,000	2,000
Total	£40,000	£35,000

Calculate the ARR and recommend which project, if any, would be selected.

Solution

	Project A	*Project B*
Average profits p.a.	$\frac{£40,000}{5}$ = **£8,000**	$\frac{30,000}{5}$ = **£7,000**
APR	$\frac{8,000}{50,000}$ = **16%**	$\frac{7,000}{50,000}$ = **14%**

Thus, based on ARR, Project A would be preferred.

Problems with ARR

ARR is simple to calculate but has several disadvantages for investment decision making, as follows:

(a) Ignores the timing of inflows and outflows

(b) Uses profit as a measure of return. Profit is calculated using accounting conventions and is not equivalent to relevant cash inflows and outflows

(c) There is no universally accepted way of calculating ARR.

Payback

Payback is a widely used investment appraisal technique. Payback is the period, usually in years, which it takes for the cash inflows of an investment project to equal the initial cash outflow. The usual decision rule is to accept the project with the shortest payback period.

Example 2

Three projects are being considered and estimates of the cash flows are as follows:

	Project X		Project Y		Project Z	
Year	**Annual Cash flow**	**Cumulative Cash flow**	**Annual Cash flow**	**Cumulative Cash flow**	**Annual Cash flow**	**Cumulative Cash flow**
Now	– £5,000	– £5,000	– £5,000	– £5,000	– £5,000	– £5,000
1	+ 2,100	– 2,900	+400	– 4,600	+ 900	– 4,100
2	+ 1,800	– 1,100	+700	– 3,900	+ 800	– 3,300
3	+ 700	–400	+ 1,800	– 2,100	+ 1,100	– 2,200
4	+ 400	–	+ 2,100	–	+ 1,000	– 1,200
5	–	–	–	–	+ 1,200	–
6	–	–	–	–	+ 950	+ 950

Payback period: Project X = 4 years
Project Y = 4 years
Project Z = 5 years.

Note: Each project requires an initial investment now of £5,000 which is an outflow, denoted by a negative sign. The positive signs denote cash inflows after 1 year, 2 years and so on.

Features of payback

(a) It is based on cash flows not profits and thus is more objective than ARR.

(b) It is a measure of liquidity not of wealth. Judged on Payback alone, Projects X and Y would be preferred to Z even though Z carries on earning after the payback period.

(c) Payback does consider the timing of cash flows but only in a crude manner. Projects X and Y are ranked equally yet there are clear timing differences.

(d) Payback is simple and easily understood and is widely used either by itself or in conjunction with other investment appraisal techniques.

11.3 Discounted cash flow (DCF)

All DCF methods use cash flows and automatically make allowance for the time value of money. As previously mentioned, accounting profits are based on conventions and are less objective than cash flows so that cash flows are preferred for decision making.

There is general acceptance that any serious investment appraisal must consider the time value of money. Sums of money arising at different times are not directly comparable. They must be converted to equivalent values at some common date and DCF methods typically use *now*, i.e. the present time, as the common date.

As an illustration of the time value of money imagine you are owed £100. Would you prefer to be repaid now or in 1 year's time? Naturally you would prefer the money now; you could use it or gain interest on it in a bank if you had it now. The sum of £100 received in a year's time is worth less than the same amount received now. Using DCF terminology the *present value* of £100 expected in 1 year is less than £100; how much less depends on interest rates and other factors.

There are two main DCF methods, Net Present Value (NPV) and Internal Rate of Return (IRR) which are described in detail later in this topic.

Discounting and present value

Scenario B Present value

Alan could see the need to express the value of all cash flows in present day terms but was unsure how this was achieved

John explained that this was done by a process known as *discounting*. The amount of the future cash flow was multiplied by a discount factor which produced the present value of the cash flow. The discount factor was always less than 1 and was found from Present Value Tables(see Table A) which showed the discount factors for various periods at different discount rates. John explained that the choice of a discount rate was a complex matter and that the Group were currently using a 15% discount rate. He showed Alan an abstract from Table A, as follows:

Period	Discount Factors at 15%
1	0.870
2	0.756
3	0.658
4	0.572
5	0.497

For example, if a sum of £8,000 was expected to be received in 3 year's time its present value (i.e. its value now) was found by multiplying £8,000 by the discount factor from the table i.e. 0.658.

∴ Present value (using a 15% rate) = £8,000 × 0.658
= £5,264

John pointed out that the fact that the present value was well below the nominal amount was due to the combined effect of having to wait 3 years for the money and the 15% discount rate. The higher the discount rate the more the discounting. The further into the future, the more the discounting.

John showed Alan some preliminary figures for an investment appraisal he was undertaking for Morden Engineering. This concerned a new die-casting machine which would enable Morden to enter the market for precision die-casting for the electronics industry. The cost of the machine was £140,000 payable now and the expected revenues and costs were:

Cash flow estimates

After	I year	2 years	3 years	4 years	5 years
	£	£	£	£	£
Revenues	90,000	150,000	250,000	160,000	100,000
Costs	65,000	110,000	170,000	110,000	80,000
Sale of machine					25,000

Quick answer questions

1. The present value, at 15%, of £8,000 received after 3 years is £5,264 as shown. What would its present value be if it was received after 2 years?, after 4 years?
2. Would the present values calculated above increase or decrease if the discount rate was altered to 20%?

3. What are the net cash flows for the proposed investment for Morden Engineering?

1. Present value of £8,000 received after 2 years at 15%

= £8,000 × 0.756 = £6,048

Present value of £8,000 received after 4 years at 15%.

= £8,000 × 0.572 = £4,576

2. Increasing the discount rate to 20% would decrease the present values.

3. Net cash flows for proposed investment:

			After		
Now	*1 year*	*2 years*	*3 years*	*4 years*	*5 years*
–£140,000	*+£25,000*	*+£40,000*	*+£80,000*	*+£50,000*	*+£45,000*

Where – = a net outflow

+ = a net inflow

It is these net cash flows which are discounted.

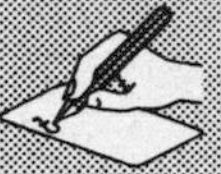

Task 2 *(answer page 187)*

(a) Calculate the NPV of the proposed investment for Morden Engineering.

(b) Calculate the Internal Rate of Return of the investment.

(c) Recommend, with reasons, whether or not the project is acceptable.

11.4 Net Present Value (NPV)

The NPV methods finds the value *in present day terms* of the project cash inflows and outflows expected to occur at different periods in the future. Because all the future cash flows are brought to their equivalent value at a common date, i.e. now, they are directly comparable and can be added together, taking note of pluses and minuses. The resulting answer is known as the Net Present Value (NPV); if positive the project is acceptable, if negative it is unacceptable.

The process by which the present value of a future sum is found is known as *discounting*. Discounting is normally carried out using discount (or present value) tables – Table A. To use the Table it is necessary to know the discount rate and when the future sum is expected to arise.

Table A shows the discount factors (or Present Value factors) for discount rates 1% to 30%, and for periods, normally years, from 1 to 25.

To illustrate the use of Table A.

What is the present value of £10,000 expected in 5 years; at 20%?, at 10%?

Expected in 5 years at 20%		
Discount factor from Table A	= 0.402	
Present value	= £10,000 × 0.402	= **£4,020**
Expected in 5 years at 10%		
Discount factor from Table A	= 0.621	
Present value	= £10,000 × 0.621	= **£6,210**

It will be seen that the higher discounting rate discounts (reduces) the future sum more heavily than the lower rate. This is a general rule.

11.5 NPV and project appraisal

A project normally consist of a series of cash inflows or outflows and the objective of project appraisal is to see whether the NPV of the project is positive or negative at the cost of capital of the company. The cost of capital is the cost of financing the project and is the rate at which the project is discounted.

Example 3

A company with a cost of capital of 10% is considering a project with the following estimated cash flows:

Now	After 1 year	2 years	3 years	4 years
– £5, 000	+ £900	+ £1,800	+ £2,400	+ £1,600

(minus represents an outflow, positive represents an inflow)

What is the NPV of the project?
Should it be accepted?

Solution

From Table A the discount factors for 10% are

1 year	2 years	3 years	4 years
0.909	0.826	0.751	0.683

NPV = – £5,000 + (0.909 × £900) + (0.826 × £1,800) + (0.751 × £2,400) + (0.683 × £1,600)
= – £5,000 + £818 + £1,487 + £1,802 + £1,093.
= **+ £200**

As the NPV of the project is positive, at the company's cost of capital it should be accepted. The £200 represents the increase in wealth that could be gained by the project, measured in present day values.

Note: The initial outlay of £5,000 does not need discounting because it is already at the present day value.

11.6 Regular cashflows

Regular cash flow patterns are commonly encountered. This means that the same amount of cash is paid out, or received, each year. An example is a lease which requires a payment of £1,200 per year for 10 years. Regular cash flows are known as *annuities* and there is a short cut method of finding their present values, using Table B.

Table B is simply the addition of the individual year's discount factors from Table A.

Take for example, the first 3 years discount factors at 12% from Table A. These are 0.893, 0.797 and 0.712 which added together equal 2.402. From Table B it will be seen that the 3 year factor under 12% is 2.402. The annuity factors from Table B are used as follows:

Example 4

What is the present value at 12% of £2,000 per year received for 3 years?

Solution

Present value = Annual amount × Annuity Factor from Table B
= £2,000 × 2.402
= **£4,804**

Alternatively and more laboriously, the individual discount factors from Table A could be used, in the normal way by multiplying each year's cash flow by the appropriate discount factor, thus:

= (£2,000 × 0.893) + (£2,000 × 0.797) + (£2,000 × 0.712)
= **£4,804**

It must be stressed that Annuity factors from Table B can only be used when the cash flows are the same each year. When the cash flows vary from year to year, the discount factors from Table A must be used.

11.7 Internal Rate of Return (IRR)

The IRR is an alternative DCF appraisal method. Instead of the answer being in £'s, as NPV, the IRR is a percentage. It can be defined as the discount rate which gives zero NPV. There is no direct method of obtaining the IRR of a project, it requires some trial and error. The normal method is to find a discount rate which gives a positive NPV and one which gives a negative NPV. It follows that some rate between the two will give zero NPV and is thus the IRR.

Example 5

Find the IRR of the project in Example 3, the cash flows of which are reproduced below.

Now	After 1 year	After 2 years	After 3 years	After 4 years
– £5,000	+ £900	+ £1,800	+ £2,400	+ £1,600

Solution

It will be recalled that, at 10%, the NPV was + £200. This will do for the positive NPV so it is now necessary to discount at some higher discount rate which will produce a negative NPV.

Try 15%

At 15% the discount factors from Table A are 0.870, 0.756, 0.658, 0.572.

Net Present Value = – £5,000 + (0.870 × £900) + (0.756 × £1,800) + (0.658 × £2,400) + (0.572 × 1,600)
= – £5,000 + 783 + 1,361 + 1,579 + 915
= **– £362**

It is clear that at some rate between 10%, giving + £200 and 15%, giving – £362, there is a rate which gives zero NPV, i.e. the IRR. The value can be found graphically or by *interpolation*, as follows:

$$\text{IRR} = \underset{(a)}{10\%} + \underset{(b)}{5\%} \times \left[\frac{\overset{(c)}{200}}{\underset{(d)}{562}}\right]$$

Notes

(a) The rate which gives a positive NPV. In this case, 10%.

(b) The difference between the two discount rates used. In this case, 15% – 10% = 5%.

(c) The difference between zero and the positive NPV. In this case 200 – 0 = 200.

(d) The total range between the positive and negative NPVs. In this case, between +£200 and –£362 i.e. £562.

If the calculated IRR is greater than the company's cost of capital the project is acceptable. In this case, 11.78% is greater than the cost of capital of 10% so the project is acceptable. If the IRR was below the cost of capital the project would not be acceptable. As an alternative to the arithmetic method shown above the IRR can also be found graphically using a Present Value Profile. Figure 11.1 plots the data from Example 5.

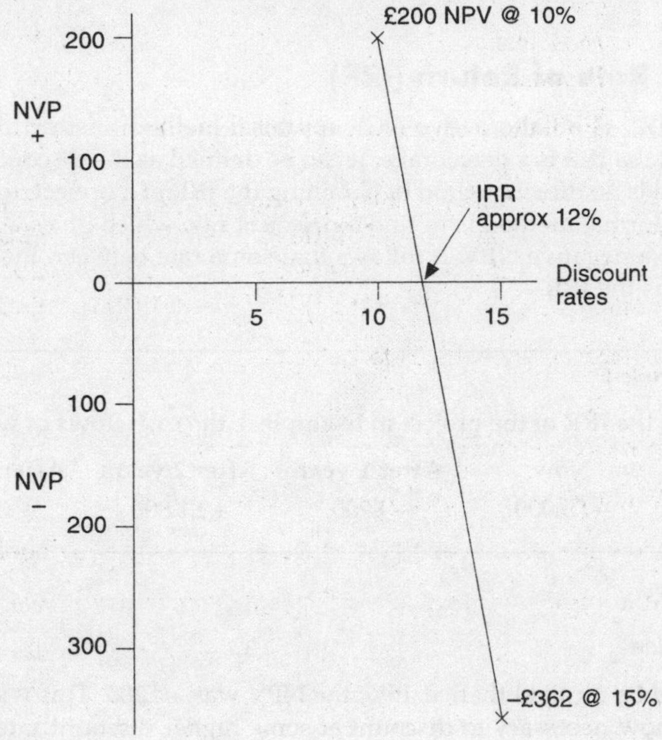

Figure 11.1 Present value profile

11.8 NPV and IRR summary

NPV and IRR are alternative DCF methods. Both values do not have to be calculated to make an investment decision. Although NPV has certain technical advantages over IRR, IRR is widely used in practice. For most projects, the methods lead to the same accept of reject decision which is summarised below.

	Accept project if	**Reject project if**
Using NPV (at cost of Capital)	NPV is positive	NPV is negative
Using IRR	IRR is greater than cost of capital	IRR is less than cost of capital

Uncertainty in investment appraisal

Scenario C Uncertainty and investment appraisal

The following day John sent for Alan and passed over the estimates regarding a project which SBP were considering. John explained that there was uncertainty about the likely costs and revenues and consequently multiple estimates with probabilities had been prepared.

Alan saw from the papers that SBP were considering setting up a plastic extrusion plant to make rain-water products. The estimated costs were as follows:

	Probability	Now £	After 1 year £
Most likely	0.7	150,000	85,000
Pessimistic	0.3	155,000	130,000

The net cash flows from sales were estimated to be:

	Probability	after 1 year	2 years	3 years	years 4–10 (per year)
Optimistic	0.2	£35,000	£90,000	£80,000	£75,000
Most likely	0.5	£20,000	£60,000	£65,000	£50,000
Pessimistic	0.3	£15,000	£55,000	£45,000	£40,000

A 15% cost of capital was to be used.

Quick answer questions

1. What is the expected value of costs required now?
2. Why can we be sure that all the cost options have been included?
3. What is the name given to the regular cash flows from sales for years 4 to 10?

1. Expected value of costs required now
= (0.7 × 150,000) + (0.3 × 155,000)
= £151,500

2. Because the probabilities of the two options listed total 1.
i.e. 0.7 + 0.3 = 1
Similarly for the sales estimates
0.2 + 0.5 + 0.3 = 1

3. Regular cash flows are known as Annuities.

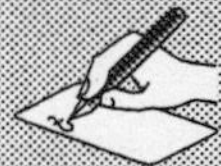

Task 3 *(answer page 188)*

1. Calculate the expected NPV of the plastic extrusion project. Is it worthwhile?
2. Calculate the best possible NPV of the project. What is the probability of this outcome occurring?
3. Calculate the worst possible outcome. What is the probability of this occurring?

Key point summary

- Long term decision making is based on similar principles to short term decision making except that the time value of money must also be considered.
- Accounting Rate of Return (ARR) is a traditional technique and is calculated thus

$$\text{ARR} = \frac{\text{average profits p.a.}}{\text{amount invested}}$$

- Payback is the number of periods' cash flows required to recoup the initial investment.
- Payback is a measure of liquidity not wealth and is widely used.
- All Discounted Cash Flow techniques use cash flows, not profits, and make allowance for the time value of money.
- The Net Present Value (NPV) is the net discounted value of all cash inflows and outflows, expressed in present day terms.
- The discount, or present value, tables show discount factors for various interest rates and periods (Table A).
- If the NPV is positive when discounted at the cost of capital the project is acceptable. If the NPV is negative, it is not acceptable.
- Annuities are regular cash flows occurring each year. They can be discounted using Table B.
- The Internal Rate of Return (IRR) is that discount rate which gives zero NPV.
- The IRR can be found graphically or by interpolation.
- NPV and IRR give the same accept or reject decision for the majority of normal projects.

Need more detail or want to pursue a topic further?

Investment appraisal	See *Management Accounting*, T Lucey, DP Publications.
Risk and uncertainty in investment appraisal	See *Quantitative Techniques*, T Lucey, DP Publications.

Performance appraisal

The need for performance appraisal is explained and various profitability measures are described. Return on Capital Employed and Residual Profit are described and compared and Ratio Analysis introduced.

Contents

Why Performance Appraisal is necessary

Scenario A Decentralisation and performance appraisal

Alan had read an article in the Financial Times which said that the Hempson Group was largely decentralised and had good performance appraisal systems. He was not too sure what this meant and thought he would ask John, the Group Management Accountant.

John explained that decentralisation meant that the authority to make decisions was dispersed round the Group rather than all decisions being taken at the centre. He explained that the Group devolved as much decision making to the operating companies as possible whilst retaining certain strategic decision making and policy control at the Holding Company. Alan asked for a few examples and John told him that financial decisions and decisions about acquisitions and disposals were typical Group decisions, being long-term and strategic, whilst decisions about, say, production methods or marketing were taken by each operating company. John emphasised that although the operating companies were largely free to conduct their affairs as they wished, they were given clear financial and other targets and told they had to keep within Group policy on a range of matters. These included; personnel practices, environmental matters, quality standards and so forth.

John explained that performance appraisal was carried out by detailed, regular reporting of the performance of each company covering sales, costs, profits, return on investment and so on. In the Hempson Group each of the operating companies had to report monthly. He explained that numerous ratios were calculated from the data supplied by the operating companies and the trends in these carefully monitored. One ratio received particular attention as it provided a convenient summary of performance. This was the Return on Capital Employed (ROCE) and was calculated in the Hempson Group as follows:

$$\text{ROCE} = \frac{\text{Operating Profits (before tax) of the individual company}}{\text{\% Capital employed in the company)}}$$

John told Alan that care was always needed with the value taken for capital employed as definitions varied between different organisations. The Hempson Group used Total Assets whilst other firms used Net Assets or some other definition. Thus when comparing the calculated ROCE of different organisations care was needed to ensure like was compared to like.

As an example John showed Alan some data for the last 5 years for Morden Engineering Ltd.

	19X1	19X2	19X3	19X4	19X5
	£'000	£'000	£'000	£'000	£'000
Profit (before tax)	147	173	152	134	141
Capital Employed	825	865	893	810	793

Quick answer questions

1. Although the Hempson Group encourages decentralised decision making, the Holding Company continues to make certain types of decisions. What do you think are the characteristics of such decisions?
2. Why do you think that the Hempson Group have formal Performance Appraisal systems for the operating companies?
3. Calculate the ROCE for Morden Engineering for each of the last 5 years.

1. The decisions that the Holding Company retain are essentially those that affect the Group as a whole. They are invariably long-term.

2. So that they can monitor the performance of each operating company on a regular, formal basis. The aim is to assess performance in relation to the financial targets set for each company.

3. **ROCE for Morden Engineering**

19X1	19X2	19X3	19X4	19X5
$\frac{147}{825} = 17.8\%$	$\frac{173}{865} = 20\%$	$\frac{152}{893} = 17.02\%$	$\frac{134}{810} = 16.5\%$	$\frac{141}{793} = 17.78\%$

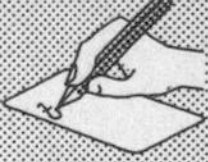

Task 1 *(answer page 188)*

1. Why is ROCE considered a useful summary of performance?
2. Why do the Hempson Group use Net Profit before tax to calculate ROCE?
3. What advantages can be obtained from decentralisation? Are there any possible disadvantages?
4. Contrast Residual Income and ROCE as measures of performance.

12.1 What is performance appraisal?

Senior managers need to be able to monitor the performance of the operating managers junior to them. They need to know whether the operating management are performing well, if they are meeting company objectives, if they are using the company's assets effectively, if they are earning target profits, if they are controlling costs and so on. Naturally much of this appraisal is done by observation and personal contact but, in addition, relevant information must be available and much of this is supplied by the cost and management accounting system of the firm. This is particularly important when there is decentralised decision making and when the organisation has a divisional structure.

12.2 Decentralised decision making and divisional structure

As organisations grow in size and complexity senior management do not have time to make all the decisions. In such circumstances, authority for certain types of decision making is delegated to subordinate management. This relieves top management of routine work and gives them more time for strategic matters. In addition, local decision making may well improve because operational management are in closer touch with day to day problems. Having increased responsibility has been found to motivate people and this factor and the need to increase efficiency has led to the growth of divisionalised organisations. Although details vary, there is typically a holding company containing some centralised services and group management and a number of operating divisions. To an extent these operate like independent companies, trading both within and outside the group. At all times group management need to ensure that the individual divisions are taking decisions that do not conflict with the objectives of the group as a whole and need to be able to monitor the performance of divisional management.

It is in these circumstances that well planned performance appraisal systems are vital.

12.3 Responsibility centres

One type of responsibility centre has already been described. This was the *cost centre*, which forms the basis of budgetary control systems. These are one form of performance appraisal, usually with the emphasis on cost items. In a full performance appraisal system the principles of responsibility accounting are developed beyond cost centres to what are known as *profit centres* and *investment centres*. Figure 12.1 summarises the types of responsibility centres.

Cost centre	**Profit centre**	**Investment centre**
Responsible for:	Responsible for:	Responsible for:
Costs	Costs	Costs
–	Revenues	Revenues
–	Profits	Profits
–	–	Profits in relation to investment

Figure 12.1 Types of responsibility centre

12.4 Profitability measures of performance

Profit is a widely used measure of performance which is familiar to management and acceptable to them. When profit is used as a measure of performance it provides a means by which division can be compared with division and one division's performance can be compared period by period. When profit is used it can be defined in various ways. Some of the more important variants are described below: including, controllable profit, divisional profit and net profit.

Controllable profit

This is defined as revenues less costs controllable at the divisional level. As this measure includes only those costs for which the local management have primary responsibility, the basis of the measure is sound and it would be a reasonable way of appraising divisional management. What costs and revenues to include depends on the amount of responsibility delegated.

The treatment of particular items is dealt with below.

- *Variable costs and revenues*

  These are items controllable by divisional management so would be included.

- *Divisional overheads*

  Again these would be included as they are controllable.

- *Depreciation and fixed asset costs*

  Normally these would be excluded as decisions on the sale and purchase are a strategic responsibility and outside the control of local management.

- *Apportioned costs*

  Frequently a portion of central administration costs are charged to the divisions. Clearly these are not controllable by the division, and are thus excluded.

Divisional profit

Also known as traceable or direct profit. This is the profit which arises from divisional operations without any apportioned central costs. It is controllable profit less depreciation and fixed asset costs. It follows that a number of costs which are identifiable with a division are not controllable by the division.

Net profit

This is the final net profit of the division and is revenues less controllable divisional costs less depreciation and apportioned costs.Although this method does show the net effect of the division on the group's results it is less useful as a means of appraising the performance of divisional management. This is because so many items are outside the control of local management.

The various types of profit are illustrated in the following example.

Example 1

The following data relate to the B division of the Alphabet Group.

	£
Sales	380,000
Variable costs	75,000
Fixed costs	
Controllable by division	38,000
Controllable centrally	29,000
Fixed assets (at cost)	450,000
Apportioned central costs	53,000

It is group policy to charge depreciation at 15% on the straight line basis. Calculate controllable, divisional and net profit for B division.

Solution

	£	£
Sales		380,000
less Variable costs		75,000
= Divisional contribution		305,000
less Divisional fixed costs		38,000
= Controllable profit		267,000
less Depreciation	67,500	
Non-controllable fixed	29,000	
		96,500
= Divisional profit		170,500
less Apportioned central costs		53,000
= Net profit		£117,500

Note: The depreciation is 15% of £450,000 = £67,500.

The calculated actual profits are used as appraisal measures in various ways. For example, actual profit is compared with planned or budgeted profit, the trend in profits is considered, the profit of one division is compared with the profit from other divisions and so on.

12.5 Performance appraisal and investment

The various types of profit shown above do not take account of the amount of investment in the division, i.e. its fixed assets. When local management are responsible both for profits and the amount of investment in the division then this should be taken into account in performance appraisal.

There are two ways this can be done. Either by calculating *residual profit* or the *return on capital employed*. Residual profit (or residual income) is profit less an interest charge calculated on the assets used by the division. Residual profit is an absolute figure, i.e. the answer is a number of £'s. Return on capital employed (ROCE) has been mentioned previously and is the ratio of profits to the capital employed by the division, i.e. the fixed assets. ROCE is a relative figure and the answer is a percentage.

These measures are illustrated below.

Example 2

The results of three divisions are shown below.

Division	X £	Y £	Z £
Trading profits for year	62,000	248,000	57,000
Fixed assets in division	225,000	2,150,000	175,000

The group has a cost of capital of 15%.

Calculate the residual profit and return on capital employed for each division.

Solution

Residual profits

Division	X £	Y £	Z £
Trading profits	62,000	248,000	57,000
less Interest on capital	33,750	322,500	26,250
Residual profit(loss)	28,250	(74,500)	30,750

Note: The interest on capital used in the division is calculated as follows:

X	=	15% of £225,000	=	£33,750
Y	=	15% of £2,150,000	=	£322,500
Z	=	15% Of £175,000	=	£26,250

Return on capital employed (ROCE)

$$\text{ROCE} = \frac{\text{Profit}}{\text{Capital employed}} \%$$

$$\text{Division X} = \frac{£62{,}000}{£225{,}000} = 27\tfrac{1}{2}\%$$

$$\text{Division Y} = \frac{248{,}000}{£2{,}150{,}000} = 11\tfrac{1}{2}\%$$

$$\text{Division Z} = \frac{57{,}000}{£175{,}000} = 32\tfrac{1}{2}\%$$

Residual Profit and ROCE give an indication how effectively the assets of the division are being used to earn profits. It will be seen that Division Y although making substantial trading profits, uses its assets much less effectively than the other divisions.

Remember that Residual Profit and ROCE are alternatives; both do not have to be calculated in practice.

12.6 Residual profits and ROCE compared

Both Residual Profit and ROCE are useful appraisal measures which allow for the impact of the amount invested. Naturally, both have certain limitations and particular advantages and disadvantages. Residual Profit is more flexible and is more likely to encourage managers to take a longer term view of asset investment and asset sales. On the other hand, Residual Profit is less useful for comparisons between investment centres nor does it relate the amount of a centre's income to the size of the investment. In this respect ROCE is a better measure of performance being a relative value.

Ratio pyramids

Scenario B Ratio pyramids

John explained to Alan that the ROCE was just one of the ratios that were calculated for each of the Group companies. He showed Alan the Ratio Chart used by Hempsons (see Figure 12.2).

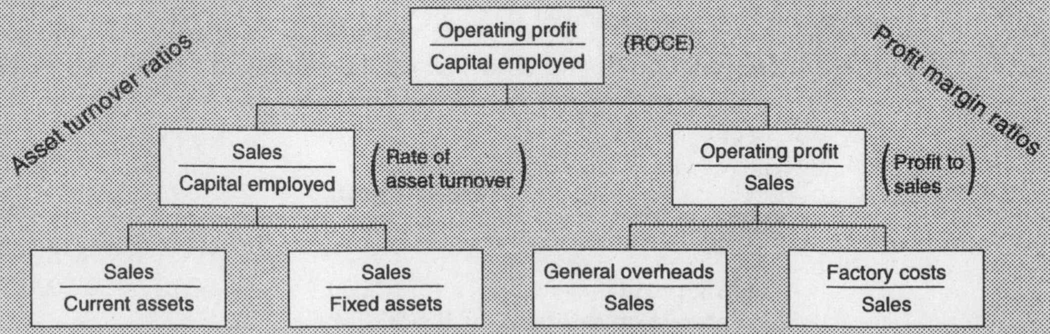

Figure 12.2 – Performance appraisal ratio chart – Hempson Group plc

John explained that the idea was to show what factors contributed to the Return on Capital Employed. In particular he pointed out that the following relationship held:

ROCE = Profit to Sales% × Rate of Asset Turnover

As an example of the procedures followed John showed Alan some data he had received from SBP Ltd. for the current financial year which had just ended.

SBP Limited
Extracts from profit and loss account
for year ended 31st December 19X5

		£m
Sales		147
less Factory costs		
Materials	53.2	
Labour	28.9	
Overheads	14.4	
		96.5
Gross profit		50.5
less General overheads		
Administration	22.7	
Marketing & distribution	18.9	
		41.6
= Net profit before tax		8.9
less Tax		2.3
= Net profit after tax		6.6

SBP Limited
Summary balance sheet as at 31st December 19X5

	£'m
Fixed assets	83
Current assets	39
Total assets	122
less Current liabilities	31
	91
Represented by	
Share capital and reserves	91

Quick answer questions

1 What was SBP's operating profit: sales percentage?

2. What was the rate of asset turnover.

3. What was the ROCE?

1. $\dfrac{\text{Operating Profit}}{\text{Sales}} = \dfrac{8.9}{147} = 6.05\%$

2. $\dfrac{\text{Sales}}{\text{Capital employed}} = \dfrac{147}{122} = 1.2$

3. ROCE = 1.2 × 6.05% = 7.3%

Task 2 *(answer page 189)*

(a) Calculate as many of the Asset Turnover and Profit Margin ratios as you can from SPB's results.

(b) Last year SBP had a Rate of Asset turnover of 1.41 and 6.38% Profit to Sales. Contrast their position last year with the current year and discuss what further analysis should be undertaken.

12.7 Ratio analysis

One important ratio, ROCE, has been described above but many others are regularly calculated during performance appraisal. They may be separated into two broad groups:

- ratios concerning *performance*

  (i.e. dealing with profits, sales, costs and asset use)

- ratios concerning *liquidity*

  (i.e. dealing with cash flows, working capital debtors and creditors)

Whatever type of ratio is calculated maximum information will be gained when the following two factors are kept in mind.

- Trends are all important. A ratio calculated for a single period is of limited value.

  What is required are results for several periods so that it can be seen whether there is a discernible trend in any ratio.

- Like must be compared with like. To be valid, comparisons of ratios should be with either, the ratios of earlier periods for the same firm or with ratios of similar sized firms in the same industry. There is considerable value in comparing ratios between different firms but, as pointed out above, great care is needed to ensure that like is being compared with like.

Scenario C **External performance appraisal**

Of course, John said, the mere preparation of reports and the calculation of ratios is only the first stage. Group Management meet the Directors of the Operating Companies on a regular basis, discuss their results and ratios, consider plans and problems and generally monitor progress. The Group regarded the formal performance appraisal systems as just one part of a two-way communication process.

Alan could see the advantage of this and looked forward to the day he would be a member of senior management. John explained that the Group used the same performance appraisal principles when they were considering the acquisition of a new company but extended the analysis to include liquidity and cash management as well as operating performance.

As an example John showed Alan some working papers containing details of Bixford Die-Casting Ltd. This is a pressure die-casting company producing non-ferrous castings for the motor and lock trades. The Hempson Group are considering making a bid for the company.

Bixford Die Casting Ltd
Profit and loss account for the years ending 31st December

	19X3	19X4	19X5
	£'000	£'000	£'000
Sales	4,800	5,050	5,340
Less Cost of sales	2,600	2,800	3,050
Gross profit	2,200	2,250	2,290
Distribution costs	460	530	495
Administration expenses	1,140	1,220	1,300
Net profit	600	500	495
Taxation	150	160	85
Profit after tax	450	340	410
Dividends	150	150	170
Retained	300	190	240

Balance sheets as at 31st December

		19X3	19X4	19X5
		£'000	£'000	£'000
Fixed assets		1,560	1,753	2,448
Current assets	Stock – raw materials	200	240	180
	Work-in-progress	250	280	210
	Finished goods	460	475	560
Debtors		900	1,190	870
Prepayments		54	56	60
Cash in hand		45	32	47
		1,909	2,273	1,927

continued

	19X3	19X4	19X5
	£'000	£'000	£'000
Creditors – due within 12 months			
Trade creditors	560	760	900
Accruals	70	86	60
Corporation tax	150	160	85
Dividends	150	150	170
Bank overdraft	479	620	670
	1,409	1,776	1,885
Net current assets	500	497	42
Net assets	2060	2,250	2,490
Share capital – 25p shares	600	600	600
Reserves	860	1,050	1,290
Due to shareholders	1,460	1,650	1,890
Creditors due more than 12 months	600	600	600
	2,060	2,250	2,490

Quick answer questions

1. Why do you think that two-way communication is necessary between Group HQ and the operating companies?
2. Do you think that all the Hempson Group Companies should be given the same ROCE target?

1. The Group must keep the management of the operating companies informed about future plans, acquisitions, key personnel changes, share issues and so on. Similarly the operating companies must keep Group informed of their plans, marketing or production plans, investment requirements and so on.

2. The Hempson Group comprises companies of different sizes and types operating in different markets. Some require major investment in Assets whilst others require much less. The comparison of ROCEs between different industries or between firms of substantially different size is virtually meaningless. Accordingly the financial targets, including the ROCE, must be tailored to suit each company having regard to size, industry, capital structure and so on.

Task 3 *(answer page 189)*

(a) Calculate what Performance ratios you can for Bixford Die-Casting Ltd.

(b) Calculate what Liquidity ratios you can.

(c) Comment on the results and trends you have found.

12.8 Liquidity ratios

Five commonly used ratios are shown below although many others are possible.

$$\textit{Current ratio} = \frac{\text{Current assets}}{\text{Current liabilities}}$$

(This ratio effectively assesses the Working Capital of the firm. Traditionally a value of 2:1 has been thought to be desirable but considerable variation is encountered.)

$$\textit{Acid Test ratio} = \frac{\text{Current assets} - \text{Stock}}{\text{Current liabilities}}$$

(Also known as the 'Quick Ratio' it concentrates on the immediate liquidity and solvency of the firm.)

$$\textit{Stock turnover ratio} = \frac{\text{Cost of goods sold in period}}{\text{Average stock in period}}$$

(This measures the conversion of stocks into Sales. In general the faster the rate, the better.)

$$\textit{Average collection period in days} = \frac{\text{Debtors}}{\text{Credit sales}} \times 365$$

(This measures how well the firm collects its debts.)

$$\textit{Average payment period in days} = \frac{\text{Creditors}}{\text{Credit purchases}} \times 365$$

(The measure of how long it takes, on average, for the firm to pay its debts.)

Example 3

Based on the data below calculate five liquidity rations

ABC Limited – Wholesalers
Balance Sheet as at 31 December 19x4

Fixed assets	Cost	Accumulated depreciation	Written down value
	£'000	£'000	£'000
Fixtures and fittings	1,800	750	1,050
Vehicles	310	134	176
	2,110	884	1,226
Current assets			
Stock		1,648	
Cash and bank		113	
Debtors		983	
		2,744	
less Creditors due within 1 year			
Tax due	87		
Proposed dividend	100		
Trade creditors	1,240	1,427	
= Net current assets			1,317
= Net assets			2,543

continued

Example 3 – continued

Represented by		
Issued share capital		
1,000,000 £1 ordinary shares		1,000
General reserve b/f	1,465	
+ Transfer for current year	78	1,543
		2,543

Solution

$$\text{Current ratio} = \frac{\text{Current assets}}{\text{Current liabilities}}$$

$$= \frac{£2,744,000}{£1,427,000}$$

$$= \mathbf{1.92}$$

$$\text{Acid Test} = \frac{\text{Current assets} - \text{Stock}}{\text{Current liabilities}}$$

$$= \frac{£2,744,000 - 1,648,000}{£1,427,000}$$

$$= \mathbf{0.77}$$

$$\text{Stock turnover ratio} = \frac{\text{Cost of goods sold}}{\text{Average stock}}$$

$$= \frac{£10,345,000}{£1,469,500^*}$$

$$= \mathbf{7.04\ times}$$

*The average stock has been calculated as follows. (Opening stock + closing stock) ÷ 2, i.e. £1,291,000 + 1,648,000) ÷ 2 = £1,469,500.

$$\text{Average collection period} = \frac{\text{Debtors}}{\text{Credit sales}} \times 365$$

$$= \frac{£983,000}{£11,162,000^*} \times 365$$

$$= \mathbf{32.14\ days}$$

*It has been assumed that all sales were on credit. If this was found not to be the case clearly some adjustment would be required.

$$\text{Average payment period} = \frac{\text{Creditors}}{\text{Credit purchases}} \times 365$$

$$= \frac{£1,240,000}{£10,897,000^*} \times 365$$

$$= \mathbf{41.53\ days}$$

*It has been assumed that purchases of goods for resale and expenses (excluding Wages, Salaries and depreciation) were all on credit.

To gain the maximum information from any ratios calculated it would be normal to calculate the same ratios for several years to assess trends and to compare the calculated ratios and trends with those from similar companies, if available.

Key point summary

- Performance appraisal systems are required so that senior managers can monitor the performance of more junior managers.
- Many organisations are separated into operating divisions with many decisions taken at local level.
- There are three categories of responsibility centres; cost centres, profit centres and investment centres.
- Controllable profit is revenues less costs controllable at the divisional level.
- Divisional profit is the profit which arises from division operations, without apportioned costs.
- Net profit is the net effect of the division on group results.
- Where performance related to investment needs to be appraised, Residual Profit or Return on Capital Employed (ROCE) may be used.
- Residual Profit is Trading Profit less an interest charge based on the assets used.
- ROCE is $\frac{\text{Profit}}{\text{Capital employed}}$ %.
- Liquidity ratios are concerned with: current assets and liabilities; stocks; cash receipts and payments; and debtors and creditors.

Need more detail or want to pursue a topic further?

Decentralisation	See *Management Information Systems*, T Lucey, DP Publications
Performance appraisal and ratio analysis	See *Management Accounting*, T Lucey, DP Publications

Developing knowledge and skills

Congratulations! You have now completed the last of the Units describing Alan's experiences. You should now develop and consolidate what you have learned by dealing with Part 3 of Section II, covering Decision making and Performance Appraisal.

You will find that some of the questions, assignments and cases draw upon the whole of your CMA knowledge, not just Decision making and Performance Appraisal.

Part 3 of Section II starts on page 230.

Answers to tasks in Section 1

Topic 1

Task 1 There are an infinite number of examples of information that might be supplied by a CMA system, e.g.

Cost of running a department
used for cost control and means of monitoring performance;

Cost of a surgical operation
used as basis for charging and for cost control;

Forecast of how a cost will behave in the future
used for budgeting and decision making;

Amount and value of scrap produced
used for estimating and materials control;

Labour efficiency statistics
used for monitoring performance and cost control;

Investment analysis for a new machine
used as a bases for decision making;

and so on.

Task 2 The general principle is that all expenditure is coded as early as possible in the CMA system. This may be when a purchase invoice is received, when wages are paid or a store issue is made.

(a) Expenditure on office sundries
Coded either on receipt of an invoice if bought specially or when a stores requisition is filled if the items are issued from stores. An indirect cost.

(b) Wages
When wages are paid or accrued. A direct cost.

(c) Usage of steel
Either on receipt of a purchase invoice or when a stocks requisition is filled. A direct cost.

(d) Expenditure on stationery
As (a) above.

Task 3 (a) In general the form of the CMA system is not defined by legislation although parts may be influenced. For example, stock valuation methods are influenced by SSAP 9 which is itself influenced by legislation.

(b) Financial accounting mostly deals with external matters and works within a legislative framework (i.e. Companies Acts, Inland Revenue and Customs Legislation for VAT).

(c) Key matters include:
Accounts payable and receivable, VAT, PAYE, Corporation Tax, preparation of published accounts, maintaining financial records, dealing with bankers etc.

Topic 2

Task 1 (a) Prime costs

Job X107 =	£258 + 482	= 740
Job W556 =	£1,479 + 3,010	= 4,489
Job 803 =	£384 + 775	= 1,159

(b) Wages for Job W556 = £1,479
$\therefore$ (152 × £6) + (81 × £x) = 1,479
$\therefore$ Wage rate in Assembly Dept. = **£7 per hour**

(c) Each job of product has to carry some of the overheads of each department it moves through. The overheads are incurred in equipping, maintaining and running departments without which products could not be made. Thus each job or product must include a proportion of the department's overheads. The usual way this is done is in proportion to the labour or machine hours that a job or product spends in a department.

Task 2 (a) Closing stock value of material 508

	£
Opening stock	11,660
less Issues (1,250 + 625 + 1,535 + 975)	4,385
	7,275

Alternatively the 555 kgs in stock are valued at the most recent prices i.e. (300 kgs × £13.20 + 255 × £13) = 7,275.

(b) Alternative systems are LIFO, Average Price, Standard Price.

(c) For example using Average Price

Opening stock = 900 kgs with a value of £11,660

$$\therefore \text{ Average price} = \frac{11{,}660}{900} = £12.95 \text{ kg}$$

Issues			£
Job S672	100 kgs @ £12.95	=	1,295
X221	50 kgs @ £12.95	=	647
L449	120 kgs @ £12.95	=	1,554
M208	75 kgs @ £12.95	=	971
			4,467

$\therefore$ Closing stock = £11,660 – 4,467 = **£1,193**

Task 3 (a) Wages charged to Jobs re Harry Smith

S552 = 3 × £6 = £18
J809 = 4 × £6 = £24
K221 = 2 × £6 = £12

(The extra £6 paid for overtime would be charged to Production overheads.)

(b) The $\frac{1}{2}$ hour waiting time is termed Idle Time.

(c) Harry Smith does receive wages for this time, i.e. £3, and this would be charged to Production overheads. The reason why idle time wages are charged to overheads is that, by definition, he was not working on a job so they cannot be charged directly yet the wages paid for this time are still part of total costs and must be charged somewhere.

Topic 3

Task 1

(a)

Cost	Apportionment basis
Heating costs	Floor area or volume
Canteen deficit	Number of people
Insurance	Capital values or floor area

(b) Working back from the overhead apportionment for rates given in the overhead summary and the total floor area of 27,000 square feet the floor area of the 7 cost centres can be deduced.

Floor area (sq feet)

Total	Grinding	Machining	Fitting	HT	Admin	Finance	Marketing
27,000	5,501	6,226	3,548	4,271	3,981	2,606	867

Note: each calculation follows the same pattern, i.e. for the Grinding CC

$$\frac{3,800}{18,650} \times 27,000 = 5,501$$

(c) Heating costs apportioned on Floor Area
Canteen deficit on number of personnel
Insurance costs on capital values.

Cost	Total	Grinding	Machining	Fitting	HT	Admin	Finance	Marketing
Heating	14,200	2,893	3,274	1,866	2,246	2,094	1,371	456
Canteen	9,410	1,866	3,001	1,460	811	1,136	487	649
Insurance	7,960	1,667	510	2,744	1,765	686	490	98

Task 2

(a) Overhead absorption invariably uses budgeted figures because job costs, intermediate results and so on are required throughout the period.

(b) The overhead absorption for non-production overheads is usually achieved by some overall percentage.

In this case a typical calculation would be:

$$\text{Non-production overheads \%} = \frac{\text{Total non-production overheads}}{\text{Total production cost}} = \frac{£50,000}{£200,000} = 25\%$$

∴ Total costs Job L551 = £670.50 + 25% = **£838**
Job X913 = £2,200 + 25% = **£2,750**

Task 3

(a) Completion of overhead summary

Cost	Grinding	Machining	Fitting	HT	Non-prod	Total
Actual	24,750	39,260	15,475	34,100	54,750	168,335
Absorbed	24,570	41,370	14,760	34,845	52,500	168,045
(under)/over absorbed	(180)	2,110	(715)	745	(2,250)	(290)

(b) The net under absorbed overheads of £290 is taken to the period end P&L account.

(c) Depreciation is a non-cash expense, the amount of which is decided by the firm.

(d) The key differences between conventional absorption costing and ABC are:

Absorption costing accumulates together all production overheads and absorbs them into costs using a single volume related base such as labour or machine hours. On the other hand ABC maintains separate cost pools, e.g. set-up costs, ordering costs etc, and absorbs these into product costs using appropriate 'cost drivers', e.g number of set-ups, number of orders etc. In general it is claimed that conventional absorption costing undercosts small volume production whereas ABC tends to charge such production with higher overheads.

Topic 4

Task 1 The differences between Job and Contract costing are summarised in the text.

Task 2

Period 1 (Normal loss)

	kgs	£	
Input material	12,500	12,500	
Labour and overheads		3,250	
	12,500	15,750	
Less Normal loss	1,875	563	(scrap sales)
	10,625	15,187	

$\therefore$ Cost of good production per kg = $\frac{15,187}{10,625}$ = **£1.429**

Period 2 (Abnormal loss)

	kgs	£	
Input material	14,000	15,400	
Labour and overheads		6,200	
	14,000	21,600	
Less Normal loss	2,100	630	(scrap sales)
Abnormal loss	300	529	*
Net good production	11,600	20,441	

$\therefore$ Cost per kg = $\frac{15,187}{10,625}$ = £1.762

* Abnormal loss transferred to P&L account at cost of good production.

Period 3 (Abnormal gain)

	kgs	£	
Input material	8,700	9,135	
Labour and overheads		2,950	
Abnormal gain	155	245	*
	8,855	12,330	
Less Normal loss	1,305	392	(scrap sales)
Net good production	7,550	11,938	

Cost of good production = $\frac{11,938}{7,550}$ = £1.58 kg.

* Abnormal gain costed at £1.58 kg, the net cost of good production.

Task 3 Total cost £26,500.

	Tonnes	Sales value £	Apportioned cost £
Aggregate	3,850	15,400	14,121
Slurry	6,750	13,500	12,379
		28,900	26,500

Topic 5

Task 1 (a) Derived cost characteristics of Dressing Dept. Costs (using High/Low)

Rates	Fixed at £15,000
Salaries	Fixed at £43,500
Materials	Variable at £3 per unit
Wages	£10,000 fixed + £2 per unit
Power	£2,500 fixed + £1 per unit

Estimated costs @ 9,750 units

	£
Rates	15,000
Salaries	43,500
Materials	29,250
Wages	29,500
Power	12,250

(b) The assumptions are linearity and consistency.

Task 2 (a) See diagram Task 2/5 below.

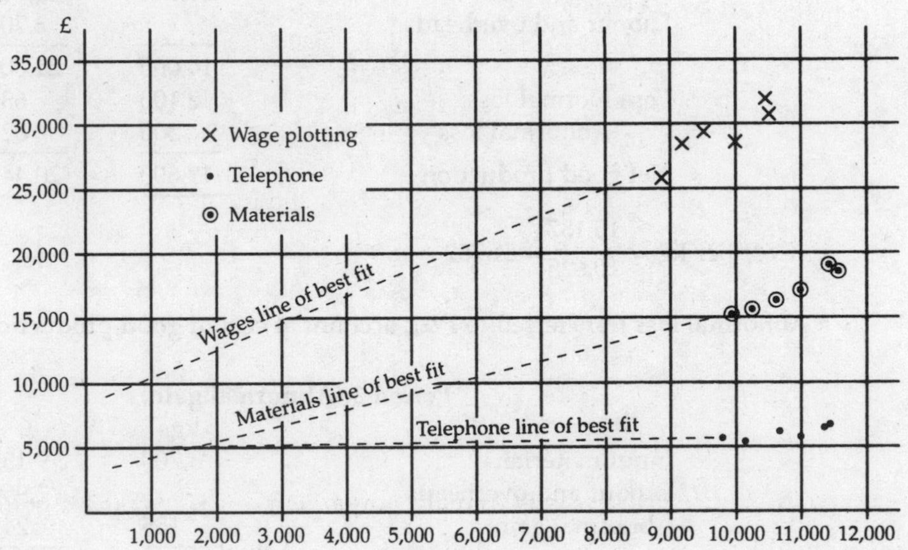

Task 2/5

Estimated characteristics from scattergraph.

Wages	£8,000 fixed + £2.5 per unit
Telephone	£5,000 fixed + 20p per unit
Material	£3,000 + £2.2 per unit

The above figures are very approximate.

(b) Using High/Low method.

	Range of cost £	Range of production units	Variable element £
Wages	4,470	1,650	2.71
Telephone	570	1,300	0.44
Materials	3,900	1,600	2.44

By deduction the fixed elements are

Wages	£5,555
Telephone	2,490
Material	6,462

(c) The results vary considerably as both methods are crude approximations only.

(d) Uncertainty, changes in prices, rates, inflation and methods, etc, etc.

Task 3 SWOT analysis (Strengths, Weaknesses, Opportunities, Threats) is a systematic way of reviewing the organisation in its competitive environment. It is a useful exercise for any organisation to carry out periodically a SWOT analysis as a prelude to detailed planning.

Topic 6

Task 1 (a)

	Period 1	Period 2	Period 3
Sales	2100	2300	2650
Closing stock	750	650	400
	2850	2950	3050
– Opening stock	440	750	650
= Production	2410	2200	2400

(b) & (c) Can be taken directly from the text.

Task 2 (a) Cost characteristics

		£
Salaries	Fixed at	9,600
Rates	Fixed at	2,850
Admin	£2,250 fixed + 15p per m.c. hour	
Wages	£9,500 fixed + 25p per m.c. hour	
Materials	Variable at 26p per m.c. hour	

(b) Budget for 36,000 hours

	£
Salaries	9,600
Rates	2,850
Admin	7,650
Wages	18,500
Materials	9,360

Task 3 (a) & (b) **Budget : Actual Comparison – Activity 36,300 hours**

	Budget	**Actual**	**Variance**	**Significant?**
	£	£	£	
Salaries	9,600	9,885	285 (A)	No
Rates	2,850	2,850	–	
Admin	7,695	8,157	462 (A)	Yes (6%)
Wages	18,575	18,020	555 (F)	No
Materials	9,438	9,816	378 (A)	No

(c) The actuals are compared with the flexed budget for 36,300 hours. With only one variance outside the ±5% range it would seem that expenditure is following the plan.

(d) In general only those items which are controllable for the budget holder.

Topic 7

Task 1 (a) July's cash receipts = £868,750 *less* received from debtors

60% × £918,000 =	550,800	
30% × £695,000 =	208,500	
8% × £810,000 =	64,800	824,100
= July's cash sales		44,650

(b) The other 2% is deemed to be Bad Debts, i.e. money due but not received.

Task 2 (a)

SBP's Cash Budget
August

	£	
Opening balance	54,650	O/D
Cash sales	75,000	
Cash from debtors	823,000	
= Total cash available	843,350	
Payments for materials	201,400	
Wages and salaries	493,136	
Overheads *	97,500	
Asset purchases	165,000	
= Total payments	957,036	
Balance	113,686	O/D

* Note that the cash flow figure is Total overheads – Depreciation, i.e. £115,000 – 17,500 = £97,500. This is because depreciation is a notional expenditure and does not create a cash flow.

(b) This shows that SBP is likely to exceed their overdraft limit slightly, Their bankers could be informed, some expenditure postponed, or they could try to obtain cash from their debtors more quickly.

(c) Except by coincidence the profit for a period is not likely to be the same as the cash flow for the period. Profits are calculated by accounting conventions based on the accruals or matching concept. Also profits are calculated using expenses which are not cash expenses, e.g. depreciation.

Topic 8

Task 1 Variance based on standard cost in 8.1 and actual results in 8.2.

(a) Materials

	£	Variances	Total variances
Wood			
Actual price	16,300	PRICE 188 (FAV)	100 ADV
less 9,160 kgs @ £1.8	16,488	USAGE 288 (ADV)	
less 1,800 × 5 × £1.8	16,200		
Glass	£		
Actual price	14,875	NIL PRICE VAR	605 FAV
less 2,975 sm @ £5	14,875	USAGE 605 (FAV)	
less 1,800 × 1.72 × £5	15,480		
Hinges	£		
Actual price	3,964	NIL PRICE VAR	4 ADV
less 3,604 × £1.1	3,964	USAGE 4 (ADV)	
less 1,800 × 2 × £1.1	3,960		

Strip	£		
Actual price	4,723	PRICE 37 (FAV)	115 ADV
less 11,900 × 0.40	4,760	USAGE 152 (ADV)	
less 1,800 × 6.4 × 0.40	4,608		

(b) Labour – machining

Actual cost	12,155	RATE 221 (FAV)	59 ADV
less 2,210 × £5.60	12,376	EFFICIENCY 260 (ADV)	
less 1,800 × 1.2 × £5.60	12,096		

Labour – assembly

Actual cost	15,880	RATE 1,155 (ADV)	490 ADV
less 3,100 × £4.75	14,725	EFFICIENCY 665 (FAV)	
less 1,800 × 1.8 × £4.75	15,390		

(c) The price and rate variances show the difference between standard prices/rates and the actual prices/rates.

The usage and efficiency shows the differences due to usage/efficiency being greater or less than standard.

Task 2 (a) Actual overheads

Actual overheads	48,500	EXPENDITURE 1,775 (ADV)	220 ADV
less Budgeted overheads (£32,550 + 9,450 × £1.5)	46,725	VOLUME 525 (FAV)	
less Recovered overheads on labour hrs (9,450 × £5)	47,250	EFFICIENCY 1,030 (FAV)	
less Recovered overheads on SHP (9,656 × £5)	48,280		

(b) Variances = – 1,775 + 525 + 1,030 = 220 ADV
= Actual overheads – standard overheads for actual production
= 48,500 – 9,656 × £5 = 220 overspent.

(c) Expenditure variance: expresses the difference between actual overheads and the flexed budgetary allowance.

Volume variance: expresses the under/over recovery of fixed overheads by working more or less than budgeted.

Efficiency variance: expresses the overhead effect of working above or below standard efficiency.

Topic 9

Task 1 (a) Relevant costs for quotation:
Steel: use replacement cost of £3.80 kg
Plastic: use resale price of £7.50 kg.

(b) Appropriate cost is the revenue foregone of £1,000 per week.

(c) The general rule is to identify the incremental cash flow change.

Task 2

(a) This is an Opportunity Cost.

(b) These costs are highly relevant and must be identified.

(c) It is a short-run decision where fixed costs are deemed to be the same for all the alternatives so are not relevant.

(d) No. Only costs which alter are relevant.

Task 3

(a)

	System 1	System 2	System 3	System 4
	£	£	£	£
Contribution	160	160	320	280
Micro-chips per unit	6	18	10	12
Contribution per micro-chip	26.67	8.88	32	23.33

(b) Ranking is Systems 3–1–4 and 2.

	Cumulative chips
Make System 3 up to demand = 5,000 × 10 =	50,000
Make System 1 up to demand = 5,000 × 6 =	80,000
Make System 4 up to demand = 2,500 × 12 =	110,000
No System 2	

(c) Contribution of best plan

	£'000
= 5,000 × 320	1,600
5,000 × 160	800
2,500 × 280	700
	3,100

Topic 10

Task 1

(a) Expected cost/unit = £(6.50 × 0.3) + (7.25 × 0.7) = 7.025
∴ Contribution = £10 – 7.025 = 2.975

Expected sales (250,000 × 0.1) + (220,000 × 0.6) + (175,000 × 0.3) = 209,500
∴ Expected contribution = £2.975 × 209,500
= £623,262

(b) Maximum contribution per unit = £10 – 6.50 = £3.50 with P of 0.3
Maximum sales = 250,000 with P of 0.1
∴ Maximum contribution = £875,000 with P of 0.03

(c) Minimum contribution per unit = £10 – 7.25 = 2.75 with P of 0.7
Minimum sales = 175,000
∴ Minimum contribution = 175,000 × £2.75 = £481,250 with P of 0.21

Task 2

It is first necessary to deduce the fixed and variable costs from the data given, thus:

Total costs increase by £1 million when sales increase by £2 million.
∴ Variable costs = 50% of sales
∴ Fixed costs = £3.75 m

(a) $\text{BEP (sales)} = \frac{3.75}{0.5} = £7.5\text{ m}$

$\text{BEP (units)} = \frac{£7.5\text{ m}}{20{,}000} = 375\text{ units}$

(b) Sales for £1.5 m profit = $\frac{3.75 \text{ m} + 1.5 \text{ m}}{0.5}$ = £10.5 m or 525 units

(c) Margin of safety = £10.5 m – 7.5 m = £3 m or 29%.

Task 3 (a) See diagram Task 3a/10 below.

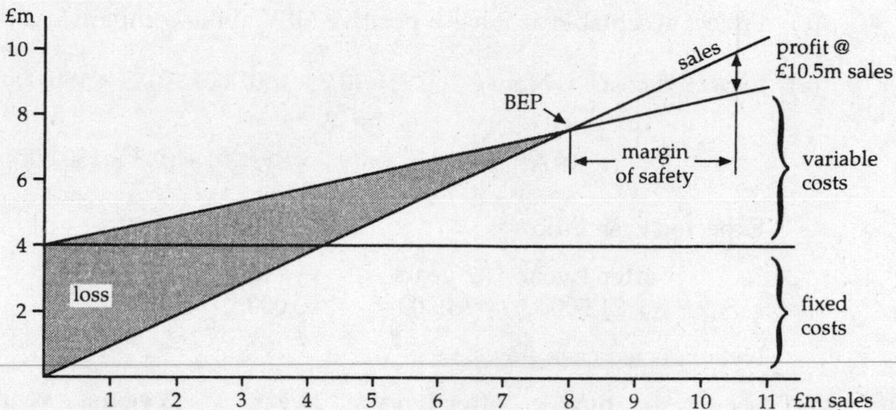

Task 3a/10

(b) See diagram Task 3b/10 below.

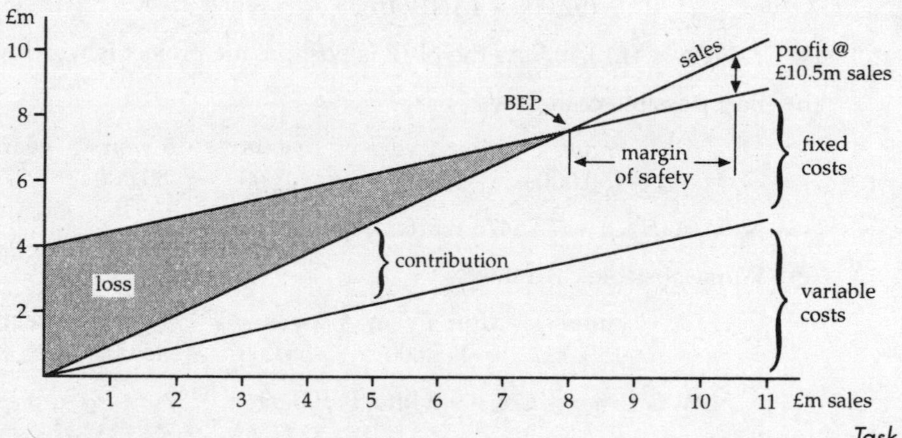

Task 3b/10

Topic 11

Task 1 (a) Cash flows are more objective, not subject to conventions and are what are actually spent.

(b) Main traditional methods are:

Accountancy rate of return = $\frac{\text{average profits p.a.}}{\text{capital invested}}$

Payback = number of period's cash flow to recoup original investment.

Task 2 (a) Net cash flows

0	1	2	3	4	5
–140,000	+25,000	40,000	80,000	50,000	45,000

∴ NPV = –140,000 + (25,000 × 0.870) + (40,000 × 0.756) + (80,000× 0.658) + (50,000 × 0.572) + (45,000 × 0.497)

= +15,595

(b) IRR of investment

NPV @ 20% = – 3,785

$\therefore$ IRR = 15 + 5 $\frac{15,595}{19,380}$

= 19.02%

(c) Project acceptable as it has a positive NPV at the company's cost of capital.

Task 3

(a) Expected costs: Now = (0.7 × 150,000) + (0.3 × 155,000)
= 151,500

After 1 year = (0.7 × 85,000) + (0.3 × 130,000)
= 98,000

Expected cash inflows:

after 1 year	2 years	3 years	years 4 to 10
21,500	64,500	62,000	52,000

Net expected cash flows:

now	after 1 year	2 years	3 years	years 4 to 10
–151,500	–77,000	+64,500	62,000	52,000

NPV @ 15% = –151,500 + (–77,000 × 0.870) + (64,500 × 0.756) + (62,000 × 0.658) + (52,000 × 4.160 × 0.658)

$\therefore$ NPV = +£13,407. As the NVP is positive the project is worthwhile.

(b) Best possible cash flows:

now	after 1 year	2 years	3 years	years 4 to 10
–150,000	–50,000	+90,000	80,000	75,000

NPV @ 15% = +£132,476 with a P of 0.14

(c) Worst possible cash flows:

now	after 1 year	2 years	3 years	years 4 to 10
–155,000	–115,000	+55,000	45,000	40,000

$\therefore$ NPV @ 15% = – £74,369 with a P of 0.09

Topic 12

Task 1

(a) ROCE relates profits earned to the capital used to earn the profits. It is a relative measure which is widely used.

(b) Frequently, net profit before tax is used for ROCE calculations rather than after tax profits because the taxation policy within a group is usually a central responsibility and to use an after-tax figure could cloud operating factors.

(c) Typical advantages:

- decisions taken locally with local knowledge
- provides motivation and development opportunities for more junior management.
- relieves strategic decision-makers of routine matters
- reduces communication problems and encourages initiative.

Possible disadvantages:

- sub-optimal decision-making
- lack of adherence to central policies
- may create stress for junior management.

(d) Residual profit is profit less an interest charge on the assets employed. It is an absolute figure as opposed to the relative nature of ROCE.

Residual profit is more flexible and may encourage a longer-term view. On the other hand it is less useful for comparisons between investment centres.

Task 2 (a) Asset turnover ratios:

$$\frac{\text{sales}}{\text{capital employed}} = \frac{147}{122} = 1.2$$

$$\frac{\text{sales}}{\text{current assets}} = \frac{147}{39} = 3.77$$

$$\frac{\text{sales}}{\text{fixed assets}} = \frac{147}{83} = 1.77$$

Profit margin ratios:

$$\frac{\text{operating profit}}{\text{sales}}\% = \frac{8.9}{147} = 6.05\%$$

$$\frac{\text{general overheads}}{\text{sales}} = \frac{41.6}{147} = 28.3\%$$

$$\frac{\text{cost of sales}}{\text{sales}} = \frac{96.5}{147} = 65.6\%$$

(b) The asset turnover has declined from 1.41 to 1.2 and the profit to sales % has declined from 6.38% to 6.05% of sales. This points to a worsening use of assets and increasing costs as a proportion of sales. Comparison should be made with as many previous periods as possible to find out the long-term trend. More detailed analysis of sales costs (item by item) should be undertaken.

Task 3 (a) Typical performance ratios include:

ROCE	$\frac{600}{1,460} = 41\%$	$\frac{500}{1,650} = 30.3\%$	$\frac{495}{1,890} = 26\%$
Profit : sales	$\frac{600}{4,800} = 12.5\%$	$\frac{500}{5,050} = 10\%$	$\frac{495}{5,340} = 9.26$
Sales : cap : emp	$\frac{4,800}{1,460} = 3.28$	$\frac{5,050}{1,650} = 3.06$	$\frac{5,340}{1,890} = 2.82$

(b) Typical liquidity ratios:

Current ratio	$\frac{1,909}{1,409} = 1.35$	$\frac{2,273}{1,776} = 1.27$	$\frac{1,927}{1,885} = 1.02$
Acid text	$\frac{999}{1,409} = 0.7$	$\frac{1,278}{1,776} = 0.72$	$\frac{977}{1,885} = 0.52$
Debtor's collection	68.4 days	86 days	59 days
Creditor's payment	49 days	61 days	67.8 days

(c) Virtually every ratio and statistic shows a worsening position. The firm is in a steep decline and seems to lack strong management. This, of course, could make it ripe for take-over.

Developing knowledge and skills

Introduction

This Section gives you a chance to apply and build upon what you have learned so far. It does so by using a mixture of cases, assignments, past examination questions and multiple choice questions. The aim is to enable you to use the principles you have learned in the real world.

Section I developed your knowledge in simple, easy stages which were largely self-contained. In the real world things are not so tidily packaged so you will find in this Section that the problems – and knowledge requirements – are more wide-ranging and draw upon numerous cost and management accounting principles. For continuity Section I was based on the experience of a trainee in a manufacturing organisation. However, it must be stressed that cost and management accounting principles are equally applicable in all types of organisation: hospitals; shops; banks; insurance companies; local and central government and many other types of service organisation, as well as manufacturing companies. Accordingly this section includes questions, cases and assignments based on a range of different types of organisation in both the service and manufacturing sectors.

Contents

How to use this section

If you are studying at a College, your Lecturer will advise you what questions/assignments/cases you should do and what sequence best suits your particular course of study.

If you are studying on your own, the following suggested study plan is recommended.

- Turn to this section as you are directed from Section I (at the ends of units 4, 8 and 12). Work through the three parts in sequence and in parallel with the units in Section I dealing with the particular topic. You will thus be confirming and extending your knowledge of a topic before moving onto something new.
- The multiple choice questions (MCQs) broadly cover the main knowledge requirements in each of the parts. Use the MCQs as a diagnostic tool to discover whether you have grasped the basics of a topic area. If not, go back over that topic until you do understand it.
- Get into the habit of referring to the appropriate study material in Section 1 (and the recommended additional reading, if necessary) as and when required. The continual cross-referencing will help to deepen your knowledge and understanding.
- Answers are provided for some of the questions in this Section. *Always* make some attempt at a question *before* looking at the answer. This is an important learning technique.

Each part contains several assignments. Usually these require you to investigate or comment on something in the real world. You may have to visit firms or organisations, write or telephone for information, or observe what is happening. Remember to be polite and patient in all your dealing with managers and staff and never forget to write a 'thank you' letter when you have finished. Dealing with assignments can be time-consuming but the process develops real practical skills and will be found to be well worthwhile.

Cost analysis and cost ascertainment

Multiple choice questions *(tick appropriate box)* ☑

1. Direct costs are costs that:
   (a) Are directly charged to a department A ☐
   (b) Can be directly identified with a product or service B ☐
   (c) Are directly under the control of a manager C ☐
   (d) Are incurred directly the factory is open. D ☐

2. Prime cost includes:
   (a) Direct materials plus total overheads A ☐
   (b) All direct costs plus factory overheads B ☐
   (c) Direct labour, direct materials and direct expenses C ☐
   (d) Direct labour plus factory overheads. D ☐

3. A cost centre is:
   (a) A unit of production or service A ☐
   (b) Any location or department which incurs costs B ☐
   (c) Part of the overhead system by which costs are gathered together C ☐
   (d) A location which controls direct costs. D ☐

4. Cost apportionment is done so that
   (a) Common costs are shared among cost centres in proportion to the benefit received A ☐
   (b) Each cost unit gathers overheads as it passes through a cost centre B ☐
   (c) Costs may be controlled C ☐
   (d) Whole items of cost are charged to cost centres. D ☐

5. Product costing is mainly concerned with
   (a) Controlling production costs A ☐
   (b) Finding the total of production costs B ☐
   (c) Analysing cost behaviour C ☐
   (d) Finding the cost of sales and valuing stock. D ☐

6. The First in First Out (FIFO) materials pricing system charges issues at:
   (a) The price of the oldest batch in stock A ☐
   (b) The price of the most recent batch in stock B ☐
   (c) The price of the first component or material used in a period C ☐
   (d) The average price of goods in stock. D ☐

7. The Last In First Out (LIFO) system
   (a) Values stocks at current values A ☐
   (b) Tends to produce realistic product costs B ☐
   (c) Makes cost comparisons between jobs easier C ☐
   (d) Understates product costs in times of rising prices. D ☐

8. Using the Average Price issuing system
   (a) Exaggerates price fluctuations A ☐
   (b) Makes cost control easier B ☐
   (c) The issue price is recalculated after each receipt C ☐
   (d) Always values stocks at the price of the oldest batch in stock. D ☐

9. Wages paid using differential piecework
   (a) Are classified as overheads A ☐
   (b) Increase as production rises B ☐
   (c) Decrease when production rises C ☐
   (d) Remain the same regardless of output. D ☐

10. A firm uses direct labour hours as a basis for overhead absorption. If large fluctuations in labour hours are experienced
    (a) This is a reason to use predetermined overhead rates A ☐
    (b) This will mean that overheads will be under or over absorbed for the year B ☐
    (c) Different amounts of overhead will be charged to jobs with the same labour hours C ☐
    (d) It will be better to use a machine hour rate. D ☐

11. A predetermined overhead rate using machine hours as a basis:
    (a) Is calculated by dividing actual overheads by budgeted machine hours A ☐
    (b) Results in the over absorption of overhead B ☐
    (c) Is inferior to a rate based on labour hours C ☐
    (d) Results in charging similar overheads to jobs with similar hours. D ☐

12. A firm recovers overheads on labour hours which were budgeted at 3,500 with overheads of £43,750. Actual results were 3,620 hours with overheads of £44,535
    (a) Overheads were under absorbed by £785 A ☐
    (b) Overheads were over absorbed by £715 B ☐
    (c) Overheads were over absorbed by £1,500 C ☐
    (d) Overheads were under absorbed by £715. D ☐

13. A firm that has under absorbed overhead at the end of the period:
    (a) Has been working inefficiently A ☐
    (b) Would be better not using predetermined rates B ☐
    (c) Incorrectly budgeted the absorption base and/or the amount of overheads C ☐
    (d) Has overspent on overheads. D ☐

14. Which of the following firms would be most likely to use job costing?
    (a) A paint manufacturer A ☐
    (b) A sugar refinery B ☐
    (c) A firm of architects C ☐
    (d) A car manufacturers. D ☐

The following data are the basis of the next 3 questions. A firm makes special switchgear to customers requirements and uses job costing. The data for a period are:

	Job No		
	X100	Y252	Z641
Opening WIP	£6,200	21,000	0
Material added in period	£15,250	0	9,000
Labour for period	£9,000	7,000	8,000

The overheads for the period were exactly as budgeted, £60,000.

15. What overhead would be added to Job No X100 for the period?
    (a) £20,000 A ☐
    (b) £22,500 B ☐
    (c) £9,000 C ☐
    (d) £24,000. D ☐

16. Job No. Y252 was completed in the period and consisted of 30 identical switch units. The firm adds 25% on to total costs to calculate the selling price. What is the price of a switch unit?
    (a) £1,167 A ☐
    (b) £2,292 B ☐
    (c) £1,896 C ☐
    (d) £1,517. D ☐

17. Jobs X100 and Z641 are the only incomplete jobs. What is the value of closing WIP?
    (a) £89,950 A ☐
    (b) £47,450 B ☐
    (c) £112,437 C ☐
    (d) £41,250. D ☐

18. The costing associated with a typical site based contract:
    (a) Means that more costs can be identified as direct A ☐
    (b) Requires some estimate to be made of interim profits B ☐
    (c) Means that the contract account will be credited with materials unused at the end of the contract C ☐
    (d) Includes all of these. D ☐

19. Which of the following firms are most likely to use process costing?
    (a) A car manufacturer A ☐
    (b) A sugar refinery B ☐
    (c) A builder C ☐
    (d) A departmental store. D ☐

20. Using process costing the amount of cost transferred to Finished Goods stock is the cost of:
    (a) The equivalent production for the period A ☐
    (b) The units started and completed during the period B ☐
    (c) The units completed during the period C ☐
    (d) The units in the opening Finished Goods stock. D ☐

21. Let O = units in opening WIP, C = units in closing WIP, S = units started in production. Then U = units completed and
    (a) U = O + S – C A ☐
    (b) U = O + C – S B ☐
    (c) U = O – C – S C ☐
    (d) U = O + S + C. D ☐

22. A process department began with no opening stocks. A total of 8,500 units was transferred in at a cost of £93,500. The cost of raw materials added was £3.50 per unit and labour costs were £5 per unit. If 6,750 units were completed and transferred out the total cost transferred out was:
    (a) £165,750 A ☐
    (b) £93,500 B ☐
    (c) £131,625 C ☐
    (d) £74,250. D ☐

23. Apportioning joint costs over joint products on either the physical unit or sales value basis is useful for
    (a) No purposes as the methods are conventions only A ☐
    (b) Decision making B ☐
    (c) Stock valuation and decision making C ☐
    (d) Stock valuation. D ☐

The following data are to be used for questions 24 and 25. A process produces three products R, S and T. Total joint costs were £17,000 and outputs and selling prices were:

R	250 kgs sold at £22 per kg
S	550 kgs sold at £19 per kg
T	450 kgs sold at £25 per kg.

24. Apportioning the joint costs on the physical unit basis gives:

(a)	R = £3,400	S = £7,480	T = £6,120	A ☐
(b)	R = £3,438	S = £6,531	T = £7,031	B ☐
(c)	R = £5,667	S = £5,667	T = £5,666	C ☐
(d)	R = £5,667	S = £4,894	T = £6,439.	D ☐

25. Apportioning the joint costs on the sales value basis gives:

(a)	R = £3,400	S = £7,480	T = £6,120	A ☐
(b)	R = £3,438	S = £6,531	T = £7,031	B ☐
(c)	R = £5,667	S = £5,667	T = £5,666	C ☐
(d)	R = £5,667	S = £4,894	T = £6,439.	D ☐

Case 1/1 *Beta Engineering Ltd*

A case dealing with job costing in a jobbing engineering company and various methods of absorbing overheads.

Beta Engineering are manufacturers of small metal fabrications. All items are made to order and quantities range from a single fabrication up to batches of 1000. Some fabrications require a substantial amount of machining or welding, others are largely hand made using simple hand tools. Because of the varying applications for the fabrications, the materials used vary widely; including special purpose alloy and stainless steels, non-ferrous metals and ordinary mild steel.

Sara Hall has recently commenced work at Beta Engineering as a Cost Clerk and is given the task of calculating the cost of each job. This is done by using the Estimate Sheet, prepared at the Quotation stage, and adjusting this for the actual materials used so as to find the actual job cost. The amount of material used is found from the Stores Issue notes.

Extracts from the Estimate Sheet for 50 stainless steel fuse holders and the subsequent Job Costs are shown below:

Estimate Sheet

			£
Labour:	500 hours @ £4	=	2,000
Materials:	150 kgs @ £8 kg	=	1,200
Overheads:	400 % of materials	=	4,800
=	Total cost		8,000
+	20% profit		1,600
=	Selling price for batch		9,600

When this batch was made Sara totalled the Issue Notes and found that 173 Kgs of material had been used and accordingly prepared the following Job Cost:

Job Cost

		£
Labour:	(as estimate)	2,000
Materials:	173 kgs @ £8 kg	1,384
Overheads:	400% of materials	5,536
=	Total cost	8,920
	Selling price	9,600
	Actual profit	£680

After only a few weeks of doing this work, Sara had serious misgivings about the system used which seems to have numerous problems.

Tasks

(a) Prepare a report to the Managing Director criticising the present system of Job Costing.

Your report must include specific comments on the method used for absorbing overheads, the problems that might arise using the present method of calculating Job Costs, and a recommendation for a better method of absorbing overheads.

(b) Outline the features you would expect to find in a good Job Costing system for a firm such as Beta Engineering.

(c) Design a more appropriate Job Cost form.

For activities (b) and (c) you should, wherever possible, find out about the systems and forms used by actual firms in your locality.

Case 1/2 *Challenge Ladders Ltd*

A case dealing with cost analysis and product costing.

Challenge Ladders have made builders' multi-section ladders for many years and have a good reputation. Alan Betts has just been appointed as the new Managing Director and wishes to diversify the product range in order to increase sales. One of the ideas being considered is a range of Loft Ladders to be marketed under the 'Rizeup' brand label in 4 standard sizes. This will require considerable investment and an important meeting has been planned with the company's bankers to discuss the whole project.

Alan Betts wishes to be well prepared and sends for you to help him with the details. Certain information has already been prepared but he thinks that more analysis is required and that some re-arrangement would make the data more understandable.

The existing information is as follows:

Planned sales and production data in first quarter.

Ladder size	Selling Price per unit	Production units	Sales units
	£		
1	150	800	500
2	130	700	450
3	100	500	400
4	75	500	350

Expected Direct costs per unit (£)

Size	Materials	Direct wages Dept. A	Direct wages Dept. B	Direct wages Dept. C
	£	£	£	£
1	18	7	5	8
2	16	5	4	3
3	13	4	2	3
4	12	4	2	3

Planned total costs for the quarter

			£
Material purchases			43,000
Production overheads:			
– Allocated	Dept. A	4,800	
	Dept. B	7,500	
	Dept. C	3,900	16,200
Apportioned overheads			21,600
Administration & selling overheads			29,600

It is the practice of the company to

(a) Apportion production overheads on departmental direct wages

(b) Value finished goods stock at prime cost plus production overheads

(c) Charge Administration and Selling overheads to products on the basis of full production cost of goods sold.

Work-in-progress is considered so small that it can be ignored.

Tasks

Prepare the following extra information for the Managing Director, supported by any explanations thought necessary.

(a) Direct Wages by product and by department

(b) Material cost by product

(c) Departmental overhead absorption rates

(d) Total production cost by product

(e) Value of closing stock of raw materials

(f) Value of closing stock of finished goods, by product

(g) Sales by product

(h) Production cost of goods sold by product

(i) Profit and Loss account analysed by product.

Case 1/3 *Utopian Hotel*

A case dealing with overhead analysis in a hotel.

The Utopian Hotel is developing a cost accounting system. Initially it has been decided to create four cost centres: Residential and Catering deal directly with customers whilst Housekeeping and Maintenance are internal service cost centres.

The following overhead details have been estimated for the next period.

	Residential	Catering	Housekeeping	Maintenance	Total
Consumable materials	14,000	23,000	27,000	9,000	73,000
Staff costs	16,500	13,000	11,500	5,500	46,500
Rent and rates					37,500
Contents insurance					14,000
Heating and lighting					18,500
Depreciation on equipment etc					37,500
					227,000

The following information is also available

	Residential	Catering	Housekeeping	Maintenance	Total
Floor area (m^2)	2,750	1,350	600	300	5,000
Value of equipment etc	£350,000	£250,000	£75,000	£75,000	£750,000
Number of employees	20	20	15	5	60

In the period it is estimated that there will be 2,800 guest-nights and 16,000 meals will be served. Housekeeping works 70% for Residential and 30% for Catering, and Maintenance works 20% for Housekeeping, 30% for Catering and 50% for Residential.

Tasks

(a) Prepare an overhead statement showing clearly allocations and apportionments to each cost centre.

(b) Calculate appropriate overhead absorption rates for Residential and Catering.

(c) Calculate the under/over absorption of overheads if actual results were as follows:

Residential:	3,050 guest-nights with overheads of £144,600
Catering:	15,250 meals with overheads of £89,250

(d) Comment briefly on possible future developments in the Utopian Hotel's cost accounting system.

CIMA Cost Accounting and Quantitative Methods

Assignments

1/1 Based on a real organisation or department, find six management tasks or functions which use information from the CMA System. Specify the types of information used.

1/2 Develop an expenditure coding system and a location/use coding system for your College. Compare what you have developed with what is actually used.

1/3 Recent developments in the National Health Service have made it essential for all Hospitals to develop CMA systems. Find out:

(a) what cost units are used in a typical hospital;

(b) how the cost of an operation is calculated.

1/4 All local authorities now have to put out a range of services to tender under what is called CCT (Compulsory Competitive Tendering).

Find out what services must be included in this scheme and what effects this is having on the authorities own costing systems.

Questions with answers

A1. (a) Describe briefly *three* methods of pricing material issues to work-in-progress frequently used in cost accounting.

(b) State the effect in times of inflation of each of the methods you have described in (a) above on:

(i) The valuation of stocks;

(ii) The cost of products made;

(iii) The profit earned.

(c) Explain why the pricing methods you have given in answer to (a) above may be unsuitable for use when prices (or estimates) are being prepared for work to be undertaken to customer's special requirements.

RSA Cost Accounting Stage II

A2. Nixan (Retail) Ltd sells only one model of portable colour television set and on 1 January 19x9 held a stock of twenty sets which had cost £80 each.

Details of purchases and sales for the first three months of 19x9 are as follows:

Date	Details of Purchases		Sales for each month	
	Sets received	Cost price per set	Sets sold	Selling price per set
		£		£
10 January	20	81		
17 January	60	70		
17 January	30	82	50	140
7 February	50	85		
20 February	30	85		
28 February	20	94	100	140
10 March	60	90		
31 March	40	97	150	150

The physical stock checks at the end of January and February agreed with the recorded quantity shown on the stock record but a similar check on 31 March revealed a deficit of two sets, presumed stolen.

For updating stock records and monthly accounting routes, all issues during a month are priced on the last day of each monthly period.

Variable selling costs are incurred at the rate of 10% on sales and fixed costs amount to £4,000 per month.

Required

(a) Calculate the month end stock valuations for January and February which would arise from pricing out monthly issues on each of the following methods:

(i) FIFO

(ii) LIFO

(iii) Weighted average

(b) Prepare a detailed Profit and Loss Account for the month of March using the weighted average basis.

LCCI Cost Accounting

A3. A small business has recently started up in precision engineering, using expensive machinery to produce components made to specific orders. Prices are being quoted on the basis of estimated total factory cost for each job plus a mark up of 100% to cover all administration/selling costs and profit.

The production budget for the current year includes the following data:

Total factory overheads	£500,000
Direct material usage	£1,000,000
Direct labour (at £4 per hour)	£200,000
Machine hours	100,000

The estimated costs and times for Job 456 are as follows:

Direct material	£1,000
Direct labour hours (at £4.50 per hour)	60
Machine hours	72

Required

(a) Calculate four possible price quotations for Job 456, using a different basis for factory overhead absorption in each case. Show details of your calculations which should be to the nearest £.

(b) State which basis should be used in these circumstances and give reasons for your choice.

LCCI Cost Accounting

A4. A machine shop has the machine capacity to produce 2,400 components each week. Each machine requires one operator, a 40 hour week is in operation and 2 grades of operator are employed. Each component is machined in four successive operations according to the following schedule:

	Operations			
	1	2	3	4
Machining time (in minutes)	20	30	10	15
Grade of Operator	A	A	B	B
Hourly Wage Rate	£4	£4	£3.20	£3.20

Required

Prepare a statement in columnar form showing (i) for each operation and (ii) in total:

(a) The number of operators required

(b) The expected weekly payroll cost

(c) The labour cost per component (to 2 decimal places of £).

LCCI Cost Accounting

A5. A furniture making business manufactures quality furniture to customers' orders. It has three production departments and two service departments. Budgeted overhead costs for the coming year are as follows:

	Total
	£
Rent and Rates	12,800
Machine insurance	6,000
Telephone charges	3,200
Depreciation	18,000
Production Supervisor's salaries	24,000
Heating & Lighting	6,400
	70,400

The three production departments – A, B and C, and the two service departments – X and Y are housed in the new premises, the details of which, together with other statistics and information is given below.

	Departments				
	A	B	C	X	Y
Floor area occupied (sq metres)	3,000	1,800	600	600	400
Machine value (£'000s)	24	10	8	4	2
Direct labour hrs budgeted	3,200	1,800	1,000		
Labour rates per hour	£3.80	£3.50	£3.40	£3.00	£3.00
Allocated overheads:					
Specific to each department (£'000s)	2.8	1.7	1.2	0.8	0.6
Service Department X's costs apportioned	50%	25%	25%		
Service Department Y's costs apportioned	20%	30%	50%		

Required

(a) Prepare a statement showing the overhead cost budgeted for each department, showing the basis of apportionment used. Calculate also suitable overhead absorption rates.

(b) Two pieces of furniture are to be manufactured for customers.

Direct costs are as follows:

	Job 123	Job 124
Direct material	£154	£108
Direct labour	20 hours Dept. A	16 hours Dept. A
	12 hours Dept. B	10 hours Dept. B
	10 hours Dept. C	14 hours Dept. C

Calculate the total costs of each job.

(c) If the firm quotes prices to customers that reflect a required profit of 25% on selling price, calculate the quoted selling price for each job.

(d) If material costs are a significant part of total costs in a manufacturing company, describe a system of material control that might be used in order to effectively control costs, paying particular attention to the stock control aspect.

AAT Cost Accounting & Budgeting

A6. A company provides a building repairs and maintenance service. A job costing system is in operation in order to identify the cost, and profit, of each job carried out. Several jobs are in progress at any one time. One such job is Job 126, which was started and completed in the month just ended.

Quantities of Material P were issued from stores to the job, as well as other materials as required. Raw material issues are priced at the end of each month on a weighted average basis. Overtime is worked as necessary to meet the general requirements of the business, and is paid at a premium of 30% over the basic rate for direct personnel. The basic rate is £6.00 per hour. Overheads are absorbed into job costs at the end of each month at an actual rate per direct labour hour. Idle time, material wastage, and rectification work after jobs are completed, are a normal feature of the business. Idle time is not expected to exceed 2% of direct hours charged to jobs. Wastage is not expected to exceed 1% of the cost of materials issued to jobs. Rectification costs are not expected to exceed 1.5% of direct costs. All such costs are not charged as direct costs of individual jobs.

Information concerning Job 125 is as follows:

Issues of Material P were 960 kilos. Issues of other materials were costed at £2,030. Of the total materials issued to the job, wastage cost £42 and materials used for rectification cost £33. The hours of direct personnel working on the job were 496. These included 37 overtime hours, 10 hours of idle time, and 12 hours spend on rectification work.

Information for all work carried out on jobs during the month is as follows:

Opening stock of Material P was 3,100 kilos, valued at £5,594. Purchases during the month were 3,500 kilos at £1.81 per kilo, and 3,800 kilos at £1.82 per kilo. 7,060 kilos of Material P were issued from stores to jobs, including 60 kilos which were subsequently wasted and 340 kilos which were used for rectification work.

Other materials issued to jobs were costed at £19,427 (including £236 wastage and £197 rectification).

Hours of direct personnel paid at basic rate were 3,640, with a further 290 hours paid at overtime rate. These total hours include 82 hours of idle time and 37 hours spent on rectification work.

Other costs incurred in the month were:

Supervisory labour	£3,760
Depreciation	£585
Cleaning materials	£63
Stationery and telephone	£275
Rent and rates	£940
Vehicle running costs	£327
Other administration	£688

Required

(a) Prepare a statement of the costs associated with Job 126.

(b) Provide, and comment upon, any additional information that may be useful in controlling the business.

ACCA Cost and Management Accounting

A7. PTS Limited is a manufacturing company which uses three production departments to make its product. It has the following factory costs which are expected to be incurred in the year to 31 December:

		£
Direct wages	Machining	234,980
	Assembly	345,900
	Finishing	134,525

		£
Indirect wages and salaries	Machining	120,354
	Assembly	238,970
	Finishing	89,700

	£
Factory rent	12,685,500
Business rates	3,450,900
Heat and lighting	985,350
Machinery power	2,890,600
Depreciation	600,000
Canteen subsidy	256,000

Other information is available as follows:

	Machining	Assembly	Finishing
Number of employees	50	60	18
Floor space occupied (m^2)	1,800	1,400	800
Horse power of machinery	13,000	500	6,500
Value of machinery (£'000)	250	30	120
Number of labour hours	100,000	140,000	35,000
Number of machine hours	200,000	36,000	90,000

Required

(a) Prepare the company's overhead analysis sheet for the year.

(b) Calculate appropriate overhead absorption rates (to two decimal places) for each department.

CIMA Accounting

A8. The Direct Service Organisation (DSO) of Vickersville District Council operates a fleet of 5 ton vans.

Information relating to the operating costs of the fleet for year ended 31 march is given below:

Number of vehicles	12
Capital cost per vehicle	£14,000
Average miles per annum, for each vehicle	20,000
Fuel consumption (miles per litre)	4
Type replacement cost per mile	£0.05
Drivers' wages per vehicle per annum	
Basic and guaranteed pay, including holidays	£9,000
Vehicle licence (each)	£300
Vehicle insurance (each)	£400
Cost of fuel per litre	£0.48

Additional information:

(i) Drivers were given a bonus and overtime pay amounting to 5% of the basic pay. Pension contributions and other fringe benefits amounted to 11% of basic pay.

(ii) It is DSO policy to depreciate all vehicles on a straight line basis over five years and to charge operating costs with notional interest at 6% per annum on the capital cost of the vehicles.

(iii) Maintenance and repairs are carried out in the DSO's own workshop which employs two mechanics at an average renumeration of £9,500 per annum. The cost of maintenance materials and spare parts was £20,000.

(iv) DSO central support costs to be charged to the vehicles were £55,000.

You are required to:

Provide suitable information on the cost of the vehicle fleet including breakdown of costs per mile.

Questions without answers

B1. (a) Distinguish briefly between job costing and batch costing.

(b) The following information is available for Job 4321, which is being produced at the request of a customer:

	Dept. A	Dept. B	Dept. C
Materials consumed	£4,000	£1,000	£1,500
Direct labour: wage rate per hour	£3	£4	£5
Direct labour hours	300	200	400

In accordance with company policy the following are chargeable to jobs:

Fixed production overhead	£5 per direct labour hour
Fixed administration overhead	80% total production cost
Profit mark-up	20% margin on selling price

Required

(i) Calculate the total cost and selling price of Job 4321.

(ii) Assume that shortly after the Job is completed the original customer goes bankrupt and the Job is not delivered. The only other possible customer is prepared to pay £9,000.

Briefly indicate, with reasons, whether you would accept the offer of £9,000.

(c) The following information is available for Z company:

	Division A		Division B	
	Year 1	Year 2	Year 1	Year 2
	£'000	£'000	£'000	£'000
Stocks				
Value at end of year	300	400	440	480
Average stock value	280	336	390	390
Value of issues during year	689	695	2,000	2,106
Holding costs	40	46.5	108	105
Debtors				
Value at end of year	657	552	1,068	1,246
Turnover	4,000	4,200	6,000	6,500

Note: all sales are on credit.

The company uses a number of performance indicators:

Indicator	Method of calculation
Operating efficiency %	Holding cost/value of issues
Activity efficiency %	Average stock value/turnover
Turnover rate (times)	Value of issues/average stock value

In addition, the company finds that debtors turnover (in days) is useful.

Required

(i) Calculate the indicators and debtors turnover for each year to 1 decimal place.

(ii) Comment briefly on your findings.

AAT Cost Accounting & Budgeting

B2. D Limited has two employees: Kay and Lee, making product E. During the week ended 28th March, both employees each worked 40 hours. Kay's rate of pay was £3.20 per hour and he produced 180 units of product E. Lee's rate of pay was £2.75 per hour and he produced 150 units. Under all the bases of payment given below each employee is guaranteed a wage based on his respective hourly rate.

Overhead is absorbed into product costs at a rate of £4 for each hour worked.

You are required to calculate:

(a) The gross wage for each employee under each of the following bases of payment:

(i) Daywork;

(ii) Piecework at a rate of £0.75 per unit;

(iii) Bonus scheme with bonus paid at £2.40 for each hour produced in excess of time taken, with time allowed at 15 minutes per unit;

(iv) Differential piecework on the following basis:

for production in a 40 hour week

For the first 100 units or less	£0.60 per unit
For the next 50 units	£0.90 per unit
For all units in excess of 150 units	£1.20 per unit

(b) The labour plus overhead cost per unit for each of the employees on each of the bases of payment you have calculated in answer to (a) above. Cost per unit should be shown to the nearest penny.

RSA Cost Accounting Stage II

B3. (a) Explain what you understand by the following terms, and briefly state the principal features of each:

Stock control

Store keeping

(b) Receipts and issues of Material X for the month of August are as follows:

	Receipts units	Total value £	Issues units
1st August	2,000	4,000	
2nd August	3,000	6,600	
3rd August	2,000	6,000	
4th August			3,000
5th August	3,000	7,500	
6th August			6,000

There were no opening stocks of Material X.

Required

Using a FIFO method of valuation, show the price charged to each issue, and the closing stock valuation at 6th August. Assume that records are maintained using a perpetual inventory system.

(c) Assume that you discover that the actual number of units of an item in stock represents 1.5 times the maximum level set for that item. Briefly explain what you might do.

AAT Cost Accounting & Budgeting

B4. The total valuation of the opening work in progress in Process 2 was £2,500. This was based on the existence of 300 units which were only 80% complete so far as labour was concerned and 60% complete for overheads.

The following information is available concerning the current period:

	Units	£
Transferred from Process 1	4,000	20,000
Labour costs incurred		7,820
Overhead costs absorbed		11,760
Transferred to finished stock		3,600

Losses do not normally occur in Process 2, but, during the current period, a machine fault resulted in 200 units being scrapped at a stage when only 50% of the conversion costs had been incurred.

Closing work in progress consisted of 500 units, which were considered to be 90% complete for labour and 80% complete for overheads.

Required

Produce detailed workings to calculate each of the following for the current period:

(i) The total cost of the units transferred to finished stock

(ii) The total cost of the abnormal loss

(iii) The total valuation of the closing work in progress.

LCCI Cost Accounting

B5. K Limited makes two products: L and M, has three production departments: N, P and Q and two service departments: R and S. The standard prime cost per unit of the two products are as follows:

		Product L			Product M		
		hours	£	£	hours	£	£
Direct material				89			77
Direct labour:							
Department	N	8	16		6	12	
	P	12	24		10	20	
	Q	15	30		14	28	
				70			60
Total				£159			£137

The follow.ing information was taken from the budget for the month of March:

Production:	Product:	L	300 units
		M	500 units
Overhead:			£
Production department		N	13,620
		P	26,720
		Q	24,660
Service department:		R	8,400
		S	14,400
Total			£87,800

The service departments are apportioned to the production departments on the following bases:

		Service department	
		R	S
		%	%
Production department:	N	20	25
	P	40	30
	Q	40	45

Using the information given above you are required to calculate:

(a) the budgeted overhead absorption rate on a direct labour hour basis for each of the three production departments;

(b) the sales price per unit of each of the products assuming a profit of 25% on total production cost is needed.

RSA Cost Accounting

B6. Stukk Chemicals Ltd manufactures a special adhesive in Process A, employing direct workers paid at £4.25 per hour and absorbing overhead at the rate of £10 per direct labour hour. At the end of this process, it is normal to produce a by-product at the rate of 6% of total input. This by-product is then processed and packed in Process B at a cost of £1.20 per kg, after which it is sold for £1.70 per kg. Process A account is credited with the net realisable value of the by-product. An additional normal loss at the rate of 4% of total input is expected in Process A in the form of a poisonous waste which requires special treatment, at a cost of £7 per kg, before it can be disposed of with safety. There is no opening or closing work in progress in either process.

Data is available for last month as follows:

Input –	Material X	18,000 kg	– at £3 per kg
	Material Y	12,000 kg	– at £1.50 per kg
Direct labour hours worked			– 2,000
By-product produced			– 1,800 kg
Adhesive produced			– 26,300 kg

Required

(i) Prepare process A's account in detail for last month, clearly indicating the cost per kg of the adhesive. Show details of any supporting calculations.

(ii) Calculate the relevant total abnormal gain or loss which will appear in the Profit and Loss Account for last month.

LCCI Cost Accounting

B7. For profit determination and stock valuation purposes, it is conventional to apportion common costs incurred prior to split off between joint products. A process produces three joint products X, Y and Z, and the following data applies:

			Sales
			£
X	400 kilos @ £12.50	=	5,000
Y	300 kilos @ £20	=	6,000
Z	200 kilos @ £25	=	5,000
			16,000

Total joint costs amount to £11,000

Required

(a) prepare statements to show gross profit per production on:
   (i) A physical units basis
   (ii) A sales value basis.

(b) Calculate gross profit percentages for each method commenting briefly upon their meaning

(c) Distinguish between joint products and by-products

(d) State how you would deal with by-products in a costing system.

LCCI Management Accounting

B8. VG Double Glazing Ltd employs sales representatives who own their own cars and who use them on company business in return for reimbursement of expenses at an agreed rate per mile travelled on company business. Records show that, after allowing for holidays, sickness and time spent at Head Office, each car is used for business on an average of 150 days in the year covering an average of 100 miles per day.

The following details have been agreed:

(a) Petrol costs £1.68 per gallon and average engine performance is 28 miles to the gallon.

(b) Oil is changed every 3,000 miles, costing £8.00 per change.

(c) Each car is serviced every 10,000 miles, costing £70.00 per service.

(d) Tyres are changed every 30,000 miles, costing £100 per set at each renewal.

(e) Each representative is to be allowed three-quarters of the following annual costs in the mileage rate calculation:

	£
Depreciation	1,400
Insurance	200
Licence	100
Garage costs	240

Required

Calculate an appropriate rate per mile for use in the above situation, presented in detail to show clearly the allowance per mile for each of the five considerations, (a) to (e) as above.

LCCI Cost Accounting

B9. LMN Limited has the following budgeted overhead costs and related data for the year to 31 March 19x9.

	Machining	Assembly	Finishing
Overhead costs	£175,500	£56,450	£98,750
Number of employees	16	7	12
Labour hours	32,540	14,000	26,000
Machine hours	30,000	2,400	Nil
Wages costs	£142,400	£43,600	£91,500
Material cost	£94,500	£32,560	£43,575

During September 19x8 Job 123 was completed. Direct costs and related data were as follows:

	Machining	Assembly	Finishing
Material cost	£1,369	£124	93
Labour cost	£608	£90	£251
Labour hours	52	30	70
Machine hours	147	25	Nil

Required

(a) Calculate an appropriate overhead absorption rate for *each* of the *three* departments (to the nearest £0.01) giving reasons for your choice of method.

(b) Use these rates to calculate

(i) the total cost of Job 123, and

(ii) the selling price if a gross profit of 40% on selling price is applied.

(c) Explain the difference between the valuation of stock under an absorption costing system and under a marginal costing system.

CIMA Accounting

B10. The manufacture of one of the products of A Ltd requires three separate processes. In the last of the three process, costs, production and stock for the month just ended were:

1. Transfers from Process 2: 180,000 units at a cost of £394,200.

2. Process 3 costs: materials £110,520, conversion costs £76,506.

3. Work in process at the beginning of the month: 20,000 units at a cost of £55,160, (based on FIFO pricing method). Units were 70% complete for materials, and 40% complete for conversion costs.

4. Work in process at the end of the month: 18,000 units which were 90% complete for materials, and 70% complete for conversion costs.

5. Product is inspected when it is complete. Normally no losses are expected but during the month 60 units were rejected and sold for £1.50 per unit.

Required

(a) Prepare the Process 3 account for the month just ended.

(b) Explain how, and why, your calculations would be affected if the 60 units lost were treated as normal losses.

(c) Explain how your calculations would be affected by the use of weighted average pricing instead of FIFO.

ACCA Cost and Management Accounting 1

Planning and control

Multiple choice questions *(tick appropriate box)* ☑

1. If the total expenditure on Cost type X was expressed as a cost per unit of the product, X would be classified as variable if:
   (a) The cost per unit changed with the level of activity A ☐
   (b) The cost per unit was affected by inflation B ☐
   (c) The cost per unit remained constant with changes in the level of activity C ☐
   (d) The total expenditure on X remained the same. D ☐

2. Using the high/low method what is the value of the variable cost based on the following data?

Cost	Units
£12,650	6,000
9,200	4,520
8,800	3,500
11,750	5,200

   (a) £1 per unit A ☐
   (b) £2.11 per unit B ☐
   (c) £2.51 per unit C ☐
   (d) £1.54 per unit. D ☐

3. From the data in (2) what is the fixed element of the cost?
   (a) £3,410 A ☐
   (b) £8,800 B ☐
   (c) £6,650 C ☐
   (d) It cannot be calculated. D ☐

4. Information feedback is
   (a) Used to calculate the profit for the period A ☐
   (b) Used to monitor the efficiency of labour B ☐
   (c) Part of the control system C ☐
   (d) To enable managers to keep abreast of business developments. D ☐

5. A fixed budget is:
   (a) One containing only fixed cost items A ☐
   (b) Designed for one activity level B ☐
   (c) One where costs are analysed into fixed and variable elements C ☐
   (d) One where the expenditure levels are fixed by senior management. D ☐

6. A flexible budget is:
   (a) The only suitable budget for control purposes A ☐
   (b) A budget analysed to fixed and variable elements B ☐
   (c) Designed to show the appropriate expenditure for the actual production level C ☐
   (d) All of the above. D ☐

7. The total budgeted expenditure for 17,000 units was £58,500 and for 17,500 units £59,875. This means that fixed costs were estimated to be:
   (a) £11,750 A ☐
   (b) £1,375 B ☐
   (c) £58,500 C ☐
   (d) £23,500. D ☐

8. A firm exactly met its budgeted output of 42,500 litres but the total expenditure of £196,200 was £12,000 over budget. Analysis showed that fixed costs of £35,500 were exactly as budgeted. What was the budgeted variable cost per litre?
   (a) £0.83 A ☐
   (b) £3.50 B ☐
   (c) £4.62 C ☐
   (d) £1.12. D ☐

9. A cash budget
   (a) Shows the expected cash shortages or surpluses in the periods ahead A ☐
   (b) Is the authorisation for a manager to spend cash B ☐
   (c) Always exactly equals the firm's cash balance C ☐
   (d) Cannot be prepared without an authorisation from a bank. D ☐

10. Depreciation is not included in cash budgets because:
   (a) It is not paid until the end of an asset's life A ☐
   (b) It cannot be known accurately until the end of an asset's life B ☐
   (c) It is not a cash flow C ☐
   (d) The same amount is charged each year so it cancels out. D ☐

11. Management by exception means that
   (a) Management are able to concentrate on items not proceeding according to plan A ☐
   (b) More attention can be given to things which happen infrequently B ☐
   (c) Only exceptionally bad performances are reported C ☐
   (d) Only exceptionally good performances are reported. D ☐

12. Budgeting and Standard Costing
   (a) Are based on similar principles A ☐
   (b) Together make up 'Responsibility Accounting' B ☐
   (c) Compare actual expenditure to target expenditure C ☐
   (d) Are all of the above. D ☐

13. A standard hour:
    (a) Is one where operatives work for 60 minutes A ☐
    (b) Is the number of hours worked above normal time B ☐
    (c) Is a measure of work content C ☐
    (d) Is any hour in which standard labour rates are paid. D ☐

14. A standard cost is
    (a) The cost that will produce maximum profit A ☐
    (b) A target cost for the period ahead B ☐
    (c) The average cost of production in the last period C ☐
    (d) Always greater than actual cost. D ☐

15. In a period 5,220 hours were worked at a total cost of £22,185. The Labour Rate Variance was £1,566 (ADV) and the Labour Efficiency Variance was £711 (FAV). How many standard hours were produced?
    (a) 5,200 A ☐
    (b) 5,400 B ☐
    (c) 5,588 C ☐
    (d) 5,421 D ☐

The following data are to be used for the next two questions.

The standard Material content of Part No. Y252 is 27 kgs at £5.75 per kg. In a period 486 units of Part No. Y252 were produced and actual material usage was 13,132 kgs at a cost of £74,852.

16. What was the Material Price Variance?
    (a) £155 (FAV) A ☐
    (b) £657 (ADV) B ☐
    (c) £575 (FAV) C ☐
    (d) £657 (FAV). D ☐

17. What was the Material Usage Variance?
    (a) £295 (ADV) A ☐
    (b) £57.5 (ADV) B ☐
    (c) £57.5 (FAV) C ☐
    (d) £295 (FAV). D ☐

The following information is to be used for the next two questions.

The standard labour content of Part No. X55 is 18 hours at £6.50 per hour. In a period 942 units were made and £110,524 wages were paid for 16,746 hours work.

18. What was the Labour Rate Variance?
    (a) £1,675 (ADV) A ☐
    (b) £1,675 (FAV) B ☐
    (c) £117 (ADV) C ☐
    (d) £117 (FAV). D ☐

19. What was the Labour Efficiency Variance?
   (a) £1,365 (ADV) A ☐
   (b) £1,675 (ADV) B ☐
   (c) £1,657 (FAV) C ☐
   (d) £1,365 (FAV). D ☐

The data below are to be used for the next four questions.

Budget for Period, Dept. XXX	
Fixed overheads	£27,495
Variable overheads	£31,850
Labour hours	6,500
Standard hours of production	6,500
Actual for period	
Fixed overheads	£29,800
Variable overheads	£31,850
Labour hours	6,450
Standard hours produced	6,550

20. What is the overhead expenditure variance?
   (a) £2,550 (FAV) A ☐
   (b) £2,305 (ADV) B ☐
   (c) £2,550 (ADV) C ☐
   (d) £2,305 (FAV). D ☐

21. What is the overhead volume variance?
   (a) £456 (ADV) A ☐
   (b) £212 (ADV) B ☐
   (c) £212 (FAV) C ☐
   (d) £456 (FAV). D ☐

22. What is the overhead efficiency variance?
   (a) £913 (FAV) A ☐
   (b) £456 (FAV) B ☐
   (c) £913 (ADV) C ☐
   (d) £456 (ADV). D ☐

23. What is the Total Overhead Variance?
   (a) £2,550 (ADV) A ☐
   (b) £2,550 (FAV) B ☐
   (c) £2,305 (ADV) C ☐
   (d) £1,849 (ADV). D ☐

The following information is to be used for the next two questions.

Output	12,000 units	15,000 units
	£	£
Production cost	46,500	52,500
Administration cost	38,000	38,000

24. If 13,500 units were sold at £7.50 each what is the contribution for the firm?
   (a) £101,250 A ☐
   (b) £74,250 B ☐
   (c) £27,000 C ☐
   (d) £84,500. D ☐

25. What are the fixed costs of the firm?
   (a) £60,500 A ☐
   (b) £38,000 B ☐
   (c) £52,500 C ☐
   (d) £46,500. D ☐

Case 2/1 *Dollbee Electronics Plc*

A case including the behavioural aspects of budgeting and the problems caused by preparing budget statements on incorrect principles.

Dollbee Electronics are manufacturers of high quality audio amplifiers and loudspeakers. The company has recently been taken over by Electronics International Inc. (EII) a multinational company operating on all continents. Hyram K. Cross of EII has been sent to review the budgeting and reporting systems used by Dollbee and finds that monthly budgets are prepared for each department. He asks to see the last budget statement for a typical department and is shown the statement for the Loudspeaker Department; whose manager is Jack Bell.

The budget statement for the last period was:

Budget Statement for period .....
Department: Loudspeaker Department

Actual Results: 12,500 units produced with 35,350 labour hours

	Actual results	**Budgeted results**	**Budget variances**
	£'000s	£'000s	£'000s
Direct materials	252	240	– 12
Direct labour	123	120	– 3
Variable prod. overhead	79	72	– 7
Fixed prod. overhead	59	56	– 3
Variable admin. overhead	41	40	– 1
Fixed admin. overhead	50	48	– 2
Total costs	604	576	– 28
Sales value of production	775	744	+ 31
Profit	171	168	+ 3

Hyram found that the budget was based on 12,000 units with a standard labour content of 2.85 hours and went to Jack Bell to find out his reactions to the budget and what use he makes of the budgeting system.

To Hyram's surprise, Jack Bell was not enthusiastic about the system and thought it of little value to a departmental manager. Jack said, 'It was introduced about a year ago by consultants who only spent about 10 minutes with me, then the budgeting system was introduced without any explanation. Frankly I think they put in a ready made system developed elsewhere. It doesn't seem to help me to run my department. For example, last month's statement showed a positive variance on profit yet I know costs have risen, though nothing like as much as the statement shows, so I would have expected to be down on budgeted profit yet according to this I am £3,000 up! It just doesn't make sense so I tend to ignore it altogether'.

After leaving Jack Bell, Hyram visited several other departments and had similar reactions from the departmental managers. Hyram decided, as a matter of urgency, to try to make the budgeting system more useful and more acceptable to the departmental managers.

Tasks

(a) Criticise the approach of the consultants who installed.

(b) Find out what behavioural objectives should, ideally be fulfilled by budgetary control systems. Do you think that the system outlined meets these objectives?

(c) Criticise the way the budget statement has been prepared.

(d) Redraft the statement in a more informative manner and give an explanation of your reasoning.

Case 2/2 *Purpose Packing Ltd*

Purpose Packing Ltd are manufacturers of special purpose racks and containers, mainly for the transport of machined components. On one of their production lines they make a gear wheel carrier out of wood and plastic. The quantities made are large and the Factory Director, John Forbes, thinks it would be worthwhile considering the possibility of installing a standard costing system. Before making a final decision it has been decided that the Accounting Department should prepare some information about current operations.

The following information is available:

Gear Wheel carrier expected unit costs

Direct materials	2 kgs wood @ £3.2 kg
	$\frac{1}{2}$ kg plastic @ £5.8 kg
Direct labour	
Preparation	1.4 hours @ £4.8 per hour
Assembly	$\frac{1}{2}$ hour @ £3.25 per hour

Budgeted total overheads for the period

	£	Labour hours
Preparation Dept.	135,000	11,000
Assembly Dept.	80,000	6,000

(Fixed overheads contained in the above are Preparation £45,000 and Assembly £35,000)

During the last period actual results were:

Output in units	8,150	
Wood usage	16,050 kgs costing	£52,965
Plastic usage	4,890 kgs costing	£27,300
Labour:		
Preparation	11,820 hours costing	£59,100
Assembly	4,300 hours costing	£15,487
Actual overheads:		
Preparation		£140,100
Assembly		£76,500

Tasks

(a) Prepare a standard cost card for a gear wheel carrier showing Prime Cost and Total Production Cost.

(b) Calculate the following variances for the period

- Direct materials variance sub–divided into Price and Usage for each material.
- Direct labour variance sub–divided into Rate and Efficiency for each type of labour.
- Total overhead variance for each department sub–divided into Expenditure, Volume and Efficiency.

(c) Comment on the possible reasons for any variances found.

(d) Calculate the under/over absorption of overheads for each department for the period.

(e) Comment on whether you think the manufacture of the gear wheel carriers is a suitable application of standard costing.

Case 2/3 *Loamshire District Council*

The Loamshire District Council operates a number of sheltered housing units, three of which have kitchens serving residents. As part of a compulsory competitive tendering exercise a cost investigation of the kitchens has been carried out, the results of which are summarised below.

	Kitchen 1	Kitchen 2	Kitchen 3
Capital costs			
Buildings	£150,000	£225,000	£120,000
Equipment	£60,000	£85,000	£50,000
Employees			
Cooks	1	2	1
Assistants	6	9	4
No. of meals produced	46,000	72,000	32,000
Food costs	£96,000	£133,000	£90,000
Direct overheads	£25,000	£38,000	£23,000

Notes

(1) Cooks are paid £15,000, assistants £10,000 per year.

(2) A supervisor/dietician is in overall charge of all three kitchens and is paid £20,000 per year.

(3) Central administrative charges of 1p per meal are to be charged to the kitchens.

(4) Buildings are depreciated on a straight line basis over 30 years and equipment over 10 years.

Tasks

(a) Prepare unit cost statements in as much detail as possible for each of the kitchens making what assumptions you think necessary.

(b) Comment on the position shown by your statements.

(c) The Council wish to exercise greater control over the costs of catering. Comment on how this might be done. Do you think Standard Costing might be of value?

(d) The Independent Catering Company have offered to take over all catering using the Council's buildings and equipment. At what price per meal do you think it would be worthwhile considering this proposal? What other factors should be considered?

Assignments

2/1 Identify six fixed costs and six variable costs in a real firm or organisation. Find out in what circumstances, if any, the fixed costs change.

2/2 Contrast the budget relationships in a public sector organisation (e.g. a college, a local authority, a hospital) with those in a typical private sector firm such as a manufacturer, a departmental store or a bank.

2/3 Investigate a firm that uses standard costing and find out:

(a) What variances are calculated.

(b) How significant variances are identified.

(c) What actions are taken when a significant variance occurs.

2/4 Many schools now operate under a freer financial system known as LMS (Local Management of Schools). Investigate what accounting records are maintained in a typical locally managed school and how the school carries out budgeting.

Questions with answers

A1. Company Z is preparing budgets for the coming year. 120,000 labour hours will be 100% level of expected productive time, but a flexible budget at 90%, 110% and 120% is required so that cost allowances can be set for these possible levels.

Budgeted cost details

1.	Fixed Cost per annum	
		£
	Depreciation	22,000
	Staff salaries	43,000
	Insurances	9,000
	Rent & Rates	12,000
2.	Variable Costs	
	Power	30p per direct labour hour
	Consumables	5p direct labour hour
	Direct labour	£3.50 per direct labour hour

3. Semi-Variable Costs

Analysis of past records, adjusted to eliminate the effect on inflation shows the following:

	Direct labour hours	Total Semi-variable cost
Last year Year 6	110,000	£330,000
Year 5	100,000	£305,000
Year 4	90,000	£280,000
Year 3	87,000	£272,500
Year 2	105,000	£317,500
Year 1	80,000	£255,000

Required

A cost budget at 100% and flexed to show cost allowances at 90%, 110% and 120% of expected level.

AAT Cost Accounting & Budgeting (part question)

A2. Kanflexus Ltd uses flexible budgets and standard costing in its control systems. The overhead costs of Machine Shop A can be analysed into four distinct behavioural groups. Extracts from the approved monthly flexible budget are as follows:

	Activity level								
in '000 machine hours	50	55	60	65	70	75	80	85	90
	Overhead costs								
in £									
Group 1	50,000	(a)	50,000	(b)	(c)	(d)	50,000	(e)	50,000
Group 2	(f)	69,250	71,000	(g)	74,500	(h)	(i)	(j)	81,500
Group 3	(k)	46,750	51,000	(l)	(m)	(n)	68,000	(o)	(p)
Group 4	24,000	(q)	28,000	28,000	32,000	32,000	(r)	36,000	40,000

The standard overhead absorption rate is based on a normal activity level of 85,000 hours per month and the flexed budget allowance used in variance analysis is based on the actual hours worked during the month.

During last month, 68,600 actual machine hours were worked in Shop A producing output equivalent to 72,200 standard hours. The total overhead incurred by Shop A for the month was £216,450.

Required

(i) In your answer book, calculate the missing figures, as indicated by a) to r) in the tabular flexible budget.

(ii) Give a concise description of the cost behavioural characteristic of each group.

(iii) Calculate the following variances for last month:
- (a) Overhead total variance
- (b) Overhead expenditure variance
- (c) Overhead volume variance
- (d) Overhead efficiency variance.

LCCI Cost Accounting

A3. E Ltd has two production departments: F and G and makes two products: H and J. The standard direct labour cost/unit of each product is based on the following data:

Dept.	Grade of labour	Standard rate per hour	Standard hours Product H	Product J
		£		
F	1	2.50	2	12
	2	3.00	4	6
G	1	2.50	8	–
	3	2.30	10	–

Actual data for the four weeks ended 26th March were as follows:

Production:	Product H	200 units
	J	300 units

	Department F		Department G	
Grade of labour	Actual hours worked	Actual wages £	Actual hours worked	Actual wages £
1	4,028	10,200	1,610	3,960
2	2,570	7,750	–	–
3	–	–	1,980	4,540

Using the information given above you are required to:

(a) Calculate the standard direct labour cost of:

(i) One unit of each product;

(ii) The total products made;

(b) Ascertain for each department the direct labour total variance;

(c) Analyse the variances in (b) above into:

(i) Direct labour rate variance;

(ii) Direct labour efficiency variance.

RSA Cost Accounting

A4. Taman Bhd produces three grades of potting compost, trade name 'Compo', by mixing three material ingredients, G, R and O, in different proportions. Budgeted cost prices of these materials are G – $0.40 per kg, R – $0.20 per kg, and O – $0.80 per kg.

There is a normal loss of 4% of total input to the mixing and filling process, at the end of which all grades of Compo emerge in sealed plastic sacks, each containing 48 kg of compost. Direct workers are paid $12 per hour and are expected to mix and fill thirty sacks per hour. An absorption rate of 400% on direct wages cost is necessary, to recover the budgeted production overheads.

Stocks at 1 May 19x9 are expected to be:

Materials (in kg)			Finished Compo (in sacks)		
G	R	O	No.1	No.2	No.3
155,000	182,500	142,500	5,000	5,500	7,500

The company plans to have decreased all stocks of raw materials by 20% at 30 April 19x0 and to have increased all stocks of Compo by 60% at the same date.

Other details are as follows:

	Compo No. 1	Compo No. 2	Compo No. 3
Standard mixes (as % of total input)			
G	50%	30%	10%
R	40%	50%	60%
O	10%	20%	30%
Sales budget (in sacks) for the year ended 30 April 19x0	50,000	40,000	60,000

Required

Prepare the following budgets for the year ending 30 April 19x0:

(i) Production

(ii) Material purchases

(iii) Production cost

LCCI Cost Accounting

A5. RS Ltd makes and sells a single product, J, with the following standard specification for materials:

	Quantity	**Price per kilogram**
	Kilograms	£
Direct material R	10	30
Direct material S	6	45

It takes 30 direct labour hours to produce one unit of J with a standard direct labour cost of £5.50 per hour.

The annual sales/production budget is 1,200 units evenly spread throughout the year.

The budgeted production overhead, all fixed, is £252,000 and expenditure is expected to occur evenly over the year, which the company divides into twelve calendar months. Absorption is based on units produced.

For the month of October the following actual information is provided. The budgeted sales quantity for the month was sold at the standard selling price.

	£	£
Sales		120,000
Cost of sales:		
Direct material used	58,136	
Direct wages	17,325	
Fixed production overhead	22,000	
		97,461
Gross profit		22,539
Administration costs	6,000	
Selling and distribution costs	11,000	
		17,000
Net profit		£5,539

Costs of opening stocks, for each material, were at the same price per kilogram as the purchases made during the month, but there had been changes in the materials stock levels, viz:

	1 October	**30 October**
	Kgs	Kgs
Material R	300	375
Material S	460	225

Material R purchases were 1,100 kgs for £35,000.
Material S purchases were 345 kgs for £15,180.

The number of direct labour hours worked was 3,300 and the total wages incurred £17,325.

Work-in-progress stocks and finished goods stocks may be assumed to be the same at the beginning and end of October.

Required

(a) Present a standard product cost for one unit of Product J showing the standard selling price and standard gross profit per unit;

(b) Calculate appropriate variances for the materials, labour and fixed production overhead, noting that it is company policy to calculate material price variances *at time of issue to production;*

(c) Present a statement for management reconciling the budgeted gross profit with the actual gross profit;

(d) Suggest a possible cause for each of the labour variances you show under (b) above, stating whether you believe each variance was controllable or uncontrollable and, if controllable, the job title of the responsible official. Please state the name and amount of each variance about which you write and explain the variance, quantifying it, where possible, in non-financial terms which might be better understood by line management.

CIMA Cost Accounting

A6. A company is preparing budgets for the year ahead for two of its raw materials that are used in various products which it manufactures. Current year material usage standards are as follows:

Kilos per thousand units of product

	Product 1	**Product** 2	**Product** 3	**Product** 4	**Product** 5
Material A	25	70	15	–	55
Material B	30	5	–	20	–

It has been decided to change standards on Material B for the following year to reflect the favourable usage variances that are occurring for that material on all products. Usage variances on Material B are 10% of standard costs.

Budgeted sales quantities for the following year are:

	Product 1	**Product** 2	**Product** 3	**Product** 4	**Product** 5
(thousand units)	600	350	1850	1200	900

Production quantities are to be budgeted in line with sales, apart from Product 5 where an increase in stock of 30% is required by the end of the budget year. Stocks of the five products at the beginning of the budget year are expected to be:

	Product 1	**Product** 2	**Product** 3	**Product** 4	**Product** 5
(thousand units)	140	80	260	180	100

Stocks of Materials A and B at the end of the budget year are to be 10% of the year's budgeted usage. Stocks at the end of the current year are expected to be:

	kilos
Material A	10,030
Material B	4,260

Required

(a) Describe the benefits that can be derived from a budgeting system.

(b) Prepare material usage and purchases budgets (kilos only) for each of Materials A and B for the year ahead.

(c) Prepare summary journal entries for the Material A stock account for the current period.

The following additional information is provided for the current period:

Material A purchases:

116,250 kilos at a cost of £280,160
(standard purchase price = £2.40 per kilo)

Production:

	Product 1	**Product 2**	**Product 3**	**Product 4**	**Product 5**
(thousand units)	580	330	1,900	1,200	800

Material A usage has been at standard.

ACCA Cost and Management Accounting

A7. AR Limited is a company which provides a shuttle airline service from London to Manchester. In addition to the flight services, it has a souvenir shop and cafeteria at each of its airstrips. The company operates a standard cost accounting system for its flight services and its standard cost card for each flight as follows:

	£
Direct wages of pilot and crew	60.00
Indirect labour costs	12.00
Fuel cost	440.00
In-flight catering	50.00
Indirect material cost	18.00
	580.00
Ground services costs absorbed	120.00
Standard cost per flight	700.00

The ground services costs are absorbed into the standard flight costs using an overhead absorption rate of 200% of direct wages. This rate comprises 60% of direct wages for variable ground services costs and 140% for fixed ground services costs. The 140% is calculated assuming an annual number of 2,000 flights.

During the year ended 31 March 19x0, the company made 1,900 flights and flight ticket receipts amounted to £2,400,000 of which £105,000 related to advance ticket sales. The amount of advance ticket sales received in the year to 31 March 19x9 was £97,000.

An extract from the company's trial balance at 31 March 19x0 showed:

		Dr £	**Cr** £
Cafeteria sales			480,000
Souvenir sales			72,000
Opening stock at 1 April 19x9:	cafeteria	16,000	
	souvenirs	3,000	
Purchases	cafeteria	233,000	
	souvenirs	44,000	
Closing stocks at 31 March 19x0 were valued at:			
Cafeteria		£15,000	
Souvenirs		£5,000	

At the end of each accounting period the management accountant of the company prepares a report which shows the variances for the current period and the year to date in respect of flight services. An extract from this report for the year to 31 March 19x0 shows the following:

		Total variance	
		£	
Direct wages of pilot and crew		12,000	Adverse
Indirect labour costs		3,000	Favourable
Fuel cost		63,000	Adverse
In-flight catering		15,000	Favourable
Indirect material cost		2,000	Adverse
Ground services costs	fixed element	14,000	Adverse
	variable element	15,000	Adverse

All of these costs are wholly variable except for the ground services costs which are semi-variable costs.

You are required

(a) to prepare a profit statement of AR Limited in as much detail as possible for the year ended 31 March 19x0, showing the actual results of the company separately for flight services, cafeteria services, souvenir services, and in total, using a columnar marginal costing format;

(b) to state what is meant by the term 'standard cost' and to discuss the use of standard costing techniques in a non-manufacturing environment such as that of AR Limited. What benefits arise from the use of such as system?

CIMA Accounting

Questions without answers

B1. PQ Limited has two production departments – machinery and assembly. Two of its main products are the Major and the Minor, the standard data for which are as follows:

		Per unit	
		Major	**Minor**
Direct materials:	Material @ £15 per kg	2.2 kgs	1.4 kgs
Direct labour:	Machining dept @ £6 per hour	4.8 hrs	2.9 hrs
	Assembly dept @ £5 per hour	3.6 hrs	3.1 hrs
Machining time		3.5 hrs	0.9 hrs

The overhead rates for the period are as follows:

Machining dept	**Assembly dept**
£16.00 per machine hour	£9.50 per labour hour

Requirement

(a) Calculate the standard production cost for each product showing clearly, as a sub total, the standard prime cost.

(b) During the period, actual results for labour were as follows:

		Major	**Minor**
Production		650 units	842 units
Direct labour:	Machining dept	2,990 hrs	2,480 hrs
		costing £18,239	costing £15,132
	Assembly dept	2,310 hrs	2,595 hrs
		costing £11,700	costing £12,975

Calculate the direct labour total variance and the rate and efficiency variances for each product and each department

(c) Explain briefly what information the above variances provide for management.

CIMA Cost Accounting and Quantitative Methods

B2. A system of budgetary control is being introduced in a manufacturing company and a budget committee has been set up under the chairmanship of the chief executive. At the first meeting, it was decided to appoint a budget officer and also to develop a budget manual.

Required

(i) List the main duties of a budget officer.

(ii) Briefly explain the general purpose of using a budget manual and list examples of the type of information it would contain.

LCCI Cost Accounting

B3. Dajini Plastics Ltd produce a wide range of plastic products. The following are the standards that apply to their largest industrial bucket:

Direct materials

1 handle $0.25
Plastic 1.25 lbs at $0.60 per lb

Direct labour

0.2 hours at $5.00 per hour

Overhead

Variable	$0.50 per bucket
Fixed	$1.00 per bucket

The budgeted monthly volume of buckets is 8,000.

The actual results for the month of May were:

Materials used

10,050 handles at $0.26 each
12,000 lbs plastic at $0.59 per lb

Labour

2,400 hours at $5.10 per hour

Overhead incurred

Variable overhead	$4,400
Fixed overhead	$7,500

10,000 buckets were produced in the month.

Required

(i) State the standard cost of the bucket

(ii) Calculate 7 variances for the month of May

(iii) Give two illustrations of how the labour efficiency variance may have arisen.

LCCI Management Accounting

B4. The increasing use of advanced manufacturing technology is causing the amount charged for depreciation of plant and machinery to be a significantly higher proportion of total manufacturing costs. Depreciation charges normally relate to the original cost of the asset and most systems include the use of a detailed plant register.

Required

(i) State why depreciation is included as part of manufacturing costs and what exactly is achieved by the normal provision of depreciation for an item of plant and machinery.

(ii) State how you would normally classify depreciation in terms of cost behaviour.

(iii) List ten items of information that you would expect to find on the plant register record for each asset.

LCCI Cost Accounting

B5. The following draft budgeted Profit and Loss Account has been prepared for Company X for the coming year.

	£'000s	£'000s
Sales		8,000
Direct Materials	2,400	
Direct Labour	2,000	
Variable Overhead	800	
Fixed Overhead	1,800	7,000
Profit		1,000

There has been a proposal from the sales department to reduce unit selling prices by 10% as this is expected to increase the volume sold by 25%. The above budgeted figures *exclude* possible cost increases that are now thought likely.

These are:

(i) Material prices may increase by 10%.

(ii) Labour rates may increase by 6%.

(iii) Fixed overheads may increase by £200,000 because a recent change in the law requiring new safety equipment.

Required

(a) Re-draft the budget after considering this proposal and the possible cost increases outlined above.

(b) Discuss the factors the firm should consider before accepting this proposal to reduce selling prices in order to increase sales volume.

(c) Calculate the contribution to sales ratio:

(i) In the original draft budget

(ii) If the sales department's plans are implemented and the possible cost increases take place.

(d) Briefly explain and give examples of the types of expenditure that might be included under the headings of:

(i) Variable overhead

(ii) Fixed overhead

(iii) Semi-variable overhead.

Show by simple charts the behaviour of costs under each heading with cost on the vertical axis and volume on the horizontal axis.

AAT Cost Accounting & Budgeting

B6. LNE Electronics Bhd makes and sells a range of electric kettles. These are marketed as models L, N and E, the current monthly budget being 1,000, 1,750 and 2,000 units respectively. All models require manufacturing operations in three production departments as indicated in the following extracts from standard specifications:

Dept.	Standard rate per direct labour hour	Standard times in minutes per unit		
		Model L	**Model N**	**Model E**
1	$14.00	72	48	36
2	$12.00	60	24	24
3	$15.20	30	15	18

There is no opening or closing work in progress in any production department. The cost department has recorded the following actual data for last month:

	Model L	Model N	Model E
Finished output (units)	900	1,800	2,100
	Dept. 1	**Dept. 2**	**Dept. 3**
Direct wages incurred	$52,800	$32,160	$25,300
Efficiency ratio	105%	100%	90%

Required

(i) Explain the term 'standard hour', clearly indicating how and for what purpose it is used.

(ii) From the data given, calculate, for each department:

(a) The direct labour rate variance

(b) The direct labour efficiency variance.

LCCI Cost Accounting

B7. (a) Define the following terms:

(i) Functional budget;

(ii) Master budget.

(b) Give three examples of functional budgets.

(c) Describe briefly the major sections of a master budget.

(d) Give two examples of a 'principal budget factor' and state how each of your examples should be taken into consideration when preparing the budgets given in (a) above.

RSA Cost Accounting Stage II

B8. Two products are manufactured by a company in one of its factories. The products comprise different mixes of two basic raw materials. One grade of direct labour is employed in the mixing process and another grade in final packaging.

Standard direct material and direct labour costs for the two products in the current period are:

	Product Y (£ per hundred units)	Product Z (£ per hundred units)
Direct materials:		
Raw material A	156.00	78.00
Raw material B	54.00	72.00
Direct labour:		
Mixing	11.25	11.25
Packaging	20.00	20.00

The current standard purchase prices of the raw materials and standard direct labour rates are:

Raw material A	£5.20 per kilo
Raw material B	£1.80 per kilo
Mixing labour	£4.50 per hour
Packaging labour	£4.00 per hour

A favourable usage variance, currently being achieved on raw material A is to be incorporated into standard for the following period. Standard material loss on raw material A of 10% input, rather than the existing standard loss of 12%, is to be included. Increases in raw material purchase prices and labour rates, of 5% and 8% respectively, are to be incorporated in the new standards for the following period.

The sales budget for the following period for Products Y and Z is as follows:

Product Y	1,700,000 units
Product Z	950,000 units

Stocks of raw materials and finished goods are budgeted as follows for the period ahead:

	Opening stocks	Closing stocks
Raw material A (kilos)	40,000	25,000
Raw material B (kilos)	95,000	90,000
Product Y (units)	190,000	200,000
Product Z (units)	150,000	125,000

Required

(a) Calculate, and show in as much detail as possible, the standard direct material and direct labour costs (per hundred units) for the following period.

(b) Establish the budgets for the following period for:

(i) production of each product *(units)*

(ii) purchases of material B *(kilos).*

(iii) mixing labour *(hours).*

(c) Describe the benefits that may be expected to result from the operation of a budgeting system.

ACCA Cost and Management Accounting

B9. (a) Planning is expressed by the budgets which are prepared, but, prior to this, it is necessary to go through a forecasting exercise.

You are required to discuss briefly *five* problems which are likely to arise when forecasting for a business.

(b) C Limited employs 300 people and has sales of £9 million. It has five producing departments, two service departments and manufactures one product.

No effective planning or financial control system has been established but after one of the directors had attended a CIMA course on 'Finance for Non-Financial Managers' he decided to introduce a budget system and performance reports related to responsibilities. Other directors and management had some reservations about the introduction of this system but they were persuaded to allow its introduction.

After the end of April, which was the first month of the current financial year, departmental performance reports were issued to all departmental supervisors. These took the form of that illustrated below for Production Department 'D' which was produced by the office manager – the senior person on the administrative staff. (A separate report was issued relating to direct material and direct labour.)

Monthly report: Department 'D' – April

	Actual	Planning budget	Variance
Units produced	1,100	1,000	100
	£	£	£
Salaries and wages	10,000	10,500	500
Indirect labour	8,000	7,000	1,000 *
Maintenance	3,500	2,750	750 *
Overhead allocated	3,000	2,750	250 *
Consumable stores	1,600	1,500	100 *
Depreciation	2,500	2,500	0
Insurance	1,100	1,000	100 *
Sundries	1,000	500	500 *
	30,700	28,500	2,200

* Note – considerable inefficiency; action should be taken to improve cost control in this department.

J, the supervisor for Department D, was not pleased on receiving her report and declared she did not have time to bother with such paperwork and, in any case, the report was inaccurate and unfair. Her comment was typical of others who had received similar reports.

You are required

(i) to state what changes ought to be made to the report and why;

(ii) to assess the situation as it now stands in May and indicate what should be done in respect of the budget system and the departmental performance reports.

CIMA Cost Accounting

B10. W Ltd has operated a restaurant for the last two years. Revenue and operating costs over the two years have been as follows:

	Year 1	Year 2
	£'000	£'000
Revenue	1,348,312	1,514,224
Operating costs		
Food and beverage	698,341	791,919
Wages	349,170	390,477
Other overhead	202,549	216,930

The number of meals served in Year 2 showed an 8% increase on the Year 1 level of 151,156. An increase of 10% over the Year 2 level is budgeted for Year 3.

All staff were given hourly rate increases of 6% last year (i.e. in Year 2). In Year 3 hourly increases of 7% are to be budgeted.

The inflation on 'other overheads' last year was 5%, with an inflationary increase of 6% expected in the year ahead.

Food and beverage costs are budgeted to average £5.14 per meal in Year 3. This is expected to represent 53% of sales value.

Required

(a) From the information given above, and using the high low method of cost estimation, determine the budgeted expenditure on wages and other overheads for Year 3. (Round your final answer for each to the nearest £000.)

(b) Calculate the gross profit (i.e. sales less food and beverage costs) percentage of sales, and the net profit percentage of sales, for each of the three years, and comment on the changes in these percentages over the period. (Round all figures to the nearest £000 or one decimal place of a %.)

ACCA Cost and Management Accounting

Decision making and performance appraisal

Multiple choice questions *(tick appropriate box)*

1. Relevant information for decision making:
   (a) Can include sunk costs — A ☐
   (b) Usually includes historical costs — B ☐
   (c) Is incremental to the decision in hand — C ☐
   (d) Includes all of the above. — D ☐

2. Three outcomes of an event are possible:

Value	Probability
£8,000	0.3
£11,500	0.5
£17,000	0.2

   What is the expected value?
   (a) £36,500 — A ☐
   (b) £11,550 — B ☐
   (c) £11,500 — C ☐
   (d) £17,000. — D ☐

3. The formula for the sales at breakeven point for a single product firm is:

   (a) $\frac{\text{Fixed costs}}{\text{Contribution/unit}} \times \text{sales price per unit}$ — A ☐

   (b) $\frac{\text{Fixed costs} \times \text{Sales value}}{\text{Contribution}}$ — B ☐

   (c) Fixed costs × $\frac{1}{\text{CS ratio}}$ — C ☐

   (d) None of these. — D ☐

4. The margin of safety is:
   (a) The difference between budgeted sales and the breakeven sales — A ☐
   (b) The difference between actual sales and budgeted sales — B ☐
   (c) Sales minus variable costs — C ☐
   (d) The difference between zero sales and breakeven sales. — D ☐

The following data are used for the next two questions.

A firm makes a single product with a marginal cost of £3 and a selling price of £5 and fixed costs of £25,000.

5. What level of sales will produce a profit of £15,000?
(a) £120,000 A ☐
(b) £20,000 B ☐
(c) £100,000 C ☐
(d) £40,000. D ☐

6. How many units will need to be sold to breakeven?
(a) 5,000 A ☐
(b) 25,000 B ☐
(c) 40,000 C ☐
(d) 12,500. D ☐

7. Which of the following would increase the per unit contribution the most?
(a) A 5% decrease in total fixed costs A ☐
(b) A 5% decrease in unit variable costs B ☐
(c) A 5% increase in selling price C ☐
(d) A 5% increase in unit volume. D ☐

The graph below relates to questions 8 to 11.

Figure MC/Sect 3

8. The distance A represents:
(a) Contribution at activity level X A ☐
(b) Profit at activity level X B ☐
(c) The amount of variable costs at activity level X C ☐
(d) The margin of safety. D ☐

9. The distance B represents:
(a) The contribution at activity level Y A ☐
(b) The amount of variable costs at activity level Y B ☐
(c) The level of sales at activity Y C ☐
(d) The profit at activity level Y. D ☐

10. Which of the following are possible causes of the changes in the graph at activity level Z?
    (a) An increase in sales value causing an increase in contribution A ☐
    (b) A decrease in fixed costs causing an increase in variable costs B ☐
    (c) An increase in total fixed costs and a decrease in variable costs per unit C ☐
    (d) An increase in total variable costs and a decrease in fixed costs per unit. D ☐

11. What do the lines C and D represent?
    (a) Fixed costs and variable costs respectively A ☐
    (b) Total costs and variable costs respectively B ☐
    (c) Variable costs and fixed costs respectively C ☐
    (d) Sales revenue and total costs respectively. D ☐

12. Marginal costing gives a different profit to absorption costing when
    (a) All production costs are fixed A ☐
    (b) Opening and closing stocks are different B ☐
    (c) All production costs are variable C ☐
    (d) There are no opening or closing stocks. D ☐

13. A firm manufactures a component with a marginal cost of £6 and a total cost of £11 based on the normal production of 50,000 components. If the firm buys in the component at £8 the change in their results will be
    (a) Costs will reduce by £150,000 A ☐
    (b) Costs will increase by £400,000 B ☐
    (c) Profits will increase by £150,000 C ☐
    (d) Profits will reduce by £100,000. D ☐

14. Which of the following are not relevant for decision making:
    (a) The cost of items bought on credit A ☐
    (b) Costs which will change in the future B ☐
    (c) Costs already spent C ☐
    (d) Costs which do not vary significantly from budget. D ☐

Use the following data for the next two questions.

A firm made 6,000 units with a total cost of £10 each. Half the costs were variable and half fixed. 5,000 units were sold at £15 each. There were no opening stocks.

15. Using marginal costing principles what was the profit for the period?
    (a) £20,000 A ☐
    (b) £25,000 B ☐
    (c) £50,000 C ☐
    (d) £5,000. D ☐

16. Using absorption costing principles what was the profit for the period?
    (a) £20,000 A ☐
    (b) £25,000 B ☐
    (c) £50,000 C ☐
    (d) £5,000. D ☐

17. A project has an IRR of 14% and the firm's cost of capital is 12%. At the cost of capital the NPV will be:
    - (a) Positive A ☐
    - (b) Zero B ☐
    - (c) Negative C ☐
    - (d) Equal to the IRR. D ☐

The following data are used for questions 18 and 19.

A firm with a cost of capital of 12% is considering a project with the following cash flows:

0	1	2	3	4
–5,000	+2,500	+2,000	+2,000	+1,500

18. What is the NPV of the project?
    - (a) 6,204 A ☐
    - (b) 1,204 B ☐
    - (c) 3,896 C ☐
    - (d) 5,000. D ☐

19. What is the project's IRR? (nearest %)
    - (a) 15% A ☐
    - (b) 28% B ☐
    - (c) 12% C ☐
    - (d) 23%. D ☐

20. The NPV of the following investment is Zero:

Cost now	£10,000
Income	£1,490 per year for 10 years

    What is the cost of capital?
    - (a) It cannot be calculated without more information A ☐
    - (b) 10% B ☐
    - (c) 18% C ☐
    - (d) 12%. D ☐

21. A firm is financed half by shares and half by loans. The cost of the shares is 18% and the cost of the loans is 10%. What would be a reasonable rate at which to discount projects?
    - (a) 18% A ☐
    - (b) 14% B ☐
    - (c) 10% C ☐
    - (d) 28%. D ☐

The following data are used for the next two questions.

A division of a group has the following results:

	£
Sales	750,000
Variable costs	275,000
Fixed costs:	
– controllable by division	135,000
– controllable centrally	98,000
Depreciation	89,000
Apportioned central costs	43,000

22. What is the controllable profit of the division?
    - (a) £340,000 A ☐
    - (b) £475,000 B ☐
    - (c) £110,000 C ☐
    - (d) £153,000. D ☐

23. What is the Divisional Profit?
    - (a) £340,000 A ☐
    - (b) £475,000 B ☐
    - (c) £110,000 C ☐
    - (d) £153,000. D ☐

The following data are used for the next two questions

Division	L	M
Trading Profit £'000s	156	2100
Assets in division £'ms	1.1	12.3

The firm's cost of capital is 12%

24. The ROCE's for the two divisions are (nearest %)
    - (a) 17% and 14% A ☐
    - (b) 10% and 10% B ☐
    - (c) 14% and 17% C ☐
    - (d) 4% and 7%. D ☐

25. The residual Profits for the two divisions are (£'000s)
    - (a) 2 and 9 A ☐
    - (b) 24 and 624 B ☐
    - (c) 156 and 2,100 C ☐
    - (d) 624 and 24. D ☐

Case 3/1 Flo-Meters Ltd

An assignment using costs for decision making where limiting factors are present.

Flo-Meters Ltd manufacture a variety of meters and testing devices. They are used in production and packing applications and measure such things as weights, volumes, pressures, moisture and so on. The meters are complex electronic devices which require skilled technicians in manufacturing, especially for calibration. They are considering a new range of grain moisture meters with three capacities; small, medium, large.

The budgeted data are

Meter capacity:	Small	Medium	Large
	£	£	£
Selling price	170	210	295
Direct materials	60	75	95
Labour cost	40	50	75
Maximum demand (units)	2,000	2,000	1,000

The labour is paid £5 per hour and variable overheads are 60% of direct labour costs. Fixed costs are expected to be £55,000 per period.

Each meter requires calibrating using skilled technicians and the number of labour hours required for calibrating each meter are:

Small	2 hours
Medium	3 hours
Large	4 hours

The skilled labour for calibration is in short supply and so, occasionally, are the direct materials.

Flo-meters wish to know if the new range of meters is worthwhile and, if so, what product mix would give the best profit.

Tasks

(a) Prepare a report for the Managing Director advising him whether production is worthwhile and what product mix should be adopted if

(i) The demand constraint applies and either

(ii) The calibration labour is limited to 9,500 hours per period or

(iii) The direct material is in short supply and is limited to £250,000 worth per period.

(b) Calculate the break-even point expressed in sales value, for each mix of sales you have advised and the margins of safety. Explain why the break-even points and margins of safety differ.

(c) Plot the recommended production mixes on separate contribution break-even charts.

Case 3/2: Cordon Bleu – Catering Packs Ltd

This an assignment covering different forms of operating statements, the treatment of fixed and variable costs and the effects of product substitutability.

Cordon Bleu are rapidly expanding specialist food suppliers to restaurants, wine bars, pubs and similar outlets. They buy, prepare and cook the ingredients which are then packaged, deep frozen and supplied to their customers who microwave or boil the meals before serving to their clients who are usually unaware that they are eating pre-packaged meals. Cordon Bleu have five main lines; Chicken Supreme, Boeuf Bourguignon, Duck a l'orange, Chili Con Carne and Chicken Kiev.

Mike Commer has recently been appointed as Managing Director of Cordon Bleu after many years experience as a Director of a major national food manufacturer. He is in the process of reviewing all aspects of operations, especially the financial and sales side which he suspects have been neglected in the formative years of Cordon Bleu, when production and packaging difficulties absorbed most of the attention of John Watson, the founder, who is now Chairman of the company.

Mike asks Bill Hope, who is the Accountant and Office Manager, to prepare a Budgeted Operating Statement for the next period showing the profitability of the main product lines. Up to now there has been no attempt to show separately the profitability of the product lines and the exercise causes Bill a great deal of work. Finally he produces the following statement which, he admits, shows a surprising result and as a consequence he recommends to Mike that he should give serious consideration to cutting out the Boeuf Bourguignon and Duck à l'orange packs to avoid the losses.

The statement produced by Bill Hope was as follows:

Cordon Bleu
Budgeted operating statement
£'000s

Product	Chicken Supreme	Boeuf Bourguignon	Duck à l'orange	Chili con Carne	Chicken Kiev	Total
Sales	1,600	1,400	2,100	950	1,900	7,950
Production costs:						
Materials	290	280	370	145	265	1,350
Labour	350	260	390	90	310	1,400
Overheads	368	366	567	122	377	1,800
	1,008	906	1,327	357	952	4,500
Packaging & transport	183	168	227	83	164	825
Advertising & office costs	322	406	550	207	415	1,900
	505	574	777	290	579	2,725
Total cost	1,513	1,480	2,104	647	1,531	7,275
Profit (loss)	87	(80)	(4)	303	369	675

Mike Commer studied the operating statement and suspected that there was more to the problem than the statement showed. Before coming to any decision he felt he needed more detail and sent for Bill Hope. After a lengthy meeting it was agreed that Bill Hope would supply the following additional information:

(a) An analysis of the fixed and variable elements of the various costs

(b) Clear guidance on the methods of allocation and apportionment used in the statement.

Fortunately Bill Hope had kept his working papers and was able to produce the required detail quite quickly. This was as follows:

Supplement to the budgeted operating statement

1. Both labour and material costs are a combination of variable costs and a surcharge of 15% and 10% respectively to absorb general fixed costs. In the case of labour this is for general production supervision and general storage and ordering costs for materials.

2. Production overheads are a combination of variable overheads recovered on the total labour cost, general fixed overheads of £830,000 recovered on labour costs and directly attributable fixed costs as follows:

Chicken Supreme	Boeuf Bourguignon	Duck à l'orange	Chili con Carne	Chicken Kiev	Total
£70,000	145,000	235,000	55,000	115,000	620,000

   The directly identifiable fixed overheads would cease if the product was discontinued.

3. Packaging and transport costs consist of £150,000 general fixed overheads absorbed on labour costs, the balance being variable costs absorbed on total material costs.

4. Advertising and Office costs have three elements: Advertising costs absorbed on sales value, general fixed overheads of £100,000 also absorbed on sales value and directly attributable fixed costs as follows:

Chicken Supreme	Boeuf Bourguignon	Duck à l'orange	Chili con Carne	Chicken Kiev	Total
£40,000	160,000	180,000	40,000	80,000	500,000

   Once again the identifiable fixed costs would cease if the product was discontinued.

Tasks

1. Comment on the position shown in the budgeted operating statement produced by Bill Hope.
2. Should the decision be taken at this stage to discontinue the two products shown making a loss? If not, why not?
3. What other information, additional to that in the Supplement, might be useful to Mike Commer in assessing the budgeted position?
4. Redraft the budgeted operating statement in a more informative manner assuming that all five products will continue.
5. Comment on your redrafted operating statement explaining why it is more informative.
6. Prepare a new budgeted operating statement assuming that Boeuf Bourguignon and Duck à l'orange are discontinued and sales of the other products continue as budgeted.
7. Comment on the new statement.
8. What decisions should be taken about the product range?

Assignments

3/1 Within any real organisation find an example of a managerial decision and investigate the information requirements, especially those from the CMA System.

3/2 Using published accounts or any other information you can find, draw a contribution Break-even chart for a real company. What assumptions have you had to make?

3/3 Obtain information about a real firm covering several years and calculate what Performance and Liquidity Ratios you can.

What do they tell you about the company?

3/4 Many directors and executives in both the public and private sectors have their pay levels determined by performance. Find an example from either sector and establish what performance indicators are used, how they are calculated, and to what extent non-financial indicators are used.

Questions with answers

A1. A company is to invest £10,000 in a new project which will have a life of 3 years. The forecasted cash inflows are:

	£
Year 1	3,000
Year 2	10,000
Year 3	4,000

The required rate of return is 10%.

The present values of £1 are:

At:	10%	25%	35%
Year 1	.9091	.8000	.7407
Year 2	.8264	.6400	.5487
Year 3	.7513	.5120	.4064

Required

(i) Calculate the net present value of the project at:
  (a) 10%
  (b) 25%
  (c) 35%

(ii) Prepare a graph from which the internal rate of return can be read. State clearly the rate your graph reveals.

(iii) By interpolation, calculate the internal rate of return

(iv) Calculate the profitability index figure of the project at 10%.

(v) State the payback of the project in years and months.

(vi) Assume the probabilities of the net present values of the project were:

Net present values	Probabilities
£	
4,000	0.5
3,000	0.3
8,000	0.2

Calculate the expected present value.

vii) State briefly what you understand by sensitivity analysis.

LCCI Management Accounting

A2. XY Ltd makes only one product, which sells at a unit price of £35. For the year just ended, during which 64,000 units were produced and sold, the following information is available:

Total fixed costs	= £560,000
Contribution to Sales %	= 40%
Analysis of total variable costs:	Direct materials 80%
	Direct labour 10%
	Variable overheads 10%

Changes in costs are expected from the start of the current year as follows:

Direct materials	= increase of 5% per unit
Direct labour	= increase of 10% per unit
Variable overhead	= reduced by £0.05 per unit
Fixed costs	= increase of £12,000

Required

(i) Calculate the net profit for the year just ended and the break-even point in units.

(ii) On the assumption that leaving the unit selling price unchanged will result in sales increasing to 66,000 units in the current year, calculate the expected profit and the break-even point in units.

(iii) On the assumption that XY Ltd increased the unit selling price to £38 for the current year, calculate how many units it needs to sell to make the same profit as last year.

LCCI Cost Accounting

A3. F Limited manufactures product G and in the year ended 31st March, 1680 units were made and sold. A statement of the sales, costs and profit for product G for the year was as follows:

	£	£
Sales		134,400
Production cost of goods sold:		
Direct material	38,140	
Direct labour	23,620	
Overhead: variable	4,620	
fixed	29,700	96,080
Other costs:		
Selling & distribution:		
variable	10,900	
fixed	7,200	
Administration, fixed	5,600	23,700
Total costs		119,780
Profit		£14,620

You are required

(a) by calculation or by a breakeven chart to ascertain the number of units to be sold to break even;

(b) to state the profit or loss if 1,100 units were sold;

(c) to calculate the number of units to be sold to make a profit of £27,200 per annum.

RSA Cost Accounting Stage II

A4. A firm produces three products and for the coming year its budget shows:

	Total	Product A	Product B	Product C
	£	£	£	£
Sales	100,000	60,000	25,000	15,000
Direct material	42,000	23,000	10,000	9,000
Direct labour	20,000	10,000	8,000	2,000
Variable overhead	10,500	4,000	5,000	1,500
Fixed overhead	15,000	7,500	6,000	1,500
Total costs	87,500	44,500	29,000	14,000
Profit (loss)	12,500	15,500	(4,000)	1,000

Fixed overheads are absorbed on the basis of a percentage on direct labour. It is suggested that Product B should be eliminated and *you are required*

(a) to re-present the above statement if product B is eliminated,

(b) produce a break-even chart for the company for the coming year, showing the break-even point based upon:

(i) the original budget

(ii) if 'B' were eliminated.

(c) to show by calculation the break-even point at the original budget level and the break-even point if Product B is eliminated,

(d) to discuss the limitations that management should be aware of when using break-even charts,

(e) to explain the term 'margin of safety'.

AAT Cost Accounting & Budgeting

A5. The budgets of the Hover and Electric Divisions for the next quarter of Lawncut Mowers plc are shown below. The Electric Division was acquired recently.

	Hover		Electric
	£'000		£'000
Sales 4,000 units at £100	400	16,000 units at £25	400
Variable cost	200		240
Contribution	200		160
Fixed cost	110		70
Profit	90		90
Capital employed	800		720

Each Division is evaluated on a profit performance measure. The manager of the Hover Division believes he could increase sales by 1,000 units if he could reduce his selling price by £5 per unit. At present he buys motors from an outside supplier for £50 each. It has now been proposed that the new Electric Division supply the motor at a price of £45, which is its variable cost. Unfortunately, every motor supplied to the Hover Division would result in five units of sale being lost to the Electric Division.

Required

(i) Discuss whether you would favour the proposal that the Electric Division should supply the motor at £45 from the position of:

(a) Lawncut Mowers plc

(b) The Hover Division

(c) The Electric Division

Note: Support your answers with suitable figures.

(ii) Calculate the return on investment to the Electric Division
   (a) With the proposal
   (b) Without the proposal

(iii) Assuming an interest rate of 10%, calculate the residual income to the Hover Division after the proposal.

LCCI Management Accounting

A6. The following information relates to three possible capital expenditure projects. Because of capital rationing only one project can be accepted.

		Project		
		A	B	C
Initial cost		£200,000	£230,000	£180,000
Expected life		5 years	5 years	4 years
Scrap value expected		£10,000	£15,000	£8,000
Expected cash inflows		£	£	£
End year	1	80,000	100,000	55,000
	2	70,000	70,000	65,000
	3	65,000	50,000	95,000
	4	60,000	50,000	100,000
	5	55,000	50,000	

The company estimates its cost of capital is 18% and discount factors are:

Year 1	0.8475
Year 2	0.7182
Year 3	0.6086
Year 4	0.5158
Year 5	0.4371

Calculate

(a) The pay back period for each project

(b) The Accounting Rate of Return for each project

(c) The Net present value of each project

(d) Which project should be accepted – give reasons

(e) Explain the factors management would need to consider – in addition to the financial factors before making a final decision on a project.

AAT Cost Accounting & Budgeting

A7. LC Electronics Ltd has a large retail store providing the use of a maximum total floor space of 20,000 square metres, which is the basis for apportioning the related total fixed expenses of £200,000 per annum.

The store is at present divided into three departments and data concerning each of these for the trading year just ended is as follows:

	Radios	Televisions	Video	Total recorders
Sales (£'000)	200	320	240	760
Gross profit margin	50%	60%	75%	–
Variable selling expenses	10% on sales	10% on sales	10% on sales	–
Floor space (sq. metres)	4,000	10,000	6,000	20,000

The Directors are keen to start selling microwave ovens which will require the use of 4,000 square metres of floor space, generating sales of £120,000 with a gross profit margin of 70% and incurring variable selling expenses at the rate of 10% on sales. The

Directors propose to replace the radio department by this new one to improve profitability.

Required

(i) For the year just ended, prepare a columnar statement which shows the gross and net profit for each department and also the total for the whole company.

(ii) Produce detailed workings to evaluate the Directors' proposal and then, basing your answers solely on considerations of revised profitability:

(a) State whether or not you support the proposal and calculate the revised total profit if it were implemented.

(b) Suggest an alternative re-allocation of the floor space which could be considered, supported by calculations of the revised total profit after implementation.

LCCI Cost Accounting

A8. Three products – X, Y and Z – are made and sold by a company; information is given below.

		Product X	Product Y	Product Z
Standard costs:		£	£	£
Direct materials		50	120	90
Variable overhead		12	7	16
Direct labour	Rate per hour	Hours	Hours	Hours
	£			
Department A	5	14	8	15
Department B	6	4	3	5
Department C	4	8	4	15

Total fixed overhead for the year was budgeted at £300,000.

The budget for the current financial year, which was prepared for a recessionary period, was based on the following sales:

Product	Sales in units	Selling price per unit
		£
X	7,500	210
Y	6,000	220
Z	6,000	300

However, the market for each of the products has improved and the Sales Director believes that without a change in selling prices, the number of units sold could be increased for each product by the following percentages:

Product	Increase
X	20%
Y	25%
Z	$33\frac{1}{3}$%

When the Sales Director's views were presented to a management meeting, the Production Director declared that although it might be possible to sell more units of product, output could not be expanded because he was unable to recruit more staff for Department B: there being a severe shortage of the skills needed by this department.

You are required

(a) (i) to show in the form of a statement for management, the unit costs of each of the three products and the total *profit* expected for the current year based on the original sales figures;

(ii) to state the profit if the most profitable mixture of the profits was made and sold, utilising the higher sales figures and the limitation on Department B;

(iii) to identify and to comment on *three* possible problems which may arise if the mixture in (a)(ii) above were to be produced;

(b) to describe briefly a technique for determining optimum levels when there is more than one input constraint.

CIMA Cost Accounting

A9. X Ltd manufactures and sells two varieties of a particular product. Selling prices and variable costs are budgeted for the following period as:

	Variety A	**Variety B**
	£/unit	£/unit
Retail selling price	5.00	6.00
Variable production cost	1.50	1.90
Other variable costs	0.30	0.30

The two varieties are sold by X Ltd direct to retailers at a basic price sufficient to provide the retailers with a gross margin 30% of sales (before discounts received). Discounts off basic price are given to retailers depending upon quantities purchased. Discount of 4% is expected on Variety A, and 5% on Variety B, in the following period.

Fixed production costs, jointly incurred by the two varieties of the product, are budgeted to total £225,000. Other fixed costs, also jointly incurred, are budgeted at £73,500.

Budgeted production and sales quantities are:

	Variety A	**Variety B**
	000 units	000 units
Production	100	150
Sales	105	140

The fixed production costs are absorbed into product costs using a predetermined rate per unit of product, based on budgeted quantities and budgeted costs. The same rate is applied to each variety of the product. Other fixed costs are shared amongst the two varieties on a similar basis, i.e. a rate per unit of product, based on budgeted quantities and costs.

Required

(a) Calculate the total revenue, gross profit and net profit that will occur in the following period:

(i) if actual results in all respects are as per budget,

(ii) if actual results are as per budget apart from production of Variety A of 105,000 units.

(b) Using marginal costing principles calculate the expected break-even sales revenue for the following period.

(c) Contrast the effect, on stock valuation and period profit reporting, of using absorption and marginal costing systems respectively.

ACCA Cost and Management Accounting

A10. Z Ltd is a retailer with a number of shops selling a variety of merchandise. The company is seeking to determine the optimum allocation of selling space in its shops. Space is devoted to ranges of merchandise in modular units, each module occupying seventy square metres of space. Either one or two modules can be devoted to each range. Each shop has seven modular units.

Z Ltd has tested the sale of different ranges of merchandise and has determined the following sales productivities.

Sales per module per week

	1 Module	**2 Modules**
	£	£
Range A	6,750	6,250
Range B	3,500	3,150
Range C	4,800	4,600
Range D	6,400	5,200
Range E	3,333	3,667

The contribution (selling price – product cost) percentages of sales of the five ranges are as follows:

Range A	20%
Range B	40%
Range C	25%
Range D	25%
Range E	30%

Operating costs are £5,600 per shop per week and are apportioned to ranges based on an average rate per module.

Required

(a) Determine the allocation of shop space that will optimise profit, clearly showing the ranking order for the allocation of modules.

(b) Calculate the profit of each of the merchandise ranges selected in (a) above, and of the total shop.

(c) Define the term 'limiting factor', and explain the relevance of limiting factors in planning and decision-making.

ACCA Cost and Management Accounting

A11.(a) The owners of a chain of retail petrol filling stations are considering opening an additional station. Initially one grade of petrol only would be sold and the normal selling price would be £0.44 per litre. Variable charges – cost of petrol, delivery and Excise Duty – total £0.40 per litre.

The fixed costs for a 4-week period are estimated to be:

	£
Rent	2,000
Rates on business premises	1,000
Wages – 5 people on shifts	3,000
Wage-related costs	400
Electricity for continuous opening (24 hour)	300
Other fixed costs	110

After establishing the site for petrol, it is intended at a later stage to develop on the same site a 'motorists shop' selling the numerous small sundry items often required by motorists. There would be no increase in staff and one cash till only would be operated.

Throughout this question, Value Added Tax is ignored.

You are required

(i) to calculate the breakeven point in number of litres and also in £s for a four-week period if (1) the above costs applied, (2) the rent was increased by 75%, (3) the rent remained at £2,000 but commission of £0.002 was given to the employees as a group bonus for every litre sold, (4) the selling price was reduced to £0.43 and no commission was paid (with the rent at £2,000);

(ii) to state how many litres would need to be sold per four-week period at £0.44 if costs were as in the original data (that is, with rent at £2,000) to achieve a profit of £700 per week;

(iii) to advise the management about the following proposal, assuming sales for a four-week period at a price of £0.44 per litre are normally (1) 275,000 litres, and (2) 425,000 litres.

The possibility of operating from 07.00 to 23.00 is being considered. The total savings for a four-week period on the original data would be £120 for electricity and one night-shift person paid £200 per week (wage-related costs £25 per week) would no longer be required. Sales would, however, reduce by 50,000 litres over a four-week period.

Workings should be shown.

(iv) to explain what would be required of the accounting system if the 'motorists shop' idea was proceeded with.

(b) Explain briefly what you understand by the terms 'contribution to sales ratio' and 'margin of safety', illustrating your answer with a diagram or graph (which is not expected to be on graph paper).

CIMA Cost Accounting

Questions without answers

B1. AFC Ltd makes only two products, called 'Ayef' and 'Efsee', in a very short manufacturing cycle, as a result of which stocks of work in progress and finished goods do not exist. Direct workers are paid at the rate of £3 per hour.

Product details are as follows:

	Ayef	**Efsee**
Direct material costs per unit	£6	£21
Direct labour hours per unit	12	6
Variable overhead per unit	£6	£6
Unit selling price	£84	£66

Total fixed costs are £125,000 per month and these are absorbed into product costs on a direct labour hour basis calculated on a budgeted monthly activity of 50,000 hours.

Monthly sales demand for the two products has suddenly increased to 3,000 units of Ayef and 5,000 units of Efsee. Steps are being taken to increase the 48,000 direct labour hours currently available, at present rates of pay, to cope with this demand. There are no other constraints and the present level of fixed costs will remain unchanged.

Required

(i) Calculate the total unit costs of each product and the net profit per unit.

(ii) On the basis of present direct labour hours, decide on the product mix which will maximise profit for next month and calculate the amount of this profit.

(iii) Calculate the amount of additional profit to be made per month if the direct labour force is increased by 20%.

LCCI Cost Accounting

B2. There are two widely accepted measures of performance used by decentralised companies, return on investment (ROI) and residual income (RI). Your company has two divisions:

	Division A	Division B
	$	$
Capital employed	200,000	500,000
Net profit	40,000	90,000

Required

(i) Calculate the ROI for each of Divisions A and B

(ii) (a) Calculate the RI for each of Divisions A and B, assuming an interest rate of 15%.

(b) Calculate the RI for each of Divisions A and B, assuming an interest rate of 20%.

(iii) Contrast the ROI and RI calculations you have made and discuss the features of each performance measure.

(iv) State and briefly discuss:

(a) Two advantages of decentralisation

(b) Two disadvantages of decentralisation.

LCCI Management Accounting

B3. HL Company has estimated the following for its operations during the year.

Sales of Product X	200,000 units
Selling and distribution overhead	£500,000
Fixed production overhead	£400,000

Standard data per unit of product X is as follows:

Materials: kilos of component BW to make 1 unit of X	5
purchase cost per kilo of Component BW	£3
Direct labour: hours per unit of product X	4
rate per hour	£10
Variable production overhead per unit of product X	£16
Selling price per unit of X	£80

Required

(i) Prepare statements which show the profit or loss for the period based on:

(a) The initial estimates of cost and standard data;

(b) A revised plan which reduces selling price by 10% and increases sales volume by 20%;

(c) An alternative plan which, through increasing advertising by £500,000, increases sales units by 10% over that originally planned.

(ii) Calculate the percentage change from the standard selling price which will cause the firm to break even.

Note: Treat each of the above requirements independently.

AAT Cost Accounting & Budgeting

B4. The Lo Hak company has $1,820,000 to invest on new capital projects next year. The final list of investments to be considered has been reduced to:

	Investment	Cost	Life (Years)	
1	Purchase the licence to manufacture a new high-technology product	$405,000	7	Annual inflows $108,000 per annum
2	Improve the existing prȯduction line conveyor system	$510,000	4	Annual cash inflows generated $210,000 per annum
3	Expand and construct new buildings & equipment	$630,000	8	Additional cash inflows $171,000 per annum
4	Replace the microcomputer facilities	$270,000	3	Cost savings $135,000 per annum

All cash inflows will commence in Year 1 except Investment 4, when the first inflows will not be received until the third year. The company's cost of capital is 15%.

The present values of $1 at 15% and 30% are:

	1	2	3	4	5	6	7	8
15%	.8696	.7561	.6575	.5718	.4972	.4323	.3759	.3269
30%	.7692	.5917	.4552	.3501	.2693	.2072	.1594	.1226

Required

Ignoring residual values:

(i) Calculate the net present values at 15% for each Investments 1-4

(ii) Prepare a profitability index and rank the investments

(iii) Which investment(s) would you reject and why?

(iv) For Investment 3, calculate the internal rate of return

(v) State the payback period for Investment 1

(vi) State 3 other factors that should be considered in making the choice of investments.

LCCI Management Accounting

B5. FGH Ltd makes only one product which sells at £40 per unit and has a budgeted total factory cost of £25 per unit, including factory overheads calculated on the basis of a normal budgeted level of activity of 50,000 units per half year.

Other details from the budget for the current year are as follows:

(1) Opening stock of finished goods – 8,000 units

(2) Work in progress will be constant throughout.

(3)

	First half year	Second half year
Production budget (units)	64,000	42,000
Sales budget (units)	48,000	56,000

(4) Fixed overheads per half year:

	£
Factory	125,000
Administration	160,000
Selling	90,000

Required

(i) Prepare a tabular statement of budgeted net profit for each half year and in total for the year:

(a) Using the absorption costing principle;
(b) Using the marginal costing principle.

(ii) Briefly explain the difference between the total net profit for the year given in your answers to (i)(a) and (i)(b).

LCCI Cost Accounting

B6. The following annual figures relate to a manufacturing company:

	£'000
Direct materials	400
Direct wages (variable)	600
Variable factory overhead	250
Fixed factory overhead	400
Fixed administration and selling expense	200
Variable selling and distribution expense	400
Sales	2,750

Required

(i) On a single graph, plot and label each item of cost separately and the total sales, to indicate the break-even point and area of profit.

(ii) On the assumption that all the above variable costs/expenses vary with the quantity of goods sold, calculate the revised break-even point (to the nearest £'000), if selling prices increased by 10%.

LCCI Cost Accounting

B7. Narburgh Ltd manufactures three products whose average costs of production are as follows:

		X	Y	Z
		£	£	£
Direct materials		57	36	54
Direct labour:	Production at £6 per hour	24	36	12
	Assembly at £3 per hour	9	12	6

Maximum potential sales for next year are:

X	12,000 units at £134 each
Y	20,000 units at £120 each
Z	16,000 units at £104 each

Unfortunately, production hours are restricted to 164,000, so the sales demand cannot be met. Assembly hours are not limited.

Required

(i) In order to maximise profits:

(a) Calculate and state the order in which product demand should be satisfied.

(b) State which product(s) would not be fully supplied and calculate the loss of contribution to the business.

(c) Calculate the anticipated profit for next year, assuming fixed costs are £644,000.

(ii) If production could be sub-contracted, give your views as to what would be the maximum acceptable price(s) for the product(s) that cannot be supplied from Narburgh's own manufacture.

LCCI Management Accounting

B8. Amendit Manufacturing Ltd opened a new factory on 1 May to produce only one standard product.

The cost accountant prepared the following budgeted Profit and Loss Account for the first three months of trading:

	May	**June**	**July**
Sales (000) units	15	20	30
Production (000 units)	20	25	30
	£'000	£'000	£'000
Sales	105	140	210
Cost of sales			
Opening stock of finished products	–	23	46
Direct production costs	60	75	90
Production overhead absorbed	32	40	48
	92	138	184
Less: Closing stock of finished products	23	46	46
	69	92	138
Production overhead under/(over) absorbed	8	–	(8)
	77	92	130
Gross Profit	28	48	80
Administration overhead	12	12	12
Marketing overhead	26	31	41
Profit/(Loss)	(10)	5	27

Additional information

(1) In the factory, total direct costs are assumed to vary with output but the overhead is assumed to be fixed.

(2) All administration overhead is assumed to be fixed but total marketing overhead contains a fixed element, the balance varying with sales.

Required

(i) Give brief but concise definitions of each of the two alternative principles, i.e. absorption costing and marginal costing.

(ii) Prepare a budgeted Profit and Loss Account for the first three months in tabular form using the alternative principle to the one used above.

(iii) List three advantages of your revised presentation in (ii) over the original one.

(iv) In what situation will profits or losses be exactly the same regardless of which principle is used?

LCCI Cost Accounting

B9. A company is currently manufacturing at only 60% of full practical capacity, in each of its two production departments, due to a reduction in market share. The company is seeking to launch a new product which it is hoped will recover some lost sales.

The estimated direct costs of the new product, Product X, are to be established from the following information:

Direct materials:

Every 100 units of the product will require 30 kilos net of Material A. Losses of 10% of materials input are to be expected. Material A costs £5.40 per kilo before discount. A quantity discount of 5% is given on all purchases if the monthly purchase quantity exceeds 25,000 kilos. Other materials are expected to cost £1.34 per unit of Product X.

Direct labour (per hundred units):

Department 1: 40 hours at £4.00 per hour.
Department 2: 15 hours at £4.50 per hour.

Separate overhead absorption rates are established for each production department. Department 1 overheads are absorbed at 130% of direct wages, which is based upon the expected overhead costs and usage of capacity if Product X is launched. The rate in Department 2 is to be established as a rate per direct labour hour also based on expected usage of capacity. The following annual figures for Department 2 are based on full practical capacity:

Overhead	£5,424,000
Direct labour hours	2,200,000

Variable overheads in Department 1 are assessed at 40% of direct wages and in Department 2 are £1,980,000 (at full practical capacity).

Non-production overheads are estimated as follows (per unit of Product X):

Variable	£0.70
Fixed	£1.95

The selling price for Product X is expected to be £9.95 per unit, with annual sales of 2,400,000 units.

Required

(a) Determine the estimated cost per unit of Product X.

(b) Comment on the viability of Product X.

(c) Market research indicates that an alternative selling price for Product X could be £9.45 per unit, at which price annual sales would be expected to be 2,900,000 units.
Determine, and comment briefly upon, the optimum selling price.

ACCA Cost and Management Accounting

B10. The directors of a family-owned retail department store were shocked to receive the following profit statement for the year ended 31 January:

	£000	£000	£000
Sales		5,000	
Less: Cost of sales		3,398	
			1,602
Wages – Departments	357		
– Office	70		
– Restaurant	26		
		453	
Delivery costs		200	
Departmental expenses		116	
Salaries – Directors and management		100	
Directors' fees		20	
Sales promotion and advertising		120	
Store capacity costs, i.e. rent, rates and energy		488	
Interest on bank overdraft		20	
Discounts allowed		25	
Bad debts		15	
Miscellaneous expenses		75	
			1,632
Net loss			(30)

Management accounting has not been employed but the following breakdown has been extracted from the financial records:

	Departments				Restaurant
	Ladies' wear	Men's wear	General	Toys	
	£'000	£'000	£'000	£'000	£'000
Sales	800	400	2,200	1,400	200
Purchases	506	220	1,290	1,276	167
Opening stock	90	70	200	100	5
Closing stock	100	50	170	200	6
Wages	96	47	155	59	26
Departmental expenses	38	13	35	20	10
Sales promotion and advertising	10	5	30	75	–
Floor space occupied	20%	15%	20%	35%	10%

The directors are considering two separate proposals which are independent of each other:

(1) Closing the Toys Department

(2) Reducing selling prices on Ladies' Wear and Men's Wear by 5% in the hope of boosting sales.

You are required

(a) to present the information for the year to 31 January in a more meaningful way to aid decision making. Include any statistics or indicators of performance which you consider to be useful;

(b) to show and explain the change in profit for a full year if the Toys Department were closed and if all other costs remain the same;

(c) to show for the Ladies' Wear and Men's Wear Departments, if selling prices are reduced by 5% and unit costs remain the same,

(i) the increase in sales value (to the nearest thousand pounds) that would be required for a full year to maintain the gross profits, in £s, earned by each of these Departments; and

(ii) the increase in (i) above expressed as a percentage of the sales for each Department to 31 January;

(d) to state your views on both the proposals being considered by the directors and recommend any alternative action you think appropriate.

CIMA Cost Accounting

B11. A retailer with a chain of stores is planning product promotions for a future period. The following information relates to a product which is being considered for a four week promotion:

Normal weekly sales (i.e. without promotion), 2,400 units at £2.80 per unit.

Normal contribution margin, 45% of normal selling price

Promotional discount, 20% (i.e. normal selling price reduced by 20% during the promotion).

Expected promotion sales multiplier, 2.5 (i.e. weekly sales units expected during the promotion is 2.5 × 2,400 = 6,000 units).

Addition fixed costs incurred to run the promotion (i.e. unaffected by the level of promotional sales) are forecast to be £5,400. Unit variable costs would be expected to remain at the same level as normal.

Required

(a) Calculate the expected incremental profit/(loss) from the promotion.

(b) Calculate the sales units multiplier that would be required during the promotion to break even compared with a no-promotion situation.

(c) Describe other factors that should be considered before making a decision regarding the promotion.

ACCA Cost and Management Accounting 1

Answers to questions in Section II

Part 1: Cost analysis and cost ascertainment

Answers to multiple choice questions (beginning on Page 193)

1	b	6	a	11	d	16	c	21	a
2	c	7	b	12	b	17	a	22	c
3	c	8	c	13	c	18	d	23	d
4	a	9	b	14	c	19	b	24	a
5	d	10	a	15	b	20	c	25	b

Answers to examination questions

A1. (a) Details can be taken from the Chapter (LIFO, FIFO and Average Price)

(b) Effect in times of inflation:

Method	*On stock valuation*	*On cost of product*	*On profit*
LIFO	understates	more realistic	more realistic
FIFO	more realistic	understates	overstates

Weighted Average produces a position between LIFO and FIFO

(c) When producing work to special requirements special materials are usually required and specific material prices used.

A2. (i) Closing stock values (given opening stock is 20 at £80 each)

	FIFO			LIFO			W.AV		
Jan	50 × 70	=	£3,500	20 × 80	=	£1,600	$\frac{£9{,}880}{130}$	=	£76
	30 × 82	=	£2,460	20 × 81	=	£1,620			
				40 × 70	=	£2,800			
	80		£5,960	80		£6,020	80 × 76		£6,080

	FIFO			LIFO			W.AV		
Feb	30 × 85	=	£2,550						
	30 × 85	=	£2,550			as above	$\frac{6{,}080 + 8{,}680}{180}$	=	£82
	20 × 94	=	£1,880						
	80		£6,980	80		£6,020	80 × 82	=	£6,560

(ii) Workings for March closing stock using weighted average

$$\frac{£6{,}560 + 9{,}280}{180} = £88$$

∴ Deficit = 2 × £88 = **£176** and Closing stock = 28 × 88 = **£2,464**

Profit & loss account for March

	£	£
Sales (150 × £150)		22,500
Opening stock	£6,560	
+ purchases	9,280	
– deficit & closing stock	(2,640)	13,200
= gross profit		9,300
Less Variable costs (10% of 22,500)		(2,250)
Fixed costs		(4,000)
Stock deficit		(176)
= net profit		£2,874

A3. (i) Four possible overhead absorption rates.

$$\text{Overhead absorption rate} = \frac{\text{total overheads}}{\text{Total of absorption base}}$$

$$\text{OAR per labour hour} = \frac{£500{,}000}{50{,}000} = £10$$

$$\text{OAR per machine hour} = \frac{£500{,}000}{100{,}000} = £5$$

$$\text{OAR Direct wages percentage} = \frac{£500{,}000}{£200{,}000}\,\% = 250\%$$

$$\text{OAR Prime cost percentage} = \frac{£500{,}000}{£1{,}200{,}000} = 42\%$$

Price quotations for Job 456

Using labour hour basis:

	£
Direct material	1,000
Direct labour (60 × £4.50)	270
= prime cost	1,270
Factory overheads (60 × £10)	600
= Factory cost	1,870
+ 100% Mark-up	1,870
= Selling price	£3,740

Using machine hour basis:

	£
Prime cost	1,270
Factory overheads (72 × £5)	360
= Factory cost	1,630
+ 100% Mark-up	1,630
= Selling price	£3,260

Using direct wages percentage:

	£
Direct material	1,000
Direct labour	270
= prime cost	1,270
Factory overheads (£270 × 250%)	675
	1,945
+ 100% Mark-up	1,945
	£3,890

Using prime cost percentage:

	£
Prime cost	1,270
Factory overheads (£1,270 × 42%)	533
	1,803
+ 100% Mark-up	1,803
	£3,606

(ii) The Machine Hour basis is likely to be the most appropriate as there is expensive machinery which will account for much of the overheads.

A4.

Operation

		1	2	3	4	Total	
Time/component(hrs)		$\frac{1}{3}$	$\frac{1}{2}$	$\frac{1}{6}$	$\frac{1}{4}$		
No of components		2,400	2,400	2,400	2,400		
= Total time (hrs)		800	1,200	400	600		
No of operatives							
(Hrs ÷ 40)	Grade A	20	30			50	
	Grade B			10	15	25	
Costs							
Grade A (Hrs × £4)		£3,200	4,800			£8,000	Grade A
Grade B (Hrs × £3.20)				1,280	1,920	£3,200	Grade B
						11,200	Total
Cost/component							
(cost ÷ 2,400)		£1.33	£2	0.53	0.8	£4.66	

A5. (a)

	Total £	A £	B £	C £	X £	Y £	Apportionment basis
				Departments			
Rent and rates	12,800	6,000	3,600	1,200	1,200	800	Floor area
Machine insurance	6,000	3,000	1,250	1,000	500	250	Machine value
Telephone charges	3,200	1,500	900	300	300	200	Floor area
Depreciation	18,000	9,000	3,750	3,000	1,500	750	Machine value
Supervisors salaries	24,000	12,800	7,200	4,000			Labour hours
Heat and light	6,400	3,000	1,800	600	600	400	Floor area
Allocated		2,800	1,700	1,200	800	600	
	77,500	38,100	20,200	11,300	4,900	3,000	
		2,450	1,225	1,225	(4,900)		
		600	900	1,500		(3,000)	
	£77,500	41,150	22,325	14,025			
Budgeted D.L.hours		3,200	1,800	1,000			
Absorption rates		£12.86	£12.40	£14.02			

(b) & (c)

		Job 123 £		Job 124 £
D. Material		154.00		108.00
D.Labour	Department A	76.00		60.80
	Department B	42.00		35.00
	Department C	34.00		47.60
Total direct cost		306.00		251.40
Overhead	Department A (20 × 12.86)	257.20	(16 × 12.86)	205.76
	Department B (12 × 12.4)	148.80	(10 × 12.4)	124.00
	Department C (10 × 14.02)	140.20	(14 × 14.02)	196.28
Total cost		852.20		777.44
Profit		284.07		259.15
Quoted selling price		1,136.27		1,036.59

(d) Detailed controls are necessary at each stage of the whole material cycle from Purchasing to material usage. For example;

Purchasing: Materials of the appropriate quality and specification should be purchased only when required and authorised. There should be an appropriate balance between price, quality and delivery.

Materials should be properly received and inspected. Storage should be secure and efficiently organised. There should be well designed documentation used at every stage. The stock control system should monitor stock levels, re-order quantities, usage rates, delivery times and so on to ensure that just enough stocks are held to service operations.

A6.

Workings

Overheads	£
Supervisory labour	3,760
Depreciation	585
Cleaning materials	63
Stationery and telephone	275
Rent and rates	940
Other admin.	688
Overtime premium*	522
Idle time*	492
Wastage*	345
Rectification*	1,035
	9,032

* Overtime premium 290 × £1.80	= £522
Idle time 82 × £6	= 492
Wastage 60 kg × £1.812 + £236	= 345
Rectification 37 × £6 hour + 340 kg × £1.812 + £197	= 1,035.

Direct labour hours = 3,640 basic + 290 overtime – 82 idle time – 37 rectification = 3,811 hours.

$$\therefore \text{Overhead absorption rate} = \frac{9{,}032}{3{,}811} = £2.367 \text{ per labour hour.}$$

Material P

			£
Opening balance	3100 kg		5,594
Purchases	3,500 kg	@ £1.81	6,335
	3,800 kg	@ £1.82	6,916
	10,400		18,845

$$\therefore \text{weighted average price} = \frac{£18{,}845}{10{,}400} = £1.812 \text{ kg.}$$

Job cost – Job 126

	£
Direct materials	
Material P 960 kg @ £1.812	1,740
Other	2,030
	3,770
less Wastage and rectification	75
	3,695
Labour: 474 hours @ £6	2,844
= Prime cost	6,539
Overheads 474 hours @ £2.367	1,122
	£7,661

(b) Useful information will be found from comparing the performance regarding such things as idle time, rectification, wastage and so on. For example:

	Job 126	All jobs
Idle time	$\frac{10}{474}$	$\frac{82}{3,811}$
	= 2.11%	= 2.15
Wastage	$\frac{42}{3,770}$	$\frac{345\ [1]}{32,220\ [2]}$
	= 1.11%	= 1.07%
Rectification	$\frac{105\ [3]}{6,539\ [4]}$	$\frac{1,035\ [5]}{53,986\ [6]}$
	= 1.61%	= 1.92%

Notes:

1 60 kg × £1.812 + £236
2 7,060 kg × £1.812 + £19,247
3 12 hours × £6 + £33
4 £3,695 + 2,844
5 340 kg × £1.812 + £197 + 37 hours × £6
6 7,060 kg × £1.812 + £19,247 – £345 – £813 + 3,811 × £6

In general performance on all jobs was below expectations although Job 126 was slightly better on idle time and rectification.

A7. (a) **Overhead analysis sheet**

Expense	Machining £	Assembly £	Finishing £	Total £	Basis
Indirect wages/salaries	120,354	238,970	89,700	449,024	allocated
Rent	5,708,475	4,439,925	2,537,100	12,685,500	area
Business rates	1,552,905	1,207,815	690,180	3,450,900	area
Heat/light	443,408	344,872	197,070	985,350	area
Mach. power	1,878,890	72,265	939,445	2,890,600	horse power
Plant Dep't	375,000	45,000	180,000	600,000	no. employees
Canteen subsidy	100,000	120,000	36,000	256,000	no. employees
Totals	£10,179,032	£6,468,847	£4,669,495	£21,317,374	

(b) **Overhead absorption rates**

Machining $\frac{10,179,032}{200,000}$ = £50.90 per machine hour

Assembly $\frac{6,468,847}{140,000}$ = £46.21 per direct labour hour

Finishing $\frac{4,669,495}{90,000}$ = £51.88 per machine hour

A8. **Cost Breakdown Vehicle Fleet**

Cost item	**Fleet cost**	**Av. vehicle cost**	**Cost/mile**
	£	**£**	**£**
Fixed costs			
Depreciation	33,600	2,800	0.14
Interest	10,080	840	0.042
Licences	3,600	300	0.015
Insurance	4,800	400	0.02
Maintenance labour	18,996	1,583	0.079
Maintenance spares	20,000	1,667	0.083
Drivers' wages	125,280	10,440	0.522
DSO central charge	22,000	4,583	0.23
	271,356	22,613	1.131
Variable costs			
Fuel	28,800	2,400	0.12
Tyres	12,000	1,000	0.05
	40,800	3,400	0.17
Totals	312,156	26,013	1.301

Part 2: Planning and control

Answers to multiple choice questions (beginning on Page 211)

1	c	6	d	11	a	16	d	21	b
2	d	7	a	12	d	17	b	22	a
3	a	8	b	13	c	18	a	23	d
4	c	9	a	14	b	19	d	24	b
5	b	10	c	15	b	20	c	25	a

Answers to examination questions

A1. Workings to find the Fixed and Variable elements of Labour Costs using the High/Low technique.

	Direct labour hrs	Total cost	Variable	Fixed
High	110,000	£330,000	£275,000	£55,000
Low	80,000	255,000	200,000	55,000
Difference	30,000	£75,000		

Variable element: £2.50 per direct labour hour.

Flexible budgets

Activity level	90% £	100% £	110% £	120% £
Depreciation	22,000	22,000	22,000	22,000
Staff salaries	43,000	43,000	43,000	43,000
Insurances	9,000	9,000	9,000	9,000
Rent and rates	12,000	12,000	12,000	12,000
Power	32,400	36,000	39,600	43,200
Consumables	5,400	6,000	6,600	7,200
Direct labour	378,000	420,000	462,000	504,000
Semi-variable				
Fixed element	55,000	55,000	55,000	55,000
Variable element	270,000	300,000	330,000	360,000
Total	826,800	903,000	979,200	1,055,400

A2 (i) (a), (b), (c), (d) and (e) £50,000, (f) £67,500, (g) £72,750 (h) £76,250, (i) £78,000, (j) £79,750, (k) £42,500, (l) £55,250, (m) £59,500, (n) £63,750, (o) £72,250, (p) £76,500, (q) £24,000, (r) £36,000.

(ii) Group
- 1 – Fixed costs £50,000 per month
- 2 – Semi–variable (MC hrs × 35p) + £50,000
- 3 – Variable (MC hrs × 85p)
- 4 – Stepped Fixed cost. Rising in £4,000 steps for each 10,000 hours.

(iii) First necessary to calculate the budget for a normal month of 85,000 hours ie

$$(e + j + o + £36{,}000) = £238{,}000$$

$$\therefore \text{OAR} = \frac{238{,}000}{85{,}000} = £2.8 \text{ per hour}$$

Variance calculations.

Actual overheads	£216,450	Expenditure variance £6,130 (ADV)	Total variance £14,290 (ADV)
Budgeted overheads (Note 1)	210,320	Volume variance £18,240 (ADV)	
Actual hours × OAR (69,600 × £2.8)	192,080	Efficiency variance £10,080 (FAV)	
SHP × OAR (72,000 × £2.8)	202,160		

Note 1: The Flexed budget allowance for 68,600 hours is:

	£	
Group 1	50,000	(Fixed)
2	74,010	(£50,000 + 68,600 × 0.35)
3	58,310	(68,600 × 0.85)
4	28,000	(7 × £4,000)
	£210,320	

A3 (a) (i) **Standard direct labour cost per product**

Dept.	Product grade		H £		J £
F	1	(2 × 2.50)	5	(12 × 2.50)	30
	2	(4 × 3)	12	(6 × 3)	18
G	1	(8 × 2.50)	20		
	3	(10 × 2.30)	23		
		Total	60		48

(ii) **Total standard labour cost of actual production**

Product	H	200 × £60	=	£12,000
	J	300 × £48	=	£14,400
				£26,400

(b) **Labour total variances for each department**

Dept. F

Actual wages	£17,950
less Standard wages for actual output	17,800*
= Total variance	£150 ADV

* In Dept. F, standard labour cost of 1 unit of H is £17 and £48 for 1 unit of J.

∴ Standard labour for actual output is (200 × £17) + (300 × £48) = **£17,800**

Dept. G	
Actual wages	£8,500
less Standard wages for actual OP*	8,600
= Total variance	100

* (200 × £43) = £8,600

(c) **Rate and efficiency variances**

Dept. F

Actual wages	£17,950	Rate variance £170 (ADV)	Total £150 (ADV)
less actual hrs at standard rates (4,028 × £2.5) + (2,570 × £3)	17,780		
less SHP × standard rate (400 × £2.5) + (3,600 × £2.5) + (800 × £3) + (1,800 × £3)	17,800	Efficiency variance £20 (FAV)	

Dept. G

Actual wages	8,500	Rate variance £79 (FAV)	Total £100 (FAV)
less actual hrs at standard rates (1,610 × £2.5) + (1,980 × £2.3)	8,579		
less SHP × standard rate (1,600 × £2.5) + (2,000 × £2.30)	8,600	Efficiency variance £21 (FAV)	

A4. Note that the Production and Materials Purchase Budget are *quantity* budgets.

(i) **Production budget (sacks)**

	Compo 1	**Compo 2**	**Compo 3**
Sales quantity	50,000	40,000	60,000
+ stock increase (i.e. 60% of opening stock)	3,000	3,300	4,500
= Production quantity	53,000	43,300	64,500

(ii) **Materials purchases budget**

	G kg		**R kg**		**O kg**
Quantity required for production					
*Compo 1 53,000 sacks: × 25 =	1,325,000	× 20 =	1,060,000	× 5 =	265,000
*Compo 2 43,300 sacks: × 15 =	649,500	× 25 =	1,082,500	× 10 =	433,000
*Compo 3 64,500 sacks: × 5 =	322,500	× 30 =	1,935,000	× 15 =	967,500
= Production requirement	2,297,000		4,077,500		1,665,500
less Stock decrease (20% of opening stock	31,000		36,500		28,500
= Purchase quantity	2,266,000		4,041,000		1,637,000

* Each sack weighs 50kgs and contains the materials in the standard mix percentages given. These have been converted to kilos per sack. For example;

Compo 1	50% G	=	50% × 50kg	=	25kg
	40% R	=	40% × 50kg	=	20kg
	10% O	=	10% × 50kg	=	5kg

(iii) **Production cost budget**

		Compo 1	**Compo 2**	**Compo 3**	**Total**
Production (sacks)		53,000	43,300	64,500	
$ per sack		**$**	**$**	**$**	**$**
1. Materials	18	954,000			954,000
	19		822,700		822,700
	20			1,290,000	1,290,000
2. Labour	0.4	21,200	17,320	25,800	64,320
3. Prod.OH	1.6	84,800	69,280	103,200	257,280
	Total	1,060,000	909,300	1,419,000	3,388,300

Note 1: The material costs per sack are calculated from the quantities in the Materials Purchase budget and the given standard prices. For example:

Compo 1	25kg	of	G	@ 0.40 per kg	=	$10
	20kg	of	R	@ 0.20 per kg	=	4
	5kg	of	O	@ 0.80 per kg	=	4
		Total				18

Note 2: Labour cost = $\frac{\$12}{30}$ = $0.40 per sack

Note 3: Production overhead = 400% of labour

= 400% of 0.4 = $1.60

A5. (a) **Standard product cost/profit**
Product J

			£
Selling price			1,200
Direct materials		£	
R : 10 kg × £30		300	
S : 6 kg × £45		270	
		£	
Direct labour 30 × £5.50		165	
= Prime cost		735	
Production overhead	$\frac{£252,000}{1,200}$	210	
= Total production cost			945
= Standard profit			255

(b) **Variances**

Direct materials – Material R

	£	
Actual issues at actual price 1,025 kg × £31.82	32,616	price £1,866 ADV
Actual issues at std. price 1,025 kg × £30	30,750	Usage £750 ADV
Standard usage at std. price 100 × 10 kg × £30	30,000	

Direct materials – Material S

	£	
Actual issues at actual price 580 kg × £44	25,520	price £580 ADV
Actual issues at std. price 580 kg × £45	26,100	Usage £900 ADV
Standard usage at std. price 100 × 6 kg × £45	27,000	

Direct labour

	£	
Actual wages	17,325	rate £825 FAV
Actual hours at std. rate 3,300 × £5.50	18,150	Efficiency £1,650 ADV
Standard hours at std. rate 100 × 30 × £5.50	16,500	

Fixed overheads

	£	
Actual cost	22,000	Expenditure £1,000 ADV
Budgeted cost	21,000	Volume £2,100 FAV
Actual hours at OAR 3,300 × £7	23,100	Efficiency £2,100 ADV
SHP @ OAR 100 × 30 × £7	21,000	

(c)

		£	£	£
Budgeted gross profit				25,500
Operating variances:		(F)	(A)	
Material price	R		1,866	
	S	580		
Material usage	R		750	
	S	900		
Direct labour rate		825		
efficiency			1,650	
Fixed overheads				
expenditure			1,000	
efficiency			2,100	
volume		2,100		
		4,405	7,366	2,961 (A)
Actual gross profit				22,539

(d)

Variance		Qty	Controllable	Responsible official	Possible cause
Lab rate	£825 (F)		yes	Personnel manager	Reduced bonus
Lab eff'y	£1,650 (A)	300 hrs (A)	yes	Production manager	Poor training

A6. (a) This can be taken from the text.

(b) Production = sales, except Product 5 where production =

Sales	900,000 units	
Plus stock increase	30,000 units	(30% × 100,000)
	930,000 units	

New standards for Material B (kilos per hundred units) are:

Product 1	2.7	(3.0 × 90%)
Product 2	0.45	(0.5 × 90%)
Product 4	1.8	(2.0 × 90%)

Material usage budget (kilos):

			Product			
Material A:	**1**	**2**	**3**	**4**	**5**	**Total**
kilos per hundred units	2.5	7.0	1.5	–	5.5	
× product (hundred units)	6,000	3,500	18,500	–	9,300	
= usage (kilos)	15,000	24,500	27,750	–	51,150	**118,400**
Material B:						
kilos per hundred units	2.7	0.45	–	1.8	–	
× product (hundred units)	6,000	3,500	–	12,000	–	
= usage (kilos)	16,200	1,575	– -	21,600	–	**39,375**

Material purchases budget (kilos)

	Material A	**Material B**
Budgeted usage (kilos)	118,400	39,375
plus/minus change in stock	1,810	(322.5)
	120,210	39,052.5

(c) Workings:

Material A usage = Production (hundred units) × standard usage per hundred units:

Product	1	5,800 × 2.5	=	14,500
	2	3,300 × 7.0	=	23,100
	3	19,000 × 1.5	=	28,500
	5	8,000 × 5.5	=	44,000
				110,100 × £2.40 = £264,240

Material A price variance:

Actual cost	£280,160
– Standard cost (116,250 × 2.40)	£279,000
	£1,160A

Journal entries:

		Dr £	Cr £
1)	Material A stock	280,160	
	Purchase ledger		280,160
	Purchases of Material A		
2)	Raw material price variance	1,160	
	Material A stock		1,160
	Price variance on purchases of Material A		
3)	Work in progress	264,240	
	Material A stock		264,240
	Issues of Material A to production.		

A7. (a)

Profit statement of AR Ltd for year ended 31 March 19x0

	Flight	Cafeteria	Souvenir	Total
	£	£	£	£
Sales	2,392,000	480,000	72,000	2,944,000
Opening stock		16,000	3,000	19,000
Purchases		233,000	44,000	277,000
Direct wages of pilot and crew	126,000			126,000
Indirect labour costs	19,800			19,800
Fuel cost	899,000			899,000
In-flight catering	80,000			80,000
Indirect material cost	36,200			36,200
Variable ground services	83,400			83,400
	1,244,400	249,000	47,000	1,540,400
Closing stock		15,000	5,000	20,000
	1,244,400	234,000	42,000	1,520,400
Contribution	1,147,600	246,000	30,000	1,423,600
Fixed ground services	182,000			182,000
Profit	965,600	246,000	30,000	1,241,600

(b) A standard cost is a predetermined cost based on objective technical estimates of what performance, usage, prices, rates etc will be in a future period. The general objective of standard costing is to assist in developing cost plans and in cost control. To be of value there should be stable conditions with accurate cost allotments and identification. Where these circumstances exist standard costing can be of the same value in a non-manufacturing environment as in certain manufacturing firms. However, in many service industries there are many common costs which are largely fixed making the value of standard costing more doubtful.

Part 3: Decision making and performance appraisal

Answers to multiple choice questions (beginning Page 230)

1	c	6	d	11	b	16	b	21	b
2	b	7	c	12	b	17	a	22	a
3	a	8	a	13	d	18	b	23	d
4	a	9	d	14	c	19	a	24	c
5	c	10	c	15	a	20	d	25	b

Answers to examination questions

A1 (i) NPV @ 10% = –£10,000 + (.9091 × 3,000) + (.8264 × 10,000) + (.7513 × 4,000)

= £3,996

NPV @ 25% = –£10,000 + (.8 × 3,000) + (.64 × 10,000) + (.512 × 4,000)

= <u>£848</u>

NPV @ 35% = –£10,000 + (.7407 × 3,000) + (.5487 × 10,000) + (.4064 × 4,000)

= <u>– £665</u>

(ii)

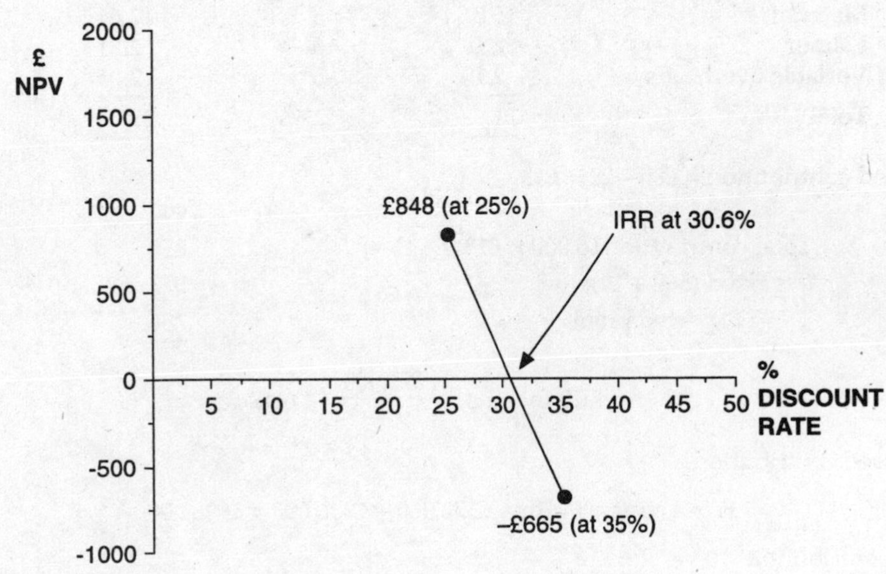

(iii) IRR by interpolation

$$= 25\% + 10\% \frac{848}{1,513} = 30.6\%$$

(iv) Profitability Index at 10%

$$= \frac{\text{NPV (or PV of cash inflows)}}{\text{investment}}$$

$$= \frac{3,996}{10,000} = 0.3996 \text{ or } \frac{13,996}{10,000} = 1.3996$$

(v) Payback is 1 year 8.4 months

(vi) Expected Present Value

	£
£4,000 × 0.5	2,000
£3,000 × 0.3	900
£8,000 × 0.2	1,600
Expected NPV	£4,500

(vii) Sensitivity analysis is a simple way of assessing risk whereby each of the factors of the problem (sales volume, sales price, cost per unit etc) are altered, one at a time, to assess the effect on the project outcome.

A2 (i) **Profit for year and break-even point**

	£'000s
Sales (64,000 × £35)	2,240
less variable cost of sales (60% sales)	1,344
= Contribution	896
less Fixed costs	560
= Profit	£336

$$\text{BEP in units} = \frac{\text{Fixed costs}}{\text{unit contribution}} = \frac{560,000}{35 - 21} = 40,000 \text{ units}$$

(ii) **Variable costs per unit**

	Last year	Change	Current year
	£	%	£
Materials	16.8	5	17.64
Labour	2.1	10	2.31
Variable overheads	2.1	–5	2.05
Total	21		22

Revised contribution = £35 – 22 = **£13**

	£'000
Total contribution 66,000 × £13	858
less Fixed (560 + 12)	572
= Expected profit	286

$$\text{BEP in units} = \frac{£572,000}{13} = 44,000$$

(iii) Required contribution

= Fixed costs + Profit = £572,000 + £336,000 = £908,000

Unit contribution = 38 – 22 = £16

$$\therefore \text{ Required quantity} = \frac{£908,000}{16} = 56,750 \text{ units}$$

A3 (a) To find contribution and profit

	£	£
Sales	134,400	
less Variable costs		
Materials	38,140	
Labour	23,620	
Variable Ohds. prod.	4,620	
Variable selling ohds	10,900	77,280
= Contribution		57,120
less Fixed costs		
Production	29,700	
S & D	7,200	
Admin.	5,600	42,500
= Profit		14,620

$$\text{Unit contribution} = \frac{£57{,}120}{1{,}680} = £34$$

$$\therefore \text{Break-even point} = \frac{\text{Fixed costs}}{\text{Unit contribution}}$$

$$= \frac{£42{,}500}{34} = \mathbf{1{,}250\ units}$$

(b) Expected profit if 1,100 units sold

	£
Total contribution = 1,100 × £34 =	37,400
less Fixed costs	42,500
= Loss	5,100

(c) Units required for profit of £27,200

$$= \frac{\text{Fixed costs + Target profit}}{\text{Unit contribution}}$$

$$= \frac{£42,500 + 27,200}{34} = \mathbf{2{,}050\ units}$$

A4 (a) Statement with B eliminated

	Total £	**A** £	**C** £
Sales	75,000	60,000	15,000
less Variable costs			
Direct materials	32,000	23,000	9,000
Direct labour	12,000	10,000	2,000
Var.ohds	5,500	4,000	1,500
= Total variable costs	49,500	37,000	12,500
= Contribution	25,500	23,000	2,500
less Fixed costs	15,000		
= Profit	10,500		

(b) See Figure A4/3/Ans following.

(c) Break-even point

			3 products			2 products
Sales			£100,000			£75,000
less Variable costs			72,500			49,500
= contribution			27,500			25,500
C/S ratio	$\frac{27,500}{100,000}$	=	$27\frac{1}{2}\%$	$\frac{25,500}{75,000}$	=	34%
Break-even point	$\frac{£15,000}{.275}$	=	£54,545	$\frac{£15,000}{.34}$	=	£44,118

(d) Main limitations

- ❒ Assumes single product or unvarying sales mix
- ❒ Assumes linear cost patterns
- ❒ Assumes that cost/revenue relationships, technology remain unchanged
- ❒ Short-term only
- ❒ Ignores uncertainty

(e) Margin of safety is the difference between normal sales and break-even point.

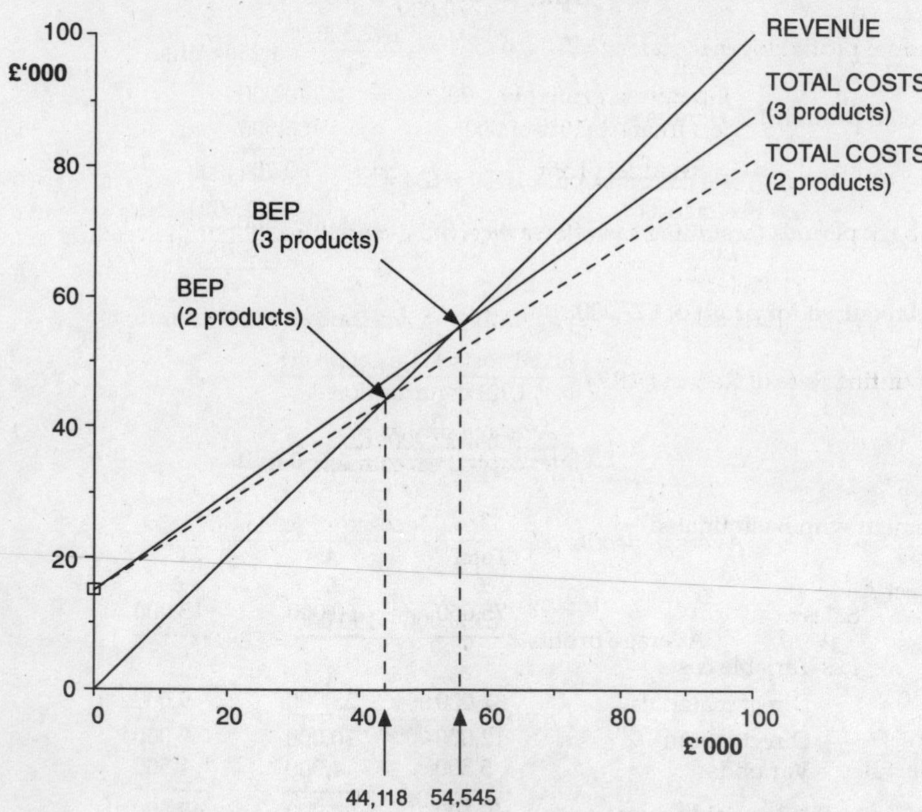

Figure A4/3/Ans Break-even chart

A5. Supply of motor at £45

(i) (a) **Position of Lawncut mowers plc**

		£
Gain in contribution from Hover sales 1,000 × £50	=	50,000 +
Loss in contribution by Electric = 5 × £10 × 1,000	=	50,000 –
		NIL

From the point of the group there is no net effect although there may be motivational or other consequences.

(b) Position of Hover Division

Gain of £50,000 contribution so clearly in favour.

(c) Position of Electric Division

Loss of £50,000 contribution so strongly against.

(ii) Return on investment Electric Division

$$\text{Before: } \frac{\text{Profit}}{\text{Capital employed}} = \frac{90{,}000}{720{,}000} = 12\tfrac{1}{2}\%$$

$$\text{After} = \frac{40{,}000}{720{,}000} = 5.6\%$$

(iii) Residual profit Hover Division

Operating profit (50 + 90)	=	140,000
less Interest (10% of 800)	=	80,000
= Residual profit	=	60,000

A6. (a) Pay back periods (assuming cash flows received evenly throughout the year)

Project	**A**	**B**	**C**
Payback	2yrs 9mths	3yrs 2mths	2yrs 8 mths

(b) Accounting Rate of Return (ARR)

$$= \frac{\text{Average profits p.a.}}{\text{Net capital investment}}\%$$

where

$$\text{Average profits p.a.} = \frac{\text{Total income} - \text{Net capital cost}}{5}$$

Project A

$$\text{Average profits} = \frac{£330{,}000 - 190{,}000}{5} = £28{,}000$$

$$\therefore \text{ARR} = \frac{£28{,}000}{190{,}000} = 14.7\%$$

Project B

$$\text{Average profits} = \frac{£320{,}000 - 215{,}000}{5} = £21{,}000$$

$$\therefore \text{ARR} = \frac{£21{,}000}{215{,}000} = 9.7\%$$

Project C

$$\text{Average profits} = \frac{£315{,}000 - 172{,}000}{5} = £35{,}750$$

$$\therefore \text{ARR} = \frac{£35{,}750}{172{,}000} = 20.8\%$$

(c) **NPV of Projects**

Project A	**Cash flows**	**Discount factor**	**Present value**
Year 0	– 200,000	1.00	– 200,000
1	+ 80,000	0.8475	+ 67,800
2	+70,000	0.7182	+ 50,274
3	+ 65,000	0.6086	+ 39,559
4	+ 60,000	0.5158	+ 30,948
5	+ 65,000	0.4371	+ 28,411
		NPV =	+ 16,992
Project B			
Year 0	– 230,000	1.00	– 230,000
1	+ 100,000	0.8475	+ 84,750
2	+ 70,000	0.7182	+ 50,274
3	+ 50,000	0.6086	+ 30,430
4	+ 50,000	0.5158	+ 25,790
5	+ 65,000	0.4371	+ 28,411
		NPV =	– 10,345
Project C			
Year 0	– 180,000	1.00	– 180,000
1	+ 55,000	0.8475	+ 46,613
2	+ 65,000	0.7182	+ 46,683
3	+ 95,000	0.6086	+ 57,817
4	+ 108,000	0.5158	+ 55,106
		NPV =	+ 26,819

(d) Assuming that 18% is the correct cost of capital Project C should be chosen as it has the largest NPV. ARR and Payback are not as reliable as NPV for investment appraisal.

(e) Numerous other factors may be considered:

- ❒ Riskiness of projects
- ❒ Effects on current operations
- ❒ Effects on staff, environment, suppliers etc.
- ❒ Reliability of estimates

and so on.

A7. (a) (i) **Profit statement**

		Radios £'000		**TVs £'000**		**VRs £'000**	**Total £'000**
Sales		200		320		240	760
Cost of sales	50%	100	40%	128	25%	60	288
= Gross profit		100		192		180	472
less Expenses							
Variable (10%)		20		32		24	76
Fixed (on space)		40		100		60	200
= Net profit		40		60		96	196

(ii) Necessary to find contribution per sq metre

	Radios	TVs	VRS	Microwaves
Sales (£'000s)	200	320	240	120
less variable costs				
Cost of sales	100	128	60	36
Variable ohds	20	32	24	12
= Contribution	80	160	154	72
Area (sq.metre)	4,000	10,000	6,000	4,000
Contribution per sq.m	£20	£16	£25.67	£18

It will be seen that the proposal to replace Radios by Microwaves is not worthwhile as the contribution per sq.m is lower and total contribution is £8,000 lower. If adopted total profit would fall by £8,000.

(b) Microwaves earn £2 per sq.m more than TVs so 4,000 sq.m could be taken from TVs and used for selling Microwaves. This would result in 4,000 × £2 = £8,000 extra profit.

A8. (a) (i)

	Product						
	X		Y		Z		
	£	£	£	£	£	£	
Direct materials		50		120		90	
Variable overhead		12		7		16	
Direct labour:							
Department A	70		40		75		
Department B	24		18		30		
Department C	32	126	16	74	60	165	
Variable prod'n cost		188		201		271	
Sales price		210		220		300	
							Total
Unit contribution		22		19		29	£
Total contribution		165,000		114,000		174,000	453,000
Fixed costs							300,000
Profit							153,000

(ii) **Department B labour hour limitation:**

Product X	7,500 × 4	30,000
Product Y	6,000 × 3	18,000
Product Z	6,000 × 5	30,000
		78,000 hours

Contribution per Department B labour hour

	X		Y		Z	
	£22/4	£5.5	£19/3	£6.33	£29/5	£5.8
Ranking		3rd		1st		2nd

Maximum sales units:

X	9,000
Y	7,500
Z	8,000

Product	Sales units	Dept B hours	Contribution £
Y	7,500	22,500	142,000
Z	8,000	40,000	232,000
X	3,875	15,500	85,250
		78,000	459,750
Fixed costs			300,000
Profit			159,750

(iii) Problems include:

Loss of goodwill caused by reduction in X sales.

Inability to increase sales of Z and Y.

Opening market to competitors.

(b) The technique referred to is Linear Programming. This is dealt with in *Quantitative Techniques* by T. Lucey, DP Publications.

A9. (a) *Workings*

Fixed production overhead absorption rate

= £225,000 ÷ 250,000 units (production)

= £0.90 per unit

Other fixed costs per unit

= £73,500 ÷ 245,000 units (sales)

= £0.30 per unit.

Unit costs and profit	Variety A £/unit	Variety B £/unit
Retail selling price	5.00	6.00
Less retailer's margin	1.50	1.80
X Ltd basic selling price	3.50	4.20
Less quantity discount	0.14	0.21
Net selling price	3.36	3.99
Less production costs		
Variable	1.50	1.90
Fixed	0.90	0.90
	2.40	2.80
Gross profit	0.96	1.19
Less other costs		
Variable	0.30	0.30
Fixed	0.30	0.30
	0.60	0.60
Net profit	0.36	0.59

(i) **Total revenue:**

	£
Variety A – 105,000 units at £3.36/unit =	352,800
Variety B – 140,000 units at £3.99/unit =	558,600
	911,400

Total gross profit:

	£
Variety A – 105,000 units at £0.96/unit =	100,800
Variety B – 140,000 units at £1.19/unit =	166,600
	267,400

Total net profit:

	£
Variety A – 105,000 units at £0.36/unit =	37,800
Variety B – 140,000 units at £0.59/unit =	82,600
	120,400

(ii) Over-absorption of production overhead will occur affecting profit. If it is assumed that the whole of the over-absorption is credited to profit for the period, the additional profit will be:

5,000 units at £0.90 per unit = £4,500.

Net profit would be £124,900. If the over-absorption is credited prior to the establishment of gross profit this becomes £271,900.

(b)

	Variety A £/unit	Variety B £/unit
Net selling price	3.36	3.99
Variable costs:		
Production	1.50	1.90
Other	0.30	0.30
	1.80	2.20
Contribution	1.56	1.79

Total contribution budgeted:

	£
Variety A – 105,000 units at £1.56/unit =	163,800
Variety B – 140,000 units at £1.79/unit =	250,600
	414,400

Contribution per cent of sales (based on budgeted sales mix) $= \frac{414{,}400}{911{,}400} \times 100\%.$

$= 45.4685\%.$

Break-even point $= \frac{225{,}000 + 73{,}500}{0.454685}$

$= £656{,}500$

Note that there are various assumptions in the above calculations so the BEP is only approximate.

(c) This can be taken from the text.

A10. (a) The allocation of modular space needs to be based on the contribution that can be generated per module.

		Contribution per module module per week		Total contribution	
		£	£	£	£
		1 module	2 modules	1 module	2 modules
Range A	(Sales × 20%)	1,350	1,250	1,350	2,500
Range B	(Sales × 40%)	1,400	1,260	1,400	2,520
Range C	(Sales × 25%)	1,200	1,150	1,200	2,300
Range D	(Sales × 25%)	1,600	1,300	1,600	2,600
Range E	(Sales × 30%)	1,000	1,100	1,000	2,200

Therefore contribution from the second module is:

Range A 2,500 – 1,350 = 1,150
Range B 2,520 – 1,400 = 1,120
Range C 2,300 – 1,200 = 1,100
Range D 2,600 – 1,600 = 1,000
Range E 2,200 – 1,000 = 1,200

Thus allocation of modules should be

Range D – 1st module
Range B – 1st module
Range A – 1st module
Range C – 1st module
Range A – 2nd module
Range B – 2nd module
Range C – 2nd module

(b) Profit

	Contribution	Operating costs	Profit
	£	£	£
Range A	2,500	1,600	900
Range B	2,520	1,600	920
Range C	2,300	1,600	700
Range D	1,600	800	800
	8,920	5,600	3,320

(c) Can be taken from the text.

A11. (a) (i) (1) Fixed costs £6,810

Breakeven sales in litres $\frac{£6{,}810}{4p}$ 170,250 litres

Breakeven sales in revenue 170,250 × 44p £74,910

(2) Fixed costs increase by £1,500

Breakeven sales in litres 170,250 + $\frac{£1{,}500}{4p}$ 207,750 litres

Breakeven sales in revenue 207,750 × 44p £91,410

(3) Fixed costs £6,810
Contribution per litre 3.8p

Breakeven sales in litres $\frac{£6{,}810}{3.8p}$ 179,210.5 litres

Breakeven sales in revenue 179,210.5 × 44p £78,852.62

(4) Fixed costs £6,810
Contribution per litre 3p
Breakeven sales in litres 227,000 litres
Breakeven sales in revenue 227,000 × 43p £97,610

(ii) $\frac{£6{,}810 + (700 \times 4)}{4p}$ 240,250 litres

(iii) (1)

		£
Reduced contribution 50,000 × 4p		2,000
Reduced costs		
Electricity	120	
Wages	800	
Wage related costs	100	1,020
Profit reduction from change in hours		980

(2) The profit reduction would be identical to that above, £980, the volume sold in the four week period being non-relevant for this particular decision, In neither case should the changed hours be introduced.

(iv) It would be necessary to identify all sales relating to the motorists shop! Bar coding and electronic tills would simplify this.

(b) Can be taken from the text.

Table A

Present value of £1 $(1 + r)^{-n}$

Periods (*n*)	Discount rates (*r*)%								
	1%	2%	4%	6%	8%	10%	12%	14%	15%
1	0.990	0.980	0.962	0.943	0.926	0.909	0.893	0.877	0.870
2	0.980	0.961	0.925	0.890	0.857	0.826	0.797	0.769	0.756
3	0.971	0.942	0.889	0.840	0.794	0.751	0.712	0.675	0.658
4	0.961	0.924	0.855	0.792	0.735	0.683	0.636	0.592	0.572
5	0.951	0.906	0.822	0.747	0.681	0.621	0.567	0.519	0.497
6	0.942	0.888	0.790	0.705	0.630	0.564	0.507	0.456	0.432
7	0.933	0.871	0.760	0.665	0.583	0.513	0.452	0.400	0.376
8	0.923	0.853	0.731	0.627	0.540	0.467	0.404	0.351	0.327
9	0.914	0.837	0.703	0.592	0.500	0.424	0.361	0.308	0.284
10	0.905	0.820	0.676	0.558	0.463	0.386	0.322	0.270	0.247
11	0.0896	0.804	0.650	0.527	0.429	0.350	0.287	0.237	0.215
12	0.887	0.788	0.625	0.497	0.397	0.319	0.257	0.208	0.187
13	0.879	0.773	0.601	0.469	0.368	0.290	0.229	0.182	0.163
14	0.870	0.758	0.577	0.442	0.340	0.263	0.205	0.160	0.141
15	0.861	0.743	0.555	0.417	0.315	0.239	0.183	0.140	0.123
16	0.853	0.728	0.534	0.394	0.292	0.218	0.163	0.123	0.107
17	0.855	0.714	0.513	0.371	0.270	0.198	0.146	0.108	0.093
18	0.836	0.700	0.494	0.350	0.250	0.180	0.130	0.095	0.081
19	0.828	0.686	0.475	0.331	0.232	0.164	0.116	0.083	0.070
20	0.820	0.675	0.456	0.312	0.215	0.149	0.104	0.073	0.061
21	0.811	0.660	0.439	0.294	0.199	0.135	0.093	0.064	0.053
22	0.803	0.647	0.422	0.278	0.184	0.123	0.083	0.056	0.046
23	0.795	0.634	0.406	0.262	0.170	0.112	0.074	0.049	0.040
24	0.788	0.622	0.390	0.247	0.158	0.102	0.066	0.043	0.035
25	0.780	0.610	0.375	0.233	0.146	0.092	0.059	0.038	0.030

Table A

Periods (n)	16%	18%	20%	22%	24%	25%	26%	28%	30%
	Discount rates (r)%								
1	0.862	0.847	0.833	0.820	0.806	0.800	0.794	0.781	0.769
2	0.743	0.718	0.694	0.672	0.650	0.640	0.630	0.610	0.592
3	0.641	0.609	0.579	0.551	0.524	0.512	0.500	0.477	0.455
4	0.552	0.516	0.482	0.451	0.423	0.410	0.397	0.373	0.350
5	0.476	0.437	0.402	0.370	0.341	0.328	0.315	0.291	0.269
6	0.410	0.370	0.335	0.303	0.275	0.262	0.250	0.227	0.207
7	0.354	0.314	0.279	0.249	0.222	0.210	0.198	0.178	0.159
8	0.305	0.266	0.233	0.204	0.179	0.168	0.157	0.139	0.123
9	0.263	0.225	0.194	0.167	0.144	0.134	0.125	0.108	0.094
10	0.227	0.191	0.162	0.137	0.116	0.107	0.099	0.085	0.075
11	0.195	0.162	0.135	0.112	0.094	0.086	0.079	0.066	0.056
12	0.168	0.137	0.112	0.192	0.076	0.069	0.062	0.052	0.043
13	0.145	0.116	0.093	0.075	0.061	0.055	0.050	0.040	0.033
14	0.125	0.099	0.178	0.062	0.049	0.044	0.039	0.032	0.025
15	0.108	0.084	0.065	0.051	0.040	0.035	0.031	0.025	0.020
16	0.093	0.071	0.054	0.042	0.032	0.028	0.025	0.019	0.015
17	0.080	0.060	0.045	0.034	0.026	0.023	0.020	0.015	0.012
18	0.069	0.051	0.038	0.028	0.021	0.018	0.016	0.012	0.009
19	0.060	0.043	0.031	0.023	0.017	0.014	0.012	0.009	0.007
20	0.051	0.037	0.026	0.019	0.014	0.012	0.010	0.007	0.005
21	0.044	0.031	0.022	0.015	0.011	0.009	0.008	0.006	0.004
22	0.038	0.026	0.018	0.013	0.009	0.007	0.006	0.004	0.003
23	0.033	0.022	0.015	0.010	0.007	0.006	0.005	0.003	0.002
24	0.028	0.019	0.011	0.008	0.006	0.005	0.004	0.003	0.002
25	0.024	0.016	0.010	0.007	0.005	0.004	0.003	0.002	0.001

Table B

Present value of £1 received annually for *n* years $\left(\frac{1-(1+r)^{-n}}{r}\right)$

Years (*n*)	Discount rates (*r*)% 1%	2%	4%	6%	8%	10%	12%	14%	15%
1	0.990	0.980	0.962	0.943	0.926	0.909	0.893	0.877	0.870
2	1.970	1.942	1.886	1.833	1.783	1.736	1.690	1.647	1.626
3	2.941	2.884	2.775	2.675	2.577	2.487	2.402	2.322	2.283
4	3.902	3.808	3.610	3.465	3.312	3.170	3.037	2.914	2.855
5	4.853	4.713	4.452	4.212	3.996	3.791	3.605	3.433	3.352
6	5.795	5.601	5.242	4.917	4.623	4.355	4.111	3.889	3.784
7	6.728	6.472	6.002	5.582	5.206	4.868	4.564	4.288	4.160
8	7.652	7.325	6.733	6.210	5.747	5.335	4.968	4.639	4.487
9	8.566	8.162	7.435	6.802	6.247	5.759	5.328	4.946	4.772
10	9.471	8.983	8.111	7.360	6.710	6.145	5.650	5.216	5.019
11	10.368	9.787	8.760	7.887	7.139	6.495	5.988	5.453	5.234
12	11.255	10.575	9.385	8.384	7.536	6.814	6.194	5.660	5.421
13	12.114	11.343	9.986	8.853	7.904	7.103	6.424	5.842	5.583
14	13.004	12.106	10.563	9.295	8.244	7.367	6.628	6.002	5.724
15	13 865	12.849	11.118	9.712	8.559	7.606	6.811	6.142	5.847
16	14.718	13.578	11.652	10.106	8.851	7.824	6.974	6.265	5.954
17	15.562	14.292	12.166	10.477	9.122	8.022	7.120	6.373	6.047
18	16.328	14.992	12.659	10.828	9.372	8.201	7.250	6.467	6.128
19	17.226	15.678	13.134	11.158	9.604	8.365	7.366	6.550	6.198
20	18.046	16.351	13.590	11.470	9.818	8.514	7.469	6.623	6.259
21	18.857	17.011	14.029	11.764	10.017	8.649	7.562	6.687	6.312
22	19.660	17.658	14.451	12.042	10.201	8.772	7.645	6.743	6.369
23	20.456	18.292	14.857	12.303	10.371	8.883	7.718	6.792	6.399
24	21.243	18.914	15.247	12.550	10.529	8.985	7.784	6.815	6.434
25	22.023	19.523	15.622	12.783	10.675	9.077	7.843	6.873	6.464

Table B

Years (n)	Discount rates (r)%								
	1%	2%	4%	6%	8%	10%	12%	14%	15%
1	0.990	0.980	0.962	0.943	0.926	0.909	0.893	0.877	0.870
2	1.970	1.942	1.886	1.833	1.783	1.736	1.690	1.647	1.626
3	2.941	2.884	2.775	2.675	2.577	2.487	2.402	2.322	2.283
4	3.902	3.808	3.610	3.465	3.312	3.170	3.037	2.914	2.855
5	4.853	4.713	4.452	4.212	3.996	3.791	3.605	3.433	3.352
6	5.795	5.601	5.242	4.917	4.623	4.355	4.111	3.889	3.784
7	6.728	6.472	6.002	5.582	5.206	4.868	4.564	4.288	4.160
8	7.652	7.325	6.733	6.210	5.747	5.335	4.968	4.639	4.487
9	8.566	8.162	7.435	6.802	6.247	5.759	5.328	4.946	4.772
10	9.471	8.983	8.111	7.360	6.710	6.145	5.650	5.216	5.019
11	10.368	9.787	8.760	7.887	7.139	6.495	5.988	5.453	5.234
12	11.255	10.575	9.385	8.384	7.536	6.814	6.194	5.660	5.421
13	12.114	11.343	9.986	8.853	7.904	7.103	6.424	5.842	5.583
14	13.004	12.106	10.563	9.295	8.244	7.367	6.628	6.002	5.724
15	13 865	12.849	11.118	9.712	8.559	7.606	6.811	6.142	5.847
16	14.718	13.578	11.652	10.106	8.851	7.824	6.974	6.265	5.954
17	15.562	14.292	12.166	10.477	9.122	8.022	7.120	6.373	6.047
18	16.328	14.992	12.659	10.828	9.372	8.201	7.250	6.467	6.128
19	17.226	15.678	13.134	11.158	9.604	8.365	7.366	6.550	6.198
20	18.046	16.351	13.590	11.470	9.818	8.514	7.469	6.623	6.259
21	18.857	17.011	14.029	11.764	10.017	8.649	7.562	6.687	6.312
22	19.660	17.658	14.451	12.042	10.201	8.772	7.645	6.743	6.369
23	20.456	18.292	14.857	12.303	10.371	8.883	7.718	6.792	6.399
24	21.243	18.914	15.247	12.550	10.529	8.985	7.784	6.815	6.434
25	22.023	19.523	15.622	12.783	10.675	9.077	7.843	6.873	6.464

Index